A
LITTLE
GIRL
IS
DEAD

ALSO BY HARRY GOLDEN

HARRY GOLDEN

A LITTLE GIRL IS DEAD

THE WORLD PUBLISHING COMPANY
CLEVELAND AND NEW YORK

Published by The World Publishing Company

2231 West 110th Street, Cleveland, Ohio 44102

Published simultaneously in Canada by
Nelson, Foster & Scott, Ltd.

Library of Congress Catalog Card Number: 65–25775

Printed in the United States of America. 2 PP 1165

Dedicated to the city of Atlanta, Georgia, which suffered the most of all Southern cities in the 1860s. In the 1950s Atlanta led the South in the resolution of the desegregation crisis, and in the 1960s it led the nation in the reapportionment process.

ACKNOWLEDGMENTS

I BEGAN TO gather material for this book twenty-five years ago when I first settled in the South, where the source material was available. But I had been absorbed with the Leo Frank story much earlier—from my days on the Lower East Side of New York when I hawked newspapers and cried out Leo Frank's fate from the headlines. In a sense, therefore, I have lived with this story all my adult life. By the time I began to write the book—March, 1964—I had mustered a small army of helpers, to all of whom I owe my thanks.

Staff members of the Georgia Department of Archives and History were most generous in their service and assistance and permitted Marre Dangar, a young Atlanta journalism student, to examine all the papers of the late Governor John M. Slaton. Miss Dangar also arranged for the photostating of each issue of Tom Watson's *Jeffersonian* in which Leo Frank is discussed.

Roger Honkanen, reporter for the Atlanta *Journal* gave me all his spare time going through back issues of the Atlanta *Constitution* and the Atlanta *Journal*.

I am grateful to the Los Angeles Public Library Staff for giving permission to my researcher, Miss Margaret Hickman, to photostat all the stories I required from the only complete file of Hearst's Atlanta *Georgian*.

The American Jewish Committee, the Anti-Defamation League, and the B'nai B'rith gave me copies of everything they had on the case; but most of all, I am grateful to the American Jewish Archives, located on the Cincinnati campus of the Hebrew Union College—Jewish Institute of Religion, which possesses a great wealth of material, all of which was made available to me: the papers of Louis Marshall, Jacob Schiff, Albert D. Lasker, and correspondence between Leo Frank and his attorneys.

Martha Huntley, my own research assistant, worked up the references from all the fifty-three books I have used in preparing this volume.

Dr. Joseph L. Morrison of the School of Journalism at the University of North Carolina, who reads all my manuscripts, once again offered important suggestions.

I am indebted to Dr. Stanley F. Chyet of the American Jewish Archives at Cincinnati, and to three Atlanta men for their graciousness in giving me some of their valuable time: Leonard Haas, Henry A. Alexander, and John M. Slaton, Jr.

Of great value to me was the work of C. Vann Woodward who wrote the definitive biography of Tom Watson; and the work of Charles and Louise Samuels who wrote the narrative of the Frank case.

And lastly, I am indebted to my eldest son, Richard Goldhurst, himself a novelist, who worked generously, brilliantly, and mightily for one long, tiring year, editing and rearranging this work.

All these research materials will be presented to the Golden Room of the Charlotte Public Library upon the publication of this book.

DRAMATIS PERSONAE

Leading Players

Leo M. Frank .... Superintendent, National Pencil Company, Atlanta, Georgia. Charged with the murder of Mary Phagan.

Mary Phagan .... Fourteen-year-old factory employee. Found murdered in the basement of the National Pencil Company the morning of April 27, 1913.

Tom Watson .... Oldtime Populist leader. Political boss of Georgia. Editor and publisher of the *Jeffersonian* magazine and the *Jeffersonian* weekly.

John Marshall Slaton .... Governor of Georgia, 1913–1915.

Jim Conley .... Factory roustabout. State's chief witness against Frank.

Hugh Mason Dorsey .... Solicitor General, Fulton County, Georgia. Frank's prosecutor.

F. A. Hooper ⎱
A. E. Stephens ⎰ .... Assistants for the prosecution.

Leonard Strickland Roan .... Trial judge.

Luther Z. Rosser .... Chief counsel for the defense.

Reuben Arnold ⎱
Herbert Haas ⎬ .... Of defense counsel.
Leonard Haas ⎰

Minor Players

John Beavers .... Chief of Police, Atlanta, Georgia.

R. P. Barrett .... Factory machinist.

John Black .... Detective assigned to the case.

Reverend Luther O. Bricker ..... Mary Phagan's pastor.

Joseph Brown .... Governor of Georgia, 1911–1913.

L. Burke .... Superintendent, Milledgeville Prison Farm.

William J. Burns .... President, Burns Detective Agency.

Annie Maude Carter .... Recipient of Jim Conley's love letters.

Fannie Phagan Coleman .... Mary Phagan's mother.

J. W. Coleman .... Mary Phagan's stepfather.

C. P. Connolly .... Journalist, *Collier's Weekly* magazine.

Britt Craig .... Reporter, Atlanta *Constitution*.

William Creen .... Convicted murderer serving a life sentence at the Milledgeville Prison Farm.

C. Brutus Dalton .... Testified he took whores into the pencil company basement.

N. V. Darley .... Pencil company foreman.

Paul V. Donehoo .... Coroner, Fulton County, Georgia.

George Epps .... Mary Phagan's supposed sweetheart.

Thomas E. Felder .... Chairman, "Citizens Committee to Solve the Phagan Mystery."

Nina Formby .... Atlanta prostitute who made deposition against Leo Frank.

Lucile Selig Frank .... Defendant's wife.

Moses Frank .... Defendant's uncle. Chief stockholder, National Pencil Company.

Mrs. Rudolph (Rhea) Frank ... Defendant's mother.

Emma Clarke Freeman .... Factory employee who testified for Frank.

Jim Gantt .... Ex-employee of the National Pencil Company. Arrested on suspicion. Witness for the prosecution.

W. H. Gheesling .... Mortician, Bloomfield's Mortuary.

M. F. Goldstein .... Judge Arthur G. Powell's law partner.

Corinthia Hall .... Factory employee who testified for Frank.

Nat Harris .... Governor of Georgia, 1915–1917.

A. H. Henslee .... Juror.

Allen Lumpkin Henson .... Assistant Attorney General, Slaton's Administration.

Ben Hill .... Judge, Fulton Superior Court. Roan's successor.

Oliver Wendell Holmes, Jr. ..... Justice, United States Supreme Court. Dissented when the Court upheld Frank's conviction.

Daisy Hopkins .... A prostitute alleged to have used the pencil company for assignations.

Bob Howell .... Vigilante in Marietta, Georgia.

Dr. J. W. Hunt .... County Physician.

O. B. Keeler .... Reporter, Atlanta *Georgian*.

Newport Lanford .... Chief of Detectives, Atlanta Police Department.

A. D. Lasker .... Chicago advertising executive. Largest contributor to Frank's defense fund.

Newt Lee .... Pencil company night watchman. Arrested.

Wheeler Mangum .... Sheriff, Fulton County, Georgia.

Louis Marshall .... Constitutional lawyer. Argued Frank's appeal before the U.S. Supreme Court.

J. C. McNaughton .... Surgeon serving life sentence for murder at the Milledgeville Prison Farm.

Rabbi David Marx .... Atlanta rabbi.

Minola McKnight .... The Selig's cook who repudiated an affidavit damaging Frank.

Sigmund Montag .... Director, also President of National Pencil Company.

Newton Morris .... Marietta's leading citizen.

Arthur Mullinax .... Arrested on suspicion.

Adj. Gen. J. Van Holt Nash ..... Commander, 5th Regiment,
                                 Georgia National Guard.
Albert S. Osborne .... Handwriting expert.
Pierre Van Paassen .... Author and foreign corre-
                                 spondent.
Judge Arthur G. Powell .... Writer of secret memoran-
                                 dum.
W. W. Rogers .... Detective assigned to the
                                 case.
Herbert Schiff .... Frank's assistant. Witness for
                                 the defense.
Harry Scott .... Private detective, Pinkerton
                                 Agency.
Mr. and Mrs. Emil Selig .... Leo Frank's parents-in-law.
William J. Simmons .... First Grand Wizard of the
                                 modern Ku Klux Klan.
Sarah Grant Jackson Slaton ..... John M. Slaton's wife.
William Smith .... Jim Conley's court-appoint-
                                 ed lawyer.
J. S. Starnes .... Detective. Witness for the
                                 prosecution.
Monteen Stover .... Factory employee. Witness
                                 for the prosecution.
Nathan Straus .... Contributor to Frank's de-
                                 fense fund.
James Woodward .... Mayor of Atlanta, 1913–1915.

Others include police authorities, detectives, editors and
reporters, members of the grand jury and trial jury, employees of the National Pencil Company, witnesses for the
prosecution and the defense, all easily identified in the narrative.

INTRODUCTION

A LITTLE GIRL IS DEAD is about an assault that took the life of a fourteen-year-old factory girl in Atlanta and of a lynching that took the life of the man the citizens of Georgia believed to be her assailant.

The Leo Frank–Mary Phagan case is familiar to many. It has absorbed the interests of historians, movie-makers, jurists, and, of course, Jews, and old-line Southerners. It has always been more than a murder story and more than a story of a lynching.

What happened to Mary Phagan was terrible. For a full generation tenant farmers, mill hands, and mountain people sang:

> Little Mary Phagan
> She went to town one day;
> She went to the pencil factory
> To get her little pay. . . .*

What happened to Leo Frank was even more terrible. Everyone felt pity for Mary, and everyone mourned her death. Many of the Georgians in 1915 sanctioned the lynching of Leo Frank despite the fact that the trial Judge thought the evidence far from conclusive; despite the fact that the Governor, one member of the prison commission, and even some members of the grand jury that returned his indictment thought him innocent;

---
* Appendix D.

and despite the fact that two justices of the United States Supreme Court rendered a minority opinion that Frank had not had a fair trial.

Governor John M. Slaton's doubt about Frank's guilt was such that he not only committed political suicide but risked his life in commuting the death sentence. Even a member of the lynch mob, with whom I spoke in 1964, was not so sure about Frank's guilt. All he would tell me was, "I was just a kid at the time."

Nothing is so important in this world as an individual's guilt or innocence. The trial is not only an every day occurrence but a literary convention at least as old as Plato's *Apology of Socrates*. The guilt or innocence of a people is the foundation of the Old Testament, and the crucifixion of the innocent Jesus the foundation of the New.

It is unlikely that anyone could be convicted in the America of the 1960s on the evidence and the testimony which convicted Leo Frank in 1913. Yet there have always been several essential mysteries to the Leo Frank case: a mystery about Frank himself; about the dynamics of his lynching and lynching generally; about the motives of Hugh Dorsey, who prosecuted Frank; and the venom which Tom Watson injected into the lynch mob.

The solution to these mysteries, however, is only half the work I want to accomplish. Leo Frank, Mary Phagan, Governor John Slaton, and Tom Watson still compel us because they lived at a crucial moment in American history. They lived at the moment when the growing pains of the new South could crush or elevate them; at a moment when the industrialization and urbanization of the last great farm region in America was beginning and was filling men with fear and hatred, fear of the stranger, hatred of the unfamiliar.

In many respects Leo Frank in America paralleled the agony of Alfred Dreyfus in France. The anti-Semitic Tom Watson from Hickory Hill, who whipped up a lynch mob with his editorials in his *Jeffersonian*, was a blood brother of editor Edouard

Drumont, of Paris, who slandered the Jews (1895–1905) in his journal *La Libre Parole.*

In August of 1915, the parallel came to an end. A lynch mob hanged Frank. Dreyfus was ultimately exonerated and freed from Devil's Island.

When a man dies his cause often dies with him. One shudders to think of the stigma forever attached to French Jews if the military court which tried Dreyfus had ordered him executed.

Think of the 23-year agitation that surged around Thomas J. Mooney and Warren K. Billings because they were still alive in San Quentin. (Mooney and Billings were radical leaders who protested America's involvement in World War I. In May, 1916, a bomb exploded among the marchers in San Francisco's "Preparedness Parade," with considerable loss of life. Mooney and Billings were convicted of the crime. The death penalty was commuted to life imprisonment, but for many years radicals in America and throughout the world marched in protest, claiming the two activist labor leaders had been framed.)

But Leo Frank was dead in 1915, and much of the interest in his case since then has been simply prurient and sensational.

Until the mid-1960s, let alone in 1913, no white man in any of the old Confederate States had ever been convicted of a capital offense on the testimony of a Negro. Yet in Atlanta, Jim Conley convicted Leo Frank. This book, about the murder of a Southern white girl, must perforce deal with the kind of lives Jews and Negroes and Southerners led then, and to some extent still do.

Only then can we understand what Georgia did to Leo Frank, Mary Phagan, John Slaton, and Jim Conley. All of them, save one, were innocent; and that guilty one was instructed by police and prosecution, with a cruel and callous indifference to the truth and disregard of the consequences.

HARRY GOLDEN

Charlotte,
North Carolina
August, 1965

PART 1

CHAPTER ONE

APRIL 26, 1913, Atlanta, Georgia. A cold gray Saturday. The weather disappoints everyone. It is Confederate Memorial Day, a legal holiday in the South, all business shut down, a parade scheduled.

The raw weather will make no difference to the widow of General Stonewall Jackson, who will accept the salute from some two hundred surviving Confederate veterans. It will make no difference to these elderly soldiers. It is a day they await all year long. Their line of march down Peachtree Street is not long, and all of them have known worse weather. Nor will the weather make any difference to the thousands of spectators crowding into Atlanta for the week-end celebration.

But the bad weather will eventually make all the difference in the world to Tom Watson, the old Populist, political boss of the state. This morning he is reading galleys. Watson publishes the *Jeffersonian* monthly and the *Jeffersonian* weekly, personal journals, which in past years have earned him enough money to buy the ante-bellum mansion he calls Hickory Hill. Hickory Hill is a sprawling plantation which most politicians in Georgia must sooner or later visit if they take their political futures seriously. Watson runs state politics, but his magazines are now in financial trouble. His anti-Catholic editorials have worn thin. Even the rednecks have grown tired of the same story of new-born infants found buried near Catholic nunneries. Watson's readership has been declining steadily since 1909.

The cloudy weather will change the political and personal fortunes of handsome Governor-elect John M. Slaton, already on the reviewing stand with Mrs. Jackson. Slaton is easily the most popular governor of Georgia since the Civil War. He has just carried one hundred and thirty-eight out of a possible one hundred and forty-eight counties in the spring election. In a state torn between contending agrarian and industrial interests, Slaton's is a significant victory.

Had it been a nice day, John M. Slaton instead of Tom Watson would have gone on to the United States Senate. Because it was a mean and blustery day, Leo M. Frank did not go to the baseball game with his brother-in-law. Instead, Frank worked through the noon hour in his second-floor office at the National Pencil Company. The next morning police would discover in the cellar of that building the mutilated body of fourteen-year-old Mary Phagan.

Leo Frank could not convince the police, the solicitor general, the jury, nor the lynch mob that he did not murder the little girl during the lonely noon hour when he attended to his weekly financial report.

The blustery cold day was only the first link in a chain of tenuous circumstances that led to the lynching of Leo Frank; to the destruction of John M. Slaton's political career; to the election of Solicitor General Hugh M. Dorsey as Governor of Georgia; and to the elevation of Tom Watson to the United States Senate.

It was the Leo Frank case that gave Watson an opportunity for a political comeback. Watson knew how to use the death of a little white Southern girl and the arrest of a Northern Jewish factory executive to exploit the fears and the frustrations of the poverty-stricken tenant farmers and millhands of Georgia. Thus for a generation to come it was not to be a Georgia led by the John M. Slatons, an industrial Georgia of the twentieth century, but a Georgia led by the Tom Watsons, its fields and meadows filled again with burning crosses, a Georgia whose city streets for the second time within a decade would overflow with howling mobs streaming past the still factories. This was the Georgia Tom Watson knew, the only Georgia in which he could survive.

This Georgia condemned Leo Frank because he was a Jew, a Yankee, a college graduate, and a "capitalist."

It doomed the innocent Mary Phagan because she was a pretty factory girl making twelve cents an hour and the daughter of a cotton-mill worker making twenty cents an hour. This Georgia banished John M. Slaton because—politician though he might have been, compromising, ambitious and perhaps even opportunistic—in his heart and being, he was still a Christian.

CHAPTER TWO

CONFEDERATE FLAGS lined Peachtree Street. Blue-and-gray bunt-
ing hung from the windows of the buildings along the way.
Grouped about the reviewing stand stood the proud battle
flags of Georgia regiments, some of them shredded and ripped
by shells fired at Shiloh and Gettysburg.

No Stars and Stripes fluttered in the cold April winds. The
last time that Georgia had voluntarily hung out the Stars and
Stripes was in '98 when a volunteer regiment entrained for
General Nelson A. Miles's Puerto Rican expedition. Atlantans
saw the flag only on those ceremonious occasions when a Democratic Presidential candidate visited the city. Certainly no one
in Atlanta would fly the Stars and Stripes on Confederate Memorial Day.

Behind the reviewing stand, which faced Atlanta's Five Point
Square, was a large red-and-white poster reading, "Watch
Atlanta Grow." These posters had become fixtures in parks,
store windows, and boulevards the year before when the Chamber of Commerce had started its campaign to "Balance Agricul-
ture With Industry."

Six blocks east of the reviewing stand, on Forsyth Street,
was one of these new industries—the National Pencil Company, housed in a dirty old four-story brick building. The company had been founded in 1907, a year after the race riots, by
fourteen Atlanta and New York businessmen, at an investment

of several hundred thousand dollars. The firm was in the old Granite Hotel building, which had once housed the Venable Theatre. The reconverted building contained machinery now. The company distributed pencils nationally, and its production and sales figures rose every year. The man directly responsible for these increases sat this morning in his office on the second floor. He was twenty-nine-year-old Leo Frank, managing superintendent of the factory.

Leo Frank had been born in Cuero, Texas, in 1884. Before he was a year old his parents had moved to Brooklyn, New York. After attending Pratt Institute, Leo Frank matriculated at Cornell University in 1902 and studied mechanical engineering.

After his graduation, he took a position as a draftsman with the B. F. Sturtevant Company of Hyde Park, Massachusetts. At the end of six months Frank returned to Brooklyn to work as testing engineer with the National Meter Company.

In 1907, his uncle, Moses Frank, majority stockholder in the newly organized pencil company, offered Leo the job of superintending the Atlanta establishment. Leo said "yes," and the uncle dispatched him at once to Germany to study the techniques and processes developed by Eberhard Faber. Eight months later, Leo Frank settled in Atlanta, where he not only superintended the factory, but tested and retested new pencil manufacturing machinery.

In 1911, Leo married Lucile Selig, daughter of a highly cultured, well-to-do Atlanta Jewish family. The Seligs were manufacturers and distributors of detergents, disinfectants, and other chemicals. The newly married couple moved into the home of the bride's parents, Mr. and Mrs. Emil Selig.

At twenty-nine Leo Frank was eight years older than Lucile and far from prepossessing in appearance. He was five feet six inches tall, and thin, but his trim appearance was spoiled by prominent eyeballs accentuated by thick eyeglasses. In the privacy of his home, in his letters to his uncle and to former classmates, he was more than articulate, even eloquent when discussing politics or music. In public he was shy and nervous. In one of his letters to his uncle, Leo sadly wrote that there was one profession in which he would never succeed—a salesman.

That he was almost immediately elected president of the Atlanta B'nai B'rith lodge followed a pattern of special sociological significance. The Jews of the South, even into the 1940's, were a single proprietary and self-employed class of retail merchants, peddlers, traveling salesmen, brokers, agents, and manufacturers. There was a small professional class and almost no "intellectuals." Leo Frank was American born, a college graduate, a German Jew—which in the Southern Jewish community of that time elected him to the elite and automatically qualified him for community leadership. Indeed, these qualifications made him a most desirable son-in-law, conferring special prestige upon his bride.

Ever since he had assumed his duties at the pencil company, Leo Frank had done all his paper work on Saturdays and holidays. Young though he was, he was rigid and inflexible, happiest when following an uninterrupted schedule—a colorless man but efficient and capable.

During the work week, he supervised production, did all the buying, repaired machinery, yet still found several hours each day to work in the company's makeshift laboratory on Bell Street trying to improve the quality of the lead used in the pencil.

This Saturday, April 26, he almost broke his routine. He had intended to see the baseball game between the Atlanta "Crackers" and Birmingham "Barons" of the Southern League, but before eleven o'clock he telephoned his brother-in-law, Charles Ursenbach, and said it was too dismal a day for a ball game and besides he had work to finish.

Only a skeleton crew stayed in the factory this Saturday. On the fourth floor, Harry Denham and J. Arthur White, the company's mechanics, were lubricating the machines and repairing the floor. E. F. Holloway, watchman and timekeeper, who never missed a Saturday, was on the third floor. N. V. Darley, who took care of the wood and all the machinery, was also at his tasks on the second floor. Alonzo Mann, the office boy, had just left.

Frank, having let his secretary go to her home in Macon on Friday, had this morning borrowed Hattie Hall, who worked for Montag Brothers, wholesale distributors of school supplies and stockholders in the National Pencil Company. Amiably, Miss Hall had agreed to help out until noon.

Leo dictated a letter to his uncle, Moses Frank, in which he discussed family affairs and local news, touching only briefly on business matters. With it he sent the week's production report.

His paragraph about sales figures was not too specific because he knew Moses Frank was in New York preparing for a European vacation. Leo did not want him worrying. Frank himself had begun to suspect that the nature of complaints the company received was beyond immediate remedy. Neither he nor any other American engineer had so far succeeded in improving the graphite used for pencils. American-developed lead remained too brittle. Customers forever complained that slight hand pressure often broke it and made sharpening pencils sometimes a futile exercise. Uncle Moses and Leo, however, deserved credit for trying. The big pencil companies, Eagle and American, had long abandoned possible solutions and imported their graphite from Eberhard Faber in Germany.

Also, production figures were down this week. On Tuesday, the factory had exhausted its supply of brass for pencil tops. Nine of the girls in this department had been laid off on Wednesday; Leo had told them they would be notified to return when the new brass shipment arrived. Three of these girls, Mattie Smith, Corinthia Hall and her friend Emma Clarke Freeman, had already stopped by to get their pay. Frank expected one or two more.

By noon, Frank had finished all his paper work except the

complicated weekly financial report. Miss Hall left. She had
started toward the stairway down the aisle made by two long
tables when she remembered she had forgotten her umbrella.
She returned for it, bid Frank another good-bye and, passing
through the aisle again, heard the noon whistles blowing.

A little after Miss Hall left, Frank, now at work on his report,
heard a tapping on his office window. It was one of the girls
who worked the machine which inserted the erasers into the
brass.

"I came to get my pay," she told Frank. "I was out Tuesday,
but I have Monday coming."

Frank asked her payroll number. She told him. He went to
the safe, opened it, and found the numbered envelope in the
payroll box. She was owed $1.20 for ten hours' work. Frank
put two fifty-cent pieces and two dimes in the envelope and
handed it to the girl.

He was bending, in the process of relocking the safe, when
she asked, "Has the brass come in yet?"

Except on one occasion, Frank always swore he said, "No,"
and swore he heard her walk away as he closed the safe. Back at
his desk he heard a muffled thump—or was it a female voice?
He rose and looked down the factory aisles, wondering about it.
Then he remembered: White and Denham on the fourth floor
were replacing rotten floor planks. Frank went back to his
paper work.

It was one of the infinite series of petty, fretful decisions that
was to cost him his life. His going back to his report probably
cost Mary Phagan her life too. If Frank's story was true, just as
he settled himself at his desk, an assailant was strangling Mary
Phagan.

Mary Phagan was born in Marietta, a small village eighteen
miles from Atlanta. On that Confederate Memorial Day, the
last day of her life, Mary Phagan was within one week of her
fourteenth birthday.

Marietta was never a pretty town. There were, to be sure, several of the old plantation houses left, but they were not in good repair. Half of these ante-bellum mansions simply housed the overseer and the office crew who managed the property. They collected the rents for absentee landlords who had long ago moved away to Atlanta or who had never seen the South but maintained offices in Chicago or New York.

In even worse disrepair were the tenant-farmer shacks which dotted the surrounding fields. Once upon a time, they had housed one-mule tenant farmers, but when the price of cotton dropped below five cents a pound, these luckless men found that neither the banks nor the seed store would advance credit on next year's crop. The farmers sold their mules to pay off their debts and left.

Those who stayed saw the withered siding of their cabins pull out from the rusty nails, and the roofs sag and eventually collapse. If these men baled any cotton, the railroads charged them such high freight rates that there was no profit left. One winter the farmers burned the cotton for fuel.

Sooner or later, the families packed their pitiful belongings and trudged toward the cities where, they had heard, there was work in the factories.

John Phagan was one of these dispossessed tenant farmers. He and his wife Fanny left Marietta one morning with their six children and walked all the way to Bellwood, just outside Atlanta, where an old neighbor took them in.

Bellwood was a mill town. Since 1900 the textile industry had been leaving New England, finding in the South the same water power, the same rail facilities, but cheaper labor. The Bellwood Mill rented John Phagan a ramshackle, three-room bungalow and let him charge food at the mill store. He worked fourteen hours a day, and at the end of the week the mill subtracted his rent and food from his paycheck. The mill even hired his children, paying five cents an hour. It was better than starving in Marietta, just better.

John Phagan was a "linthead," a mill worker in a mill town, returning to his cramped, crowded home every night covered with lint as though sprayed for some grotesque charade. He died in 1911.

Within the year, Fanny Phagan married another linthead, J. W. Coleman, who was kind and good to her children. Life was a little better by 1913. For one thing, Mrs. Coleman's children were not constrained to work in the mills. They were old enough to work in the factories in Atlanta, as Mary did, who worked for the pencil company.

Mrs. Coleman remembered awakening Mary that April 26. Mary had worked one day the week before and the girl wanted to go downtown, collect her money, and see the parade. Mary Phagan was a pretty girl, almost voluptuous. She had played Sleeping Beauty in a church play two weeks before. She gave promise of growing into a beautiful woman. Mrs. Coleman had some hope for her.

Mary ate a breakfast made from leftovers: cold cabbage and bread. Then she dressed in her pathetic finery and set off for downtown Atlanta carrying a pretty mesh bag and a gaily colored parasol of which she was inordinately proud.

She boarded the English Avenue streetcar at the beginning of its run. Motorman W. M. Matthews and Conductor W. T. Hollis said hello to her. Both swore later that she had traveled all the way to Atlanta alone.

It was near noon when she got off the streetcar and went down Hunter Street and over to the factory entrance on Forsyth Street. Herbert Schiff, who usually paid off the girls, wasn't in, but Leo Frank was. She wouldn't have to wait. She wanted to see the parade. Already Peachtree Street was jammed with milling spectators. Jingling the money in the brown envelope, Mary Phagan started down the aisle. Within moments that pretty smile faded apprehensively. Later that night, the police found her shoes in the basement and the next morning, her parasol in the elevator shaft. No one ever found her mesh bag.

Toward one o'clock, Frank went up to the fourth floor and found White and Denham, along with Mrs. White, who had brought her husband's lunch.

"I'm leaving for a while," said Frank. "Are you coming back, Mrs. White, or can I lock the factory until three?"

There was no chance that Leo would let Mrs. White remain to let herself out. Leo locked the factory when he left, and no one unlocked it after him. He was the superintendent, and he unfailingly performed his duties. Mrs. White knew as much. She said she was going. She left while Leo briefly instructed the two mechanics. On her way out she saw a shape—she was sure it was a Negro—sitting on a box under the stairs near the front door. It was the sweeper, she decided. She passed into the street.

A few minutes later, Frank himself left on his way home for lunch. His wife Lucile and her mother were going to the opera matinee that afternoon, and he would have to hurry. Mr. and Mrs. Emil Selig, Frank's in-laws, with whom he lived, had their home on East Georgia Avenue. He was home in time to tell the two women he hoped the performance would be good. He ate with his father-in-law. Minola McKnight, the Selig's colored maid, said he arrived at the table by one twenty. After his meal, Frank took a catnap and then caught the Washington Street trolley. On the trolley he talked with Julian Loeb, his wife's cousin. He got off at Hunter Street, watched the parade, and was back in the factory by three o'clock.

He went to work again on the financial report. It would absorb him for the rest of the afternoon.

A little after he had arrived, Denham and White finished work on the fourth floor and went downstairs to punch out. Arthur White asked for a two-dollar advance on his wages, which Frank gave him. Now Frank was alone in the factory, and remained alone until four o'clock when Newt Lee, the new night watchman, appeared.

Lee was tall and dark, the first Negro the National Pencil Company had hired for so responsible a position. Turnover in personnel among watchmen and sweepers had always been rapid, and replacing them was time consuming. Frank and his assistant, Herbert Schiff, had decided three weeks ago to take a chance on Newt Lee.

Lee had proved responsible. Frank had told him yesterday to be sure to report for work at four in the afternoon. Here he was.

"I thought I would be at the ball game," said Frank. "I won't need you now. You can amuse yourself for a couple of hours but be back here around six."

"I could take a nap in the packing room," said Lee. Although only three weeks on the job, Lee already knew his boss. He didn't tell him about the old cot in the packing room on which he intended to sleep. Frank would have had it removed.

"Go on downtown," said Frank. "Have a good time there."

A little after six Lee returned and Frank gave him explicit instructions about his rounds, even inserting a new tape in the clock the watchman punched on the hour and on the half-hour. Newt made his first punch and began his rounds on the first floor while Frank cleared up his paper work.

From the saloon across the street, John M. Gantt approached the factory, greeted Lee, and said he wanted to retrieve a pair of shoes he had left in his locker.

"I can't let anyone into the building after six," said Lee.

Frank came out, and when he saw Gantt, leaped back in alarm. Frank had fired this lanky giant two weeks before when he found Gantt's payroll accounts one dollar short.

A nervous man, and an exceptionally timid one, Frank thought Gantt had come for trouble. But Gantt told him about the shoes.

"I think I saw a pair of black shoes swept out," said Frank.

"I left two pairs of shoes in that locker," said Gantt. "A brown pair *and* a black pair."

"Take him upstairs, Newt," Frank agreed. "But as soon as he gets his shoes, show him out." With that, Frank left the factory, not waiting for the two to return.

Gantt reclaimed his shoes. They were right where he had said they were, in his locker, a brown pair and a black pair.

Frank stopped at Jacob's Pharmacy on the way home and bought his wife a box of candy. He was at the Selig's at six twenty-five. Unaccountably, he picked up the hall telephone and had the operator ring his office. There was no answer. If Lee was punctual, Frank thought, he should be at the time clock now, punching in. Ten minutes later Frank tried again. Still no answer. At seven Frank heard Lee pick up the phone. "Is everything all right?" Frank asked.

He had no way of knowing he had uttered a sentence irrevocably damning himself. He was never able to explain convincingly why he made that call, any more than he was able to account convincingly for his time between noon that day and one o'clock.

CHAPTER THREE

"YES," SAID NEWT LEE, "everything is all right." He hung up and continued through the huge brick building, where machines and tables loomed like ghostly beasts until his lantern shone on them. It took Lee twenty minutes to make his rounds. He could make the rounds more quickly by elevator, but on week-ends the power box was usually locked. On this Saturday Lee tramped the stairs from the top floor to the basement trap-door.

Lee had made fifteen tours from the time Frank telephoned him until 3:30 A.M., at which time, instead of flashing his lantern along the walls of the cellar through the trap-door, he descended the ladder in order to go to the "colored" toilet.

The basement contained several boilers with the furnaces to fire them. Box after box of imperfectly manufactured pencils lay piled haphazardly about. Some of them had spilled their contents on the floor. Packing crates lined the walls. Several tons of coal were banked against the chute. Lee let his lantern play about the basement.

Something in the corner caught his eye, frightening him.

It was a holiday. That was it. Someone had thrown a bunch of rags there to startle him. "Some devilish boys are playing a trick on me," he said aloud, approaching the bundle.

His lantern shone on the lifeless body of a young girl.

Newt, panic welling within him, bent to examine the body

which lay atop a slag heap, cheek down. Her hair was matted with blood. He saw one of the cords which were used to tie the pencil boxes knotted about her throat so tightly it had sliced evenly into the flesh. Not tied quite so tightly around her throat there was also a bandage, torn from her underclothes. Her tongue protruded.

Newt stumbled back, swinging the lantern over the girl. Her dress was flung about her hips, and for the first time, Newt realized that he had come upon the most terrifying experience that can befall a Southern Negro: he had found the violated body of a white woman.

He clambered up the ladder and ran moaning to the second-floor telephone. He asked for Mr. Frank. When the operator said there was no answer, he begged for the police, sobbing.

Sergeant L. S. Dobbs of the Atlanta police took the call at headquarters. He heard the caller tell him there was a body of a woman in the cellar of the National Pencil Factory. Dobbs knew it was murder. Over the past years, thirteen Negro women had been reported murdered in Atlanta, and their assailant or assailants had never been found. In the beginning it had been easy enough to announce, "The nigger women are killing themselves." Who in Atlanta cared about a nigger whore?

But then one of the newspapers pointed out to the city that a murderer who could cut up Negro women could also cut up white virgins. If it wasn't one thing, thought Dobbs, it was another; everybody was down on the police.

"Another one of them nigger murders," Dobbs said to Detectives W. W. "Boots" Rogers, John Black, and J. S. Starnes. They went out to the car parked directly in front of the station. In the back seat, they saw Britt Craig, a reporter for the Atlanta *Constitution*, sleeping off his usual Saturday night drunk.

The police liked Craig. He bought them moonshine, and although he drank a good measure himself, still no other newspaperman ever did as much. No other reporter glamorized the patrol officers as Craig did. The cops tipped Craig off to a couple of good stories every year. "Let's take him along," said Dobbs. "A nigger murder on a Saturday night is better than nothing."

They were taking Britt Craig to the biggest story ever to hit Atlanta.

They were at the factory in fifteen minutes. Newt Lee admitted them. The night watchman was shaking so much that Rogers had to support him as he led them to the basement by the ladder.

The lantern shook as Newt Lee shone it on the dead girl. Rogers took it from him and held it steady. The girl lay prone, her face twisted to the left. Her face had been pocked and torn by splinters and cinders as though someone had dragged her over the floor by her feet. A blow on the back of her head had broken the scalp and she had bled profusely. One of her eyes was blackened and swollen. Bending closer, the detectives could see her mouth was clogged with cinders. At this moment even the detectives were shaking: "Great Jesus in the morning," shouted Detective Starnes, "it's a white woman."

The cord which strangled her sliced deeply into the flesh of her throat. The straight end lay neatly between the two heavy braids of hair along her back, as though placed there deliberately. The clumsy bandage, torn from her petticoat, partially covered her head and face as if to conceal the method of murder.

Her arms were bruised and on her left wrist was a gold bracelet which, too, had cut into her flesh apparently from the pressure of a heavy grip. She was dressed in a one-piece pongee dress of lavender, simply made and cut at the bodice and trimmed at the sleeves with lace. Blood and urine covered her clothes. Her skirt had been tossed above her hips and the detectives could also see blood on the backs of her legs. She wore black stockings and a black gunmetal shoe was on her right foot.

Mary Phagan was four feet ten inches in height and weighed one hundred and five pounds. She bore no identification. Dobbs told Rogers they would check the list of missing girls back at the station.

The police began playing their flashlights over the black interior of the cellar. Detective Black found one of the girl's shoes. Craig, already writing the story in his head, suddenly bent beside the dead girl and came up with two scraps of paper. They were penciled notes.

The first, written on a leaf of white scratch paper, read: "he said he wood love me and land down play like night witch did it but that long tall black negro did buy his slef."

The second, written on the brown carbon sheet of an order blank, read: "mam, that negro hire doun here did this i went to make water and he push me doun that hole a long tall negro black that hoo it was long sleam tall negro i wright while play with me."

Starnes shone his light on the trembling Newt Lee. Newt was a tall slim Negro, very dark.

"Symbolic retribution," said Craig. "Girl, murdered in pencil factory, identifies her killer. What a story." From that moment on, he felt that the crime would make his career.

Newt Lee, in growing terror, tried to make out the shapes of the four men opposite him, all of whom were shining their lights in his face. In a bare, rasping voice, Newt fairly screamed, "It look like ĥe trying to put it off on me!"

But his protests were in vain. They were going to arrest him. Even as he wailed they put the handcuffs on him while Rogers went to summon the mortuary ambulance and the police wagon. By dawn, Newt Lee would be in jail, "on suspicion."

CHAPTER FOUR

THE SELIGS had entertained several after-dinner guests that Saturday. The company made up two foursomes of bridge. While play went on, Frank sat on the sofa reading. Leo Frank always read certain magazines every week and liked reading them best at a certain time on Saturday night. Once he interrupted the bridge games to read everyone an anecdote about a baseball umpire. At ten thirty he excused himself and went upstairs to bed.

It seemed to him the telephone rang several times around three in the morning. Before he could rouse himself from sleep it stopped and Frank thought he had dreamed it—until the insistent rings awakened him Sunday morning around seven.

"I want you to come down to the factory right away," said a husky voice.

"Has there been a fire?" asked Frank.

"No. A terrible tragedy."

"I'll be there as soon as I dress and have my breakfast."

"You'll have to come now. We'll send a car. We're the police."

Frank hurried but he had not finished dressing when Detectives Starnes, Rogers, and Black came up the walk to the house. Lucile Frank admitted them. Frank, still lacking tie, cuff links, and vest, met them in the foyer.

"We're the police," Starnes said, introducing himself. "Do you know Mary Phagan?"

The presence of the detectives, the peremptory question unsettled Frank. "No," he stuttered, "I don't."

"A little girl with long hair down her back?" Starnes pursued.

Frank kept shaking his head no.

"Did you pay off a girl like that yesterday?" Rogers asked.

"Maybe," Frank said. "I would have to check. The girls have payroll numbers."

"We'll give you the chance to check. That little girl was murdered in your factory yesterday."

Frank quailed. The factory was an extension of himself.

"What is it, Leo?" called Lucile Frank, now at the top of the stairs.

"A little girl is dead," Frank said.

"We want you to identify her," Starnes said.

"Yes, yes, certainly," Frank said. "Let me finish dressing and have my breakfast."

"We have a damn murder on our hands and you want breakfast," snapped Starnes. "We're going now. Come on." And he took Frank by the arm.

Crowded into the police car, they drove to the Bloomfield undertaking establishment.

It never occurred to Leo Frank, his lawyers, or his friends that there was anything unusual about this episode. It is true that the revelation that the police were acting suspiciously this morning might not have impressed the jury; it is true that Frank's defenders and friends might have recoiled from the implications of such unusual police action; and it may well be true that Frank had his own reasons for ignoring it. But if the defense counsel had been able to ask, "Why did you need a factory superintendent to identify a dead girl? What was wrong with her mother? Or her brothers? Or her stepfather? Why Leo Frank?" they would have put a much different cast on the case.

Both Frank and the police swore to the foregoing dialogue, the police insisting they asked him who Mary Phagan was when they were in the car (which makes their story all the more suspect), and that on the way to the factory Leo Frank agreed to go to the mortuary first.

By what virtue did the Atlanta police boldly tell a factory executive who made $60 a week (in the days when twenty cents an hour was an average wage) to come with them *right now?* And why didn't Leo Frank say, "I beg your pardon. I'm going to put on my tie and my cuff links and my vest before I go, and I'll have my coffee too"? What choice would Starnes, Black, and Rogers have had? They had neither a search warrant nor a warrant for Leo Frank's arrest. They would have waited. No, there was a reason why they acted so arbitrarily and there was a reason why Leo Frank acceded to their rudeness.

Every police officer testified he was nervous, but all men are nervous when confronted by three policemen. The police mean business of one sort or another. They bullied him because they knew something or thought they knew something.

Four hours before, they had found the corpse of a murdered girl; they already knew her name, knew she worked for the National Pencil Company, knew she had gone to Atlanta for her pay, knew everything except whether she had, in fact, been paid yesterday noon.

Since they were not in the dark as to the identity of the victim, they did not need Leo Frank to tell them it was Mary Phagan in the mortuary. Only one white girl had been on the missing women list compiled during the day at the precinct house. Besides, one of the girls who worked in Mary Phagan's department, Grace Hicks, had already identified the body.

Starnes, Black, and Rogers were interested now in the identity of her assailant, her killer. How could they know Leo Frank paid off the girls when Herbert Schiff, Frank's assistant, always met the payroll save on rare occasions, like yesterday, when he was ill?

Someone had to have told them. Someone had to have told them it was Mary Phagan in the cellar; yes, she had worked for the National Pencil Company; yes, she was going downtown to collect her pay and would get it from Mr. Frank, the superintendent of the factory himself. That someone was Mary; these must have been the precise facts she told her mother, Fanny Phagan Coleman. And Fanny Phagan Coleman, directly or indirectly, in anguish or in guile, put a dangerous obsession in the minds of the three policemen. The new factories were suspect institutions in Georgia; "a Jewish convent as lascivious as a Catholic monastery," Tom Watson wrote some months later. The police were confronted with a murder, yes, but they, Southern white males, had also stumbled upon another threatening situation. Here was a Jewish superintendent from the north with nearly one hundred Southern white girls at his mercy.

This nervous man with the protruding eyeballs had told them he did not know Mary Phagan. Maybe he did and maybe he didn't. He was a factory superintendent. He ought to know some of the girls, they thought. But his wife climbing the stairs, in hearing distance, made unlikely the chance of his admitting he knew any of the girls.

The police took Frank to the mortuary instead of to the factory. They wanted to take him to Bloomfield's because they wanted to see his reaction when they showed him the body. He might give himself away.

Unknowingly, Leo Frank helped prepare the case against himself. He went along. He was a nervous man, given to tearing his hair when shipments were late, wringing his hands when assistants made mistakes, moaning over inconveniences; a young man who liked to dramatize his authority. He was certainly nervous this morning. Perhaps there was a secret about relationships he had with these daughters of lintheads and sharecroppers working the pencil machines, making twelve cents an hour.

Bloomfield's undertaking establishment was a commerical enterprise, one room of which was set aside as the city morgue. It was to this small side room that W. H. Gheesling, funeral director and embalmer, led Frank and the policemen. Gheesling had removed Mary from the cellar at four that morning. He thought she had been dead about fifteen hours.

When Gheesling, after maneuvering the table between Detective Black and Frank, removed the sheet, everyone could see the cord still tight around Mary Phagan's throat. Gheesling turned her face sideways and silently pointed to the two-inch wound in the back of her head.

Frank did not look long. He breathed heavily and stepped away. "That's the little girl I paid off yesterday," he said.

"Is it Mary Phagan?" asked Starnes.

"I don't know," said Frank. "I'll have to check my records. She didn't tell me her name."

Policemen were swarming over the factory and street when the officers with Frank drew up to the front door at 8:20 A.M. Frank saw N. V. Darley, one of his employees, and hailed him. The five—Starnes, Dobbs, Black, Frank, and Darley—rushed upstairs to the office. Here Frank looked over his records and finally, categorically, revealed what no one thought was any longer a mystery, the dead girl was Mary Phagan.

By this time, Detectives Starnes, Black, and Rogers had been joined by Newport Lanford, their chief.

"Show Mr. Frank where the body was found," said Lanford. "Maybe he can help us there, too."

It was finally clear to Frank that these detectives did not like him. Their dislike could not help but make him apprehensive. With Darley, he pushed by them and walked to the elevator which worked on a power switch from a box which Frank thought was locked. He trembled as he tried to operate it. Then he remembered it was unlocked because the insurance company had insisted on its accessibility. The detectives crowded him. He never got the elevator going. Darley had to step in front of him and raise the gate and pull the plunger to take them to the cellar.

There were several policemen already in the basement. "Right there," said one of them, pointing to the cinder pile. "That's where she was."

Another policeman showed Frank and Lanford the girl's shoe and hat and her umbrella. "We found the umbrella in the shaftway," said the officer named Lassiter.

"Now," said Lanford, "what about this door?"

The cellar door, which rolled, was ajar. One of the staples that held its lock in place was broken. The door was covered with bloody handprints. As Frank kept staring at it, his face whitened and his body quivered.

"That door is always kept locked," said Frank. He walked to it and tried replacing the staple. His hand was shaking. He kept fumbling. Darley did it for him.

For the next hour, Frank and Darley led the policemen over the four-story structure, pointing out every stairway, closet, and lavatory. The police speculated aloud whether the girl had been killed on one of the other floors. Someone had dragged her face down. But nothing any place else in the factory was amiss.

"Do you have any idea who did it?" asked Frank.

"We've arrested Newt Lee," said Lanford.

"I'm going to have to tell the owners about this," said Frank. Seizing the initiative at last, he asked, "Do you mind if I go now?"

"No," said Chief Lanford, "not at all. But we want to talk to you this afternoon."

Ordinarily, Sigmund Montag, a director of the pencil company, might have replied to news of a murder in his factory with the complaint, "I've worked hard all my life. All my life, and now this." But not this morning. Something about Leo's demeanor, his flushed and apprehensive excitement, his fear, made

Sig conciliatory. "Look, Leo," he said, "of course the police went
to see you. This is a horrible thing. And it happened in our
factory. We have to help them every way we can."

"They seem to think I know something about this murder,"
said Leo.

"Do you? Do you know anything about it?" asked Montag.

"No," said Leo. "Nothing. I know nothing."

"Tell them that. See it from their side. They have a vicious
crime on their hands. From our standpoint, I just hope it
wasn't this night watchman, this Newt Lee."

Montag was making sense. Of course. The factory was involved. Frank would have to do all he could to help. It would
be hard on the National Pencil Company if it was Newt Lee.
What a mistake in judgment Frank had made in hiring him.

Early that Sunday afternoon Frank went downtown to the
Bloomfield Mortuary again. By this time, the murder had spread
an epidemic of excitement throughout Atlanta. If anyone needed
proof of how serious a crime Atlanta thought this was, one
needed to go no further than Bloomfield's. There was already a
line of people stretching to the street, all waiting to go into the
mortuary room and say a prayer over Mary Phagan. Frank saw
several of the girls who worked with her. They were crying. He
also met N. V. Darley again and Herbert Schiff. The three of
them waited their turn in the ever growing queue. Save for the
factory girls, who whispered and sniffled and cried, nobody said
anything. Frank viewed the body, now prepared for burial, and
then he and Darley and Schiff went downtown to police headquarters.

All Sunday afternoon, Chief Lanford and the other detectives
kept questioning Frank. And all Sunday afternoon, Frank kept
listing his movements on Saturday. But he could not satisfy
Lanford's curiosity about the telephone call to Newt Lee Saturday night.

"I just called him to see if everything was all right," said
Frank.

"But you just said you didn't usually call on Saturday nights," pushed Lanford.

"He was a new man," said Frank.

"Why didn't you call him last Saturday? He was newer then."

Frank could only shrug.

Lanford let him go. Frank went home, afraid and worried. His own predicament he thought he could resolve. But perhaps the predicament of the National Pencil Company was more serious. The murder was bound to affect them all. There were dangerous prospects ahead.

Monday morning, April 28, there was the police car again, John Black driving it, this time accompanied by Detective John Haslett.

"We want you down at headquarters right away," said Haslett.

"What's happened?" Frank asked, blinking in the bright April sunshine.

"Lanford wants to talk to you. Newt Lee's been saying things."

Leo Frank stood talking earnestly with these two men, not knowing they were putting his head into a noose and kicking the old, yellow kitchen table from his bound feet. These two detectives and the apparatus they served had determined not Leo Frank's actual guilt but how convenient it would be if he were guilty.

These policemen did not proceed cold-bloodedly, like assassins stalking important prey, nor did they proceed in outrage. They proceeded on the compelling assumption that this unpleasant young man, standing so amazed on the bright green lawn, had—even if he had not killed Mary Phagan—perhaps wanted to violate her.

The crime was so typically a Southern murder, a murder mixed with fantasy and fear, that it gained significance only if an alien had willed and perpetrated it. Here before them was their alien—a Northerner, a factory executive, a Jew, and by this time, they knew he was a college graduate, too. They, not he,

sensed the symbolic proportions of the crime. So vast were these
proportions, he must have killed the girl. Leo Frank must have
done it, for only if he had been the villain, only if he were
properly punished, could these Georgians act out the neurotic
fantasies that kept them chained to their meager past and to
their even more meager future.

"Newt Lee is saying things," said Haslett, knowing even as
he said it that Newt Lee had nothing to say. Newt Lee never incriminated Leo Frank. The police hoped Newt Lee would say
things, they may have even believed he *had* said things, but in
his confusion and fright all Newt Lee could repeat was the story
of how he had found the body.

There would, of course, be someone finally to seal the state's
charge against Leo Frank. Neither Haslett nor Black nor Starnes
nor Lanford knew of him at this moment. As the police drove
Leo Frank to headquarters, one of the factory girls, Mary Pirk,
in hysteria and tears, was accusing Jim Conley, the Negro
sweeper, of the murder.

CHAPTER FIVE

ONCE DIVINING the man who *ought* to have committed the crime, police have two reasons and only two reasons for ever trying to convict that man. The prime reason for conviction is their own certainty that the man is guilty. Unfortunately, policemen are no smarter than the best of us. It is not hard to convince one's self of a man's guilt, particularly if the man is by nature an "unpleasant" man, as Leo Frank was. The second reason the police succeed is that circumstances arrange themselves in so convincing a manner that convicting an innocent man is easier than it ought to be.

The police who took Leo Frank down to Chief Detective Newport Lanford's office again that morning acted in good faith. They had to arrest someone, bring in someone; the reporters were watching. These officers thought they sat beside the murderer, a murderer trying to evade punishment by spinning lies, insisting on a story so artless it provided him no alibi but, on the contrary, made their own work harder. They were sure they had penetrated to the depths of his guilty being. It was only natural, therefore, that they would spin their own lies in order to catch him. They said Newt Lee had implicated him in the crime, an implication which was not then, nor ever, true. It was Leo Frank's misfortune that as soon as one of these lies broke down as admissible evidence or bent before the weight of common sense, the police could invent another. It was Frank's misfortune because he could never dispense with his own lies or errors.

The reporter, Britt Craig, had come upon an important crime. It was important because it was an archetypical crime: the young virgin violated in the wood by the dark assailant, the primordial fear of the American South. Of course it had not been a wood, it had been a coal cellar, but this was industrial Atlanta, and a coal cellar satisfied one of the essential conditions of the myth.

Because it was industrial twentieth-century Atlanta, the conventions of the legend had been complicated. The young virgin had not cried out; instead, she had supposedly left two penciled notes. She had not been tendering aid to the isolated, she had come to collect her pay; she was no aristocratic innocent, but she was innocent enough to earn only twelve cents an hour.

From then to this day, no one has ever believed Mary Phagan wrote those notes. No assaulted girl, even though she works in a pencil factory, gathers her senses enough to describe her attacker. Mary never wrote the notes while she was being attacked because she would have been lying supine, and she never wrote the notes after her assailant left her because by then she had been garroted. Even presuming that somehow she had written those semiliterate messages, certainly her killer would have confiscated them.

It is obvious her killer wrote those notes and wrote them for a purpose. And the only two purposes he could have had were simultaneously to call attention to himself and divert suspicion from himself, the first an unconscious wish, the second a practical gesture. Such ambivalence is rare in murderers. The police thought this killer was a rare one. They looked for the rare man instead of the rare criminal. Leo Frank was just rare enough.

The police officers would soon discover that several facts impinged upon the boundaries of the myth. The autopsy report would reveal Mary Phagan had not been raped. But even then these policemen would not be ready to collapse the myth. Robbery, for instance, would never enter their minds. A Southern white girl lying on a slab in the morgue could mean only one thing—sex, with a fight to the death for her honor.

Chief Lanford kept Frank waiting. Finally, he put his hand through the door and barked, "Come here." In the office, Lanford produced the time slip which Frank had removed from the clock Sunday morning on which he had scribbled Sunday's date.

"Notice anything about it?" Lanford asked.

Frank studied it. Maybe there was something irregular about Lee's punches. Even if there weren't, Frank was apprehensive enough about his own predicament to say there was.

Before he could pursue this possibility, there was a banging at Lanford's door.

Frank heard, "That man is my client and I am going in that room. Keep me out, and I will get a writ of *habeas corpus.*"

The voice belonged to one of the best-known lawyers in Atlanta, Luther Z. Rosser, who had just arrived at Police Headquarters with young Herbert Haas, the lawyer who represented the Montag Brothers. The Montags had asked Haas to represent their interests in the case, and since Haas expected to be in court Monday afternoon he had asked the help of Rosser. Rosser was a criminal lawyer, and he knew that when the police took a man into a room alone, that man was a suspect; a suspect needs counsel.

Like Frank, both Haas and Rosser were primarily interested in stemming the scandal the murder occasioned. None of them ever correctly estimated how perilous Frank's position was, not then, not during the trial, not when they made their appeals.

"I didn't know this man had a lawyer," Lanford said. "What's he need a lawyer for?"

"You make no statement," Rosser said to Frank, "unless I am present."

Alerted by the discussion, Police Chief John Beavers came to

Lanford's office. Beavers knew enough about the law and lawyers to realize they wouldn't waive any rights. Beavers asked Frank to make a statement, and Frank did so to a police stenographer.

While Frank was dictating, Rosser pointed out to Beavers and Lanford how foolishly incredible their suspicions were. Mary Phagan must have fought her attacker, the lawyer said. She must have clawed and scratched. Frank didn't have a mark on him. The longer the police wasted their time chasing the innocent Leo, the less chance they had of catching the murderer.

As soon as Frank had finished his statement, Lanford and Beavers asked him if he had any cuts or scratches.

Without a word, Frank rose from his chair, took off his coat, vest, and shirt and showed the police he was unmarked.

"Nothing on him," said Rosser proudly.

"This is the suit I wore Saturday," said Frank. "If I had killed her my clothes would be covered with blood."

"Not necessarily," Lanford said. "Could have changed your shirt and underwear."

"All my shirts are still at home," Frank said.

"Why don't you see if there's any blood on them?" Rosser urged.

Off Frank went accompanied by two detectives as well as Rosser and Haas. It never occurred to Beavers or Lanford that a murderer might not save his bloodied clothes.

This was the only moment since the trip to the mortuary Sunday morning that the police doubted Frank was their man. Rosser had almost succeeded in allaying their suspicions. In fact, while Frank went off with one search party to the Selig home, two other detectives went out to Newt Lee's shack.

Since bloodstains would incriminate the murderer, these policemen took along a home-brewed mixture that they spread by hand on one of Newt Lee's old shirts.

Confronting Lee later with his mysteriously bloodstained shirt, the police listened to Lee say, sobbing, that it was his shirt all right but that he hadn't worn it in a year. A little later, a city chemist told the police department that not only were the stains not blood, but they had been spread by hand.

When Frank reached his home, he had to tell Lucile. She had been all the while unsuspecting of the net her husband felt tightening about him. He had told her he was eager to save the factory from scandal, and she believed this was the reason the police were continuing to claim so much of his time.

"They want to inspect your dirty laundry?" she asked incredulously. (She meant also, "This doesn't happen to nice people.") Lucile Selig Frank did not at that time, nor for a few months thereafter, realize how her every gesture would be construed by the inflamed citizenry of Atlanta. She would perform perfectly innocent actions at her husband's instructions, and these could always be interpreted as signs she knew him to be guilty.

In alarm, she led the police and her husband to the laundry bag in the bedroom. Fate was teaching her its first lesson: its decisions are hard and arbitrary, and there are no appeals. It was all too bewildering. Lucile was a plump Jewish girl who liked to play bridge and who felt proud because her college educated husband was president of the Atlanta B'nai B'rith.

The police officers went through all of Frank's laundry, laying it out on the bed piece by piece, cataloguing each item.

Nothing.

When the two policemen left, Frank knew they were still keeping an eye on him. He told Lucile at their noon-hour dinner, "They are harrassed. It's all a mistake. Not serious enough to keep me from the factory."

She wanted to cry.

Leo said, "Not now. Please. I've got to get to the factory. This whole episode has really broken down our production schedules."

His schedules were far more awry than he suspected, because

when he reached the offices of the National Pencil Company, he
found no one at work.

"The women were hysterical," Darley told him. "We had to
send them home. They weren't getting anything done."

"What made them so frantic?" the surprised Frank asked. No
matter what happened, schedules were important.

Darley explained. A machinist, R. P. Barrett, who operated a
lathe on the second floor, near the women's dressing room, insisted he had found blood spots by his machine as well as five
strands of hair on one of the lathe's handles. The word spread
throughout the factory: here Mary Phagan was murdered.
Barrett had started his search when one of the factory girls told
him Mary had been killed in the metal department of the factory. A few days later Barrett would find a discarded pay envelope and insist this, too, was Mary Phagan's.

At Barrett's lathe, with a flashlight, Frank and Darley examined the discovery. The five blood spots, not one as large as
a fingernail, lay under a white substance called haskoline, a
cleaning compound. Frank bent and scraped at them. Dirt or
oil stains. Microscopic analysis later revealed that only one of
the spots contained blood and only a miniscule amount at
that. By that time, however, Leo Frank was fighting a losing
battle. Today, Monday, April 28, the police would come and
chip away the spots and insist that Mary Phagan had been
killed on the second floor.

This last absurdity, the blood, convinced Frank that he
would have to protect himself. He was frightened. He asked Sig
Montag if the pencil company could hire a private detective to
help assemble and understand what evidence there was. A private detective ought to be able to produce objective data to
dispel what these silly incriminating coincidences portended.

Montag agreed. That afternoon Frank got in touch with the
local Pinkerton Agency, which dispatched Detective Harry Scott
to the factory.

The Atlanta ordinances directed that private detectives work in conjunction with the police, a fact that Frank waved off. He would have done well to have thought about it. Harry Scott, a detective with no better equipment than Starnes or Black, was dependent upon them for all of his information.

Frank should have dismissed him when Scott confessed he hadn't read the papers, that he didn't know what stage the case had reached. Harry Scott thought precisely like the rest of Atlanta, and the rest of Atlanta, reading the papers, thought Leo Frank was the killer.

The first thing Frank told Scott was that Starnes and the other officers suspected him. He wanted to clear his name and absolve the pencil company from any notoriety. Scott proceeded to question him about his movements and actions that Saturday.

Either Frank hurried when he told Scott about his last conversation with Mary Phagan or Scott lied later about what Frank said. When Mary Phagan asked if the brass had come in, Scott testified Leo Frank answered, "I don't know." If Leo Frank had said, "I don't know," there was a chance, in fact a strong probability, that he and Mary Phagan had gone to see if the brass shipment had indeed arrived or not. Frank also told Scott too casually, or Scott lied, about what time Frank had left the building: Scott told the jury Frank left at ten minutes after one, when it was crucial to Frank's defense that the jury believe he left at one o'clock or a little before.

Frank never understood the detective he had engaged. Here was a man whose importance in life was guarding payroll deliveries, catching pilferers, or checking on embezzlements. Suddenly he was hired to track down a murderer; and he wanted to catch a murderer; and he would catch the man the police told him was the murderer because it was easier that way. If Frank did not have enough millstones around his neck, he certainly did after he hired Harry Scott—a millstone he hung upon himself.

On Tuesday morning, Frank was back at his routine, sending out the orders to the different factory departments. The girls were back at work, and the full administrative staff about its duties. The office boy, Alonzo Mann, brought Frank one of the extras that the *Constitution* was constantly publishing. Britt Craig's story on the front page said that Leo Frank would be arrested that day.

Frank had expected as much. He showed no surprise when Detectives Scott and Black arrived and said they needed him at headquarters.

The police station was filled with reporters and photographers, and a gang of the curious had gathered on the front steps to see "the strangler," as the murderer by this time was called. They hissed at Frank as the detectives pulled him in. The police fingerprinted him, stored his wallet and his watch in the police safe, and led him to a cell. He would see daylight again and see different places and know moments of strong, sure hope, but that mob at the steps should have convinced him that his life was forfeit.

Leo Frank knew some hope that midnight. Starnes came to his cell and asked, "Want to talk to Newt Lee? We can't get anything out of him, but you're his boss. Maybe he'll tell you."

Frank would speak to Newt Lee. Frank thought Newt Lee was the killer. No one else had been in the factory that afternoon but Newt Lee. He followed Starnes along the cell block to an office from the other side of which two men brought in the weary Negro. Newt Lee sat in an armchair, and one of the policemen affixed his handcuffs to the bottom of a chair. What a futile errand, thought Frank, looking at the bowed, frightened man. "Newt, you'd better tell them everything you know," he said.

"Look at me, Mr. Frank," Lee said, tears streaming down his cheeks, "handcuffed. Handcuffed all the time."

"Well, they've got me, too," said Frank.

"Before God, I don't know anything," said Lee.

CHAPTER FIVE

"If you do," said Frank, "you'd better tell them or we will both go to hell."

Lee's sobs brought the policemen back. As Starnes led him to his cell, Frank could hear the police badgering Lee, beating, and berating him. Frank resolved he would not talk or cooperate with any of these detectives again.

CHAPTER SIX

LUTHER OTTERBEIN BRICKER was the pastor of the First Christian Church in Bellwood, Georgia; Mary Phagan, one of his parishioners. Thirty years after her death, in a letter to a friend which he allowed published in the *Shane Quarterly* for April 1943,[1] Dr. Bricker remembered the passions which enflamed him and all Atlanta.

His first impression, he says, on learning that Mary had been murdered and that the night watchman, Newt Lee, had been arrested for the crime was that the Negro's life was a poor price for the little girl's.

He continues:

> "But, when the police arrested a Jew, and a Yankee Jew at that, all of the inborn prejudice against the Jews rose up in a feeling of satisfaction, that here would be a victim worthy to pay for the crime.
>
> "From that day on the newspapers were filled with the most awful stories, affidavits and testimonies, which proved the guilt of Leo M. Frank beyond the shadow of a doubt. The police got prostitutes and criminals, on whom they had something, to swear anything and everything they wanted them to swear to. And reading these stories in the

---

[1] Luther Otterbein Bricker, *Shane Quarterly*, April, 1943, Butler University, Indianapolis, Ind.

paper day by day, there was no doubt left in the mind of the general public but that Frank was guilty. And the whole city was in a frenzy. We were all mad crazy, and in a blood frenzy. Frank was brought to trial in mob spirit. One could feel the waves of madness which swept us all.

"Had I been a member of the jury that tried Frank I would have assented to the verdict of guilty, for the jury did exactly as I wanted it to and I applauded the verdict."

Rev. Bricker came to Frank's defense before the lynching, convinced he was innocent, an action which almost lost him his pulpit. No one can understand what happened to Leo Frank, however, unless one can see that though the Reverend Bricker was a brave man, compassionate, filled with pity, yet he spoke with the voice of sin.

The week Leo Frank was arrested, three Negroes were lynched in Georgia for outrages as mild as shooting off a gun while drunk, talking back to a white man, and ogling Sunday school teachers out on a picnic. The curse of the South, its tragedy, is echoed by the Reverend Bricker.

Of course a Negro wasn't worth the game. Rev. Bricker could believe a Negro capable of murder, but he could not believe that punishment of a mere Negro could expiate or atone for a Mary Phagan. Dr. Bricker couldn't believe this because he couldn't bring himself to believe that the passions that bring a Negro to murder are human passions. A Negro was subhuman. No one in the Georgia of 1913 had to bring a Negro to trial to punish him. Lynching was simpler.

The black man intruded across the entire spectrum of Southern life. That intrusion corrupted the South, made it poor, intolerant, and often destroyed its urge toward justice. Atlanta wanted something more than a mere Negro on whom to wreak vengeance.

When Mary Phagan didn't come home that Saturday night, J. W. Coleman, her stepfather, went to Atlanta and waited un-

til the Bijou Theatre let out, hoping that the young girl might
be among the departing audience. Arriving back in Bellwood,
he and the girl's mother tried to allay their anxiety by surmis-
ing Mary had gone to visit her grandmother some miles away,
as she did occasionally. A little before five o'clock, Sunday
morning, Helen Ferguson, a neighbor, ran to the Coleman house
crying that Mary Phagan had been murdered. The Ferguson
girl had a telephone call from her friend, Grace Hicks, who had
identified the body at Bloomfield's.

Long before the detectives called at Leo Frank's home that
Sunday morning, they knew who the dead girl was.

When J. W. Coleman rushed in a neighbor's car to the police
station, early Sunday morning, April 27, he passed the National
Pencil Company. He was in time to see policemen leading a
handcuffed Newt Lee to a wagon. Coleman went on to the mortuary to cry and shake and nod yes, that was his little step-
daughter on the slab. He wanted to kill the man who did this.
So did the mob which had begun gathering at the factory. Although there was more muttering than overt action, the mood
of Atlanta was even at that early hour a lynch mood.

The newspapers encouraged this mood, exploited it, played
upon the murder day after day to please their readers. And in
the end, as the Reverend Bricker so poignantly pleaded, the papers, too, became an oppressive force against the fortune and
the very life of the factory superintendent.

Britt Craig, who had accompanied the police to the factory
to discover the dead girl, broke the story early Sunday in the
Atlanta *Constitution*. It wasn't a big story; it ran a column and
a half. But it was a singularly important story.

For almost ten years Atlanta had agonized over murdered
women. In 1906, the rumor that two white women had been
wantonly murdered by Negroes set off the worst race riot America has ever suffered. Mobs surged through the streets, pulling
innocent Negroes off streetcars and trampling them to death,
invading the Negro section to murder men, women, and chil-

dren. Armed mobs roamed through Atlanta's streets for over a week, breaking into stores to steal the guns. When the National Guard finally restored order, no one had ever found the murdered women.

Then in 1911, the rumors became epidemic again and persisted. Admittedly, there were women murdered, Negro and white women, but not out of racial tensions. And there never were as many murdered as Atlantans insisted.

Britt Craig, however, saw a real woman, ripped and torn by an assailant. Here in the coal cellar was the nightmare. Another woman murdered. Would the police secure a conviction? Britt Craig's editor saw his chance. The *Constitution*'s editorial that Sunday demanded Mary Phagan's killer. On Tuesday, the day Leo Frank was arrested, the *Constitution*'s editorial declared, "The detective force and the entire police authorities of Atlanta are on probation in the detection and arrest of this criminal with proof. To justify the confidence that is placed in them and the relation they are assumed to hold toward law and order, they must locate this arch-murderer. If ever the men who ferret out crime and uphold the law in Atlanta are to justify their function, it must be in apprehending the assailant and murderer of Mary Phagan."

The other newspapers were baying at the police, too. It was not the sort of climate to encourage dispassionate, professional police work. It was just the atmosphere which would pressure the police into mass arrests. Which it did. All in all, the police arrested seven men for the crime before the week was out.

There were three newspapers in Atlanta in 1913: the *Constitution*, the *Journal*, and the *Georgian*, the latter owned by William Randolph Hearst. The *Georgian* was a year old, and Hearst's brand of journalism had not yet captured the readership he wanted. A circulation war between the three tugged at readers. None of the three had achieved supremacy.

But Foster Coates, Hearst's editor, knew little Mary Phagan

would sell newspapers. He never suspected, perhaps, that she would sell newspapers for three solid years, that she would sell at least one book a decade and inspire three movies about her fate; but Foster Coates did know she would sell papers the week of April 29–May 3, 1913.

Henry Adams claimed the Blessed Virgin was a dynamo, engendering love and reverence. The American Virgin, once despoiled, is no less a dynamo, engendering rancor and hate.

Foster Coates had been scooped on Sunday, but he put Mary Phagan on pages one, two, three, and four on Monday, and she was to stay on the front page from April 27 until June 4, a period of thirty-nine days. She moved inside the paper briefly, but re-emerged when Frank's trial started in late July.

"Body Dragged by Cord After Terrific Fight"; . . . "Girl's Grandfather Vows Vengeance"; . . . " 'I Could Trust Mary Anywhere,' Her Weeping Mother Says." These are but three of the headlines that filled the *Georgian* Monday.

"In the room where Mary Phagan was attacked and paid out her young life to the brutality of her assailant, across the floor where her limp form was dragged, down the stairs and down through the trap door into the dirty basement where her body was found" was the kind of reporting guaranteed to bring twenty thousand people to view her body at Bloomfield's Mortuary.

There was also news, for the police had arrested two more suspects by Monday night. One was John M. Gantt. Frank had told the police of Gantt's visit to the factory Saturday afternoon to claim his shoes. In their careening search for any information that would justify an arrest the police and reporters had converged upon Mrs. F. C. Terrell, Gantt's half-sister. They beset her with questions. All the reporters were aping Hearst. They offered her money. To get rid of them Mrs. Terrell said she hadn't seen Gantt at home Saturday and thought he was on his way to California.

Coincidentally, poor Gantt was arrested in Marietta carrying a little sleeping bag. Within a day, Mrs. Terrell recanted, confessing that the police and the reporters had driven her to near-hysteria; besides she was drunk when she told the story. Gantt was innocent. The recantation didn't save Gantt from three bad nights in the jail, plus the annoying and frightening notoriety of a murder charge while the police checked his story.

In their chase for suspects, the police also rounded up an unemployed streetcar conductor named Arthur Mullinax and charged him, too, with Mary Phagan's murder. Mullinax was arrested on the word of one Edgar Sentell, who told police he knew Mary Phagan well and had seen her at 10:00 P.M. as Mullinax's escort near the pencil company.

Both Dr. J. W. Hurt, county physician, and W. H. Gheesling, the mortician, had determined almost at once that Mary Phagan had been dead at least twelve hours before her body was discovered. Yet it would take these careless policemen almost a week before they realized Mary Phagan had never left the factory after she got her pay, that she was dead by one o'clock that Saturday.

Arthur Mullinax had some bad moments, too, though he was able to produce his sweetheart, sixteen-year-old Pearl Robinson, and his landlady, Emma Rutherford, as alibi witnesses. Fortunately for him, too, a streetcar conductor remembered transporting young Mullinax and his girl friend Pearl that Saturday night.

For no reason at all the police also arrested Gordon Bailey, the factory elevator operator, a young colored boy not yet twenty, called "Snowball."

Gordon Bailey could see the rough mill workers gathered sullenly outside the factory. He could sense the prevailing outrage. He could even sense the desperate policemen, goaded by a city fascinated, and in a strange way delighted, by the atrocity. Gordon Bailey, in his cell, could hear the mutterings of the small mob of men who waited all day long outside police headquarters. Being a Negro released from jail in a Southern town is a dangerous business to this day. The police of Atlanta were taking Bailey's life in their hands in 1913.

On Tuesday, of course, the headlines centered on Frank's arrest, the *Georgian* reporting that "the strangler" had been captured and running a retouched picture of Frank, under the caption "Monster." He was shown without glasses, which emphasized the protruding eyeballs, and his lips had been made thicker.

On page four of the *Georgian* that day was a ten-inch story describing the pictures of nudes which decorated the walls of the National Pencil Company. These so-called nudes consisted of a smiling girl adorning a calendar in Frank's office. The *Georgian* reporter went so far as to invent Leo Frank's admission that the factory was a bawdy house: "In a plant of this size where 170 people are employed and among them a large number of girls, it is quite probable that some of them were approached by some of the men working in the shop."

Whether Leo Frank was guilty or not, one of his obvious motivations that moved him from Sunday morning until his trial was his passion to save the reputation of the National Pencil Company. He had hired a Pinkerton detective, he had conferred with Montag Brothers about the possible scandal, and he had worried aloud to his assistants about the notoriety the factory might acquire. He never would have admitted that the men and girls in his employ played fast and loose. In December of 1912, Leo Frank summarily fired one Ed Bourne because he caught him taking a swig of whiskey on the job. It might well be that some amatory adventures were initiated in his factory, but that was because Leo Frank did not know about them. He simply would not have tolerated such conduct. The pencil company was his life.

So the worst thing that can happen to a man under suspicion of murder, the worst thing that can happen to a police force, the worst thing that can happen to duly elected officialdom had happened: the newspapers had taken over. The reporters were competing with the cops, uncovering stories before the detectives, hoarding "scoops," improving on them for their readers. The reporters were no longer in the first row of the audience; they were the stage managers.

Thirteen years later Herbert Asbury, a reporter for the *Georgian* was to tell about the Frank case in an article for H. L. Mencken's *American Mercury*, for January, 1926. In "Hearst Comes to Atlanta" Asbury wrote:

> "Foster Coates [the editor] made a blunder when Frank was accused of the crime and taken to police headquarters. He put an extra on the street, of course—and wrote a banner line for it which said without qualification that the strangler had been arrested! The type was even larger than we used when we tried to convince the citizenry that there was news when there was none. The line was a blunder of the sort that is made every day in newspaper offices, but it had far-reaching consequences. . . ."

The far-reaching consequences were that the *Georgian* set the pace for the *Constitution* and the *Journal*. These two papers tried to keep up. But it was the *Georgian* that first attracted the attention of outsiders. At a board meeting of the American Jewish Committee in May, 1913, a letter from a Southern member was read in which it was charged that, "The *Georgian* has convicted the president of the Atlanta B'nai B'rith without a trial."

Asbury points out that an editor on the *Constitution* and one on the *Journal* were Jews. They were also, for that matter, unaware and irresponsible. Since Hearst was decorating his papers in New York, Chicago, and elsewhere with Happy Passover Greetings, it was only a matter of time until some of these Jewish advertisers told Hearst they were shocked, and the *Georgian* changed its posture, eventually demanding a new trial. By that time, it was too late. By that time Tom Watson was explaining to the Atlantans the reason for the *Georgian*'s change

of heart. He said that William Randolph Hearst was really a
half-Jew, taking his orders from Nathan Straus of R. H. Macy.
The *Georgian* was singularly inept about the Frank case. It
lost this circulation contest, and a few years later, Hearst folded
the sheet. The *Georgian* antagonized the merchants by inflam-
ing the populace. The curious who came to Atlanta spent all
their time reading the extras which followed one another onto
the streets. In 1926, Asbury was still convinced of Frank's guilt.
But that is because he helped assess it. Both the *Georgian* and
the *Constitution* assumed Leo Frank's patent guilt, and though
the *Journal* remained tentative, it invented its own brand of
sensationalism and morbidity.

Each day the reporters added up the rewards offered by the
state, the city, private corporations, and individuals, which
eventually amounted to $4,300. No one ever collected a penny
of it. It was a reward which elicited more perjured testimony
than any ever offered.

Mary Phagan was buried on Tuesday, April 29, in Marietta,
where she was born.

"A thousand persons saw a minister of God raise his hands
to heaven today and heard him call for divine justice. Before
his closed eyes was a little casket, its pure whiteness hidden by
the banks and banks of beautiful flowers. Within the casket lay
the bruised and mutilated body of Mary Phagan, the innocent
young victim of one of Atlanta's blackest and most bestial
crimes," wrote one anonymous newspaperman.

Viewing the coffin and hearing the supplication for vengeance, Mrs. Coleman screamed and fell into the arms of her
husband. Mrs. Lizzie Phagan, Mary Phagan's aunt, also pierced
the air with a shriek and collapsed. W. J. Phagan, the girl's
grandfather, sat with tears streaming down his cheeks. Her
brothers, Benjamin Phagan, a sailor on the battleship *Joshua,*
and Charles comforted Ollie, Mary's sister. The funeral in
Marietta thronged with mill workers and tenant farmers, the

dispossessed of Atlanta. For the next decade there was always a procession of these marginal people through the graveyard to Mary Phagan's grave. To these poor exploited and abused factory hands and farmers, Mary was more than purity outraged. She was a symbol of their own oppression. If they could avenge her, they could avenge themselves.

One can only say of Mary Phagan, "God rest her." In death, sadly enough, she was attended by more concern than any ever thought to show her and other girls in her position.

Mary Phagan's inquest opened Wednesday morning, April 30, at nine o'clock, in the room of the Board of County Commissioners. Paul V. Donehoo, Atlanta's coroner, impaneled a jury of six men, whose purpose was to hear testimony and decide whether those persons under suspicion should be held for grand jury indictment.

Two police officers, Anderson and Brown, were the first witnesses. They had come to the factory to relieve Dobbs, Rogers, Starnes, and Black. Anderson offered a description of how the body was mutilated and told how Britt Craig had entrusted the two notes to him.

Brown's testimony incriminated Newt Lee. Newt Lee had told the officers he had found the body of a white woman, but Brown said determining the girl's color was impossible; she was face down and until he rolled back her stocking he could not tell whether she was white or colored.

While Brown was testifying, Benjamin Phagan, the young seaman, rose in the back of the room. Soundlessly he stared at the sad pile of his sister's clothes which lay indifferently heaped on a chair. As the audience and the witnesses, one by one, began to look at him, he put his hands to his head, uttered a muffled scream, and ran from the room.

Coroner Donehoo called Newt Lee next. Lee swore he had not touched the body. He knew it was a white woman, he declared, because her hair was different from a black woman's.

He said the body was face up when he found it, a confusion
he never resolved. Either he did not remember the position of
Mary Phagan's body when he found it or he did move the body
and worried lest he be punished for touching a white woman
even though she was dead.

Donehoo adjourned the inquest for the noon-hour recess.

In the afternoon, Coroner Donehoo summoned R. P. Barrett,
the mechanic who had found the bloodstains and the strands
of hair, as well as subsequently finding the torn and unidentified
pay envelope. This witness had already announced his can-
didacy for the reward money.

Frank M. Berry, assistant cashier of the Fourth National
Bank, was sworn as a handwriting expert. He told Coroner
Donehoo that his twenty-three years of service as teller more
than qualified him. Handed the murder notes, he rose from
the witness chair and walked to the window, where he held
them to the light. Then he compared them with handwriting
samples the police had taken from Newt Lee and Leo Frank.
Portentously he announced that the two notes bore a slight re-
semblance to Newt Lee's handwriting. (While Berry dramat-
ically displayed his expertise, the *Georgian*, in its eighth extra
of the day, informed the public, "Newt Lee's Guilt Proved.")

Mary Phagan's stepfather, J. W. Coleman, succeeded to the
witness chair. He described his anxiety of Saturday night, his
trip downtown on Sunday morning to identify the body, and
concluded with the observation that "Mary often said things
went on at the factory that were not nice and that some of the
people there tried to get fresh. She told most of those stories to
her mother."

The sensation of the day was the testimony of George Epps,
a boy who came to the inquest barefooted and introduced himself as Mary Phagan's sweetheart.

"How old are you, son?" asked Donehoo.

"Fifteen—going on sixteen."

"Do you work, or go to school?"

"I work at a furniture store. In the afternoon I sell papers."

"Did you know Mary?"

"Yes, sir; I certainly did. We were good friends."

"When did you last see her alive?"

"Saturday morning, just before dinner, when we came to town together on a streetcar."

"Did you arrange to meet her that afternoon?"

"Yes, sir! We were to have met at two o'clock in Elkins and Watson's Drug Store at Five Points. We were going to see the parade and go to the moving picture show."

"When you and Mary were riding to town, did you talk any?"

"We talked a whole lot. She said she was going to the pencil factory to draw the wages due her. She said she didn't have but $1.60 [sic] coming to her, but wanted that mighty bad."

"Did you both get on the car at the same time?"

"No! She was on first. When I got on she motioned for me to come and sit beside her. While we were coming to town she began talking about Mr. Frank. When she would leave the fac- tory on some afternoons, she said, Frank would rush out in front of her and try to flirt with her as she passed. She told me that he had often winked at her and tried to pay her attention. He would look hard and straight at her, she said, and then would smile. She called him Mr. Frank. It happened often, she said."

"How was the subject of Mr. Frank brought up?"

"She told me she wanted me to come down to the factory when she got off as often as I could to escort her home and kinder protect her."

What no one bothered to tell Atlanta was that George Epps was only fourteen; that testimony proved Mary Phagan went to town on the trolley alone and that Epps was later to become Atlanta's legendary liar.

Epps's surprise testimony convinced the *Constitution,* which forthwith accused Frank. And the *Constitution* convinced Atlanta.

This testimony also set Soliciter General Hugh Mason Dorsey to thinking. Wednesday night, after Donehoo had adjourned the inquest until the following day, Hugh Dorsey realized what the Phagan case was: in the words of Charles and Louise Samuels, who wrote one of the definitive studies of the Frank case in *Night Fell on Georgia,*[2] he recognized the chance of a lifetime. If he could convict Leo Frank, there was probably no office in the State to which he could not succeed.

Hugh Mason Dorsey, this April night in 1913, was forty-two years old and had been solicitor general for the Fulton County Court for a little over a year. He had been graduated from the University of Georgia and from the University of Virginia Law School. He was ambitious, smart, and tough. And people usually underestimated him.

The first thing he did was to summon Chief of Police Beavers and Chief of Detectives Lanford to tell them he was taking over the investigation of the case. Since they had just come from a similar session with Mayor James Woodward, they were too exhausted to offer opposition. Next Dorsey asked Coroner Donehoo to postpone the inquest until he could exhume Mary Phagan's body and find out what time Saturday or Sunday she died. Donehoo acceded. Dorsey rounded up two hundred witnesses on Thursday, the greatest number ever sworn for a coroner's inquest in Georgia up to that time. Donehoo swore them in en masse the next afternoon and promptly adjourned.

Dorsey told Atlanta, "The burden of convicting the perpetrator of this horrible crime, whoever he may be, will fall directly on my shoulders, and I don't propose, for that reason, to let the case drift along."

The inquest had so far uncovered certain facts, as the papers

2 Charles and Louise Samuels, *Night Fell on Georgia,* Dell Publishing Co., New York, N.Y., 1956.

were quick to report. It was on Wednesday that Mullinax and Gantt were cleared by witnesses who provided each with unassailable alibis. Regretfully, the police turned them loose while remanding Leo Frank and Newt Lee to the county jail, called ominously the Fulton Tower.

While the papers speculated from Thursday through Monday about new clues, Dorsey started questioning the two hundred witnesses Donehoo had summoned, looking for the ones who would expand on Leo Frank's "degeneracy." Thus Dorsey conceived his strategy. It wasn't an ingenious strategy; Atlanta believed it already.

Joseph Brown, Georgia's outgoing Governor, issued a plea on Sunday, May 4, urging Atlanta's citizens to let the law take its course, promising that the guilty would be punished and the innocent freed. The Governor was alerted to the possibility of a lynching which might lead again to another race riot, and had advised Adj. Gen. J. Van Holt Nash to ready officers and men of the Fifth Regiment, Georgia National Guard. The following day Atlanta's Mayor Woodward issued a statement: "I want to appeal to the people of Atlanta not to be misled by the sensational reports in the newspapers."

On Sunday night, Mary Phagan's grave was opened and an autopsy performed. Dorsey, after consultation with the county physician, was able to tell the police what they should have known all along; that the young girl had probably died within an hour after eating her bread and cabbage. She was dead by 12:30 P.M. Saturday.

The police were still making arrests. They asked authorities in Houston, Texas, to hold Paul Bowen of Georgia. The previous Saturday and Sunday, Bowen had stayed at the St. Jean Hotel in Atlanta, where his next door neighbors heard him muttering over and over again, "Why did I do it?" Bowen was well educated, a boy of good family who had gone to Houston to see a girl. A Texas judge freed him shortly thereafter, by which time, of course, the Atlanta cops had forgotten all about

him. The episode probably pleased Dorsey. It occupied the
police and kept them out of his way.

On Monday, May 5, Donehoo again convened the inquest.

Lemmie Quinn gave his testimony. Quinn, a lean and wiry
country boy, was the foreman of the department Mary Phagan
worked in. He swore he had been in Leo Frank's office that
Saturday noon. "I wanted to see Frank," he told the Coroner.
"I wanted to tell him 'Howdy do.' I knew he would be in the
place. He is always there on Saturdays. It was about twelve
fifteen or twelve twenty when I arrived at the building. I saw
no one out front or as I went upstairs to the office. Frank was
at his desk. He appeared very busy. I stepped in and said, 'Well,
I see you work even on holidays. You can't keep me from coming around the building on Saturdays either. How do you feel?'
He said he was feeling good. He didn't appear agitated or
nervous. I didn't want to disturb him so I left."

Quinn had quite suddenly remembered seeing Frank. When
he stepped in to tell the police about this important visit, he
reported they were annoyed, so annoyed that they kept pepper-
ing questions at him for more than an hour before they let
him go. Chief of Detectives Lanford insisted Quinn had taken
a bribe to testify in Frank's behalf. Quinn announced he would
punch anyone in the nose who said he was bribed, though he
did remember his crucial visit awfully late in the day.

Mr. and Mrs. Selig, Frank's in-laws, testified that Frank had
arrived for luncheon at the time he said he did and that he
departed when he said he did.

Frank was the last witness. He took the stand at 2:15 P.M.
and submitted to Donehoo's questions until 6:15 that night.
He answered precisely and without hesitation, detailing the
movements he made as he had already detailed them to Lanford
and Beavers and as he was to detail them again and again.

After he stepped down, Police Chief Beavers drove Frank
back to the Tower. It is more than possible that Frank did
know now the gravity of his situation. Though insulated in the

Fulton Tower, he must have suspected he was being readied as a scapegoat.

On the day of his arrest, when his wife Lucile rushed to see him at police headquarters, he instructed her not to come until he asked for her. The papers made much of her absence, hinting she knew of his guilt. But it is more reasonable to believe, since she stood by him steadfastly during the trial and afterwards—and for the rest of her life—that she was simply obeying Frank's wishes.

On her solitary visit, when Lucile Frank had to wait three hours to see her husband, the reporters badgered her. Frank's ordering her not to come was to spare her anguish.

On Tuesday, May 6, and Wednesday, May 7, the inquest was again postponed. Dorsey wanted to make a second exhumation of Mary's body, and he was still in the process of winnowing out "good" witnesses from "bad."

Dorsey never explained the reason for this second exhumation. A Bertillon expert, who was supposedly able to identify fingerprints, accompanied Dorsey to the grave and laboratory. The papers speculated that the solicitor general wanted to check the fingerprints on the dead girl's throat.

The Bertillon expert, P. A. Flak, remained only a day and spent his time dusting the murder notes. He told Dorsey that the reporters and police had so manhandled them that he could find nothing.

Just what Dorsey was looking for never became plain until fifty years later when Pierre van Paassen * in his book *To Number Our Days* described his own interest in the Leo Frank case.[3] In a visit to Atlanta in 1922, Van Paassen became interested in the tragedy that befell Leo Frank. It moved him to a study of all the old evidence. Van Paassen had settled himself in the courthouse, reading the records, when he came upon a sheaf

---

* *Who's Who in America.*

[3] Pierre van Paassen, *To Number Our Days*, Charles Scribner's Sons, New York, N.Y., 1964, pp. 237–38.

of papers and a number of X-ray photographs showing teeth indentations. "The murdered girl," says Van Paassen, "had been bitten on the left shoulder and neck before strangulation. The bites were deep enough to leave an impression (a fact no newspaper or police officer reported). Those indentations did not correspond with the X rays of Leo Frank's set of teeth which were what the envelope contained."

It was to check these X rays with the impression on Mary Phagan's shoulder that Dorsey reopened the grave. They didn't check. Dorsey obviously suppressed this. Had he not suppressed it, it is doubtful it would have made any difference. The skids were greased, as the last day of the inquest proved.

Newt Lee and Leo Frank testified again briefly.

By this time, the coroner's jury knew that Newt Lee and Frank had been remanded to the Tower and knew also that Hugh Dorsey was preparing the grand jury. If the six men on the coroner's jury didn't think they had the guilty man in court, they weren't thinking at all.

Frank repeated his story, and Newt Lee his. Donehoo called Pinkerton Detective Harry Scott, who noted darkly, among other things, that he would not commit himself on the evidence he had gathered but it was, he was sure, conclusive.

Detective Black followed Scott. His testimony was as non-committal, but was also filled with menacing hints. The police had a "chain of evidence," he said, which established that Leo Frank was in the factory when Mary Phagan arrived and was attacked. Either Newt Lee or Frank, he went on, was the last man to see her alive. He concluded with the observation that Leo Frank, on arrest, was far more nervous than Newt Lee.

Now for the motive.

Donehoo paraded but three of Dorsey's two hundred witnesses. The first of these was Nellie Pettis, a sister-in-law of one of the girls employed in the factory.

"Do you know Leo Frank?" asked Donehoo.

"I have seen him once or twice."

"When and where did you see him?"

"In his office at the factory when I went to get my sister-in-law's pay."

"What did he say to you that might have been improper on any of these visits?"

"He didn't exactly say—he made gestures. I went to get sister's pay about four weeks ago, and when I went into the office of Mr. Frank I asked for her. He told me I couldn't see her unless I 'saw him' first. I told him I didn't want to 'see him.' He pulled a box from his desk. It had a lot of money in it. He looked at it significantly and then looked at me. When he looked at me, he winked. As he winked, he said, 'How about it?' "

The next witness was Mrs. C. D. Donegan, who two years earlier had worked for three weeks as a factory forelady.

"State your observations of Frank's conduct toward the girls and women of the plant."

"I have noticed him smile and wink at the girls in the place. That was two years ago," Mrs. Donegan replied.

"Did you make a statement to the detectives of the undue familiarity you witnessed?"

"I told them that I had seen Frank flirt with the girls and women—that's all I said."

As this testimony continued, Mr. J. W. Coleman, who had attended every one of the sessions of the inquest, straightened up from his slouch in the corner and fixed his eyes on Frank, who sat attentively behind the coroner. Coleman never took his eyes off that central figure. The intensity of gaze was not only dramatic, but electric. Everyone began to stare at Frank.

Still another ex-employee was called—a Miss Nellie Wood. If the jury had begun to suspect that these witnesses were acting out a grudge against their former employer, Miss Wood confirmed their suspicions by admitting it.

"Do you know Leo Frank?" came the question.

"I worked for him for two days."

"Did you observe any misconduct on his part?"

"Well, his actions didn't suit me. He'd come around and put his hands on me when such conduct was entirely uncalled for."

"Is that all he did?"

"No. He asked me one day to come into his office, saying that he wanted to talk to me. He tried to close the door, but I wouldn't let him. He got too familiar by getting so close to me. He also put his hands on me."

"Where did he put his hands?"

"He barely touched my breast. He was subtle with his approaches and tried to pretend that he was joking, but I was too wary for such as that."

Tom Blackstock was the last of these witnesses. He was an employee of the National Pencil Company, hired six weeks before the murder.

"Do you know Leo M. Frank?"

"Yes."

"How long have you known him?"

"About six weeks."

"Did you ever observe his conduct toward female employees of the factory?"

"Yes, I've often seen him picking on various girls."

"Name some."

"I can't exactly recollect names."

"What was the conduct you noticed particularly?"

"I saw him feel the girls."

"See it often?"

"A half-dozen times, maybe. He generally was seen to become familiar while he was touring the building."

"Can't you name just one girl?"

"Yes. Magnolia Kennedy."

"Did you see him act with undue familiarity toward her?"

"No. I heard talk about it."

"Before or after the murder?"

"Afterwards."

"When did you observe this misconduct of which you have told?"

"Sometime ago."

"Did you hear complaints around the plant?"

"No, the girls tried to avoid him."

At 6:30 P.M., the jury went into executive session to hear the testimony of Dr. J. W. Hurt, county physician, on the specific causes of Mary Phagan's death. The doctor talked for twenty minutes.

Donehoo convened the witnesses to hear the jury findings:

> "We, the coroner's jury, empaneled and sworn by Paul Donehoo, coroner of Fulton County, to inquire into the death of Mary Phagan, whose dead body now lies before us, after having heard the evidence of sworn witnesses, and the statement of Dr. J. W. Hurt, County Physician, find that the deceased came to her death from strangulation. We recommend that Leo M. Frank and Newt Lee be held under charges of murder for further investigation by the Fulton County grand jury.
> (signed)
> HOMER C. ASHFORD—FOREMAN
> DR. J. W. HURT—
> COUNTY PHYSICIAN"

J. W. Coleman moved from his corner and approached the jury box. With a tremulous hand, tears streaming down his face, he went from juror to juror, shaking hands with each and murmuring words of gratitude.

Luther Z. Rosser, Frank's attorney, watched the process and scoffed. Dorsey had tenuous evidence with which to argue for indictment. Frank had been in the factory when Mary Phagan came to get her pay, a fact he admitted. Perhaps Frank was a lecher, a fact he would stoutly deny. But neither of these seemed sufficient reasons for a grand jury to vote an indictment.

What Luther Rosser didn't know was that Hugh Dorsey had

an ace up his sleeve. The police had found a material witness whose testimony was enough to guarantee an indictment. More than that—a fact which even Hugh Dorsey didn't yet know— the police had arrested another suspect, who would guarantee that Frank would be convicted. The material witness was Monteen Stover, and the suspect was Jim Conley.

CHAPTER SEVEN

WHEN HUGH DORSEY began manipulating the Frank case, he hired his own detectives. They worked for him ten days and quietly withdrew. While none of them found any clues, a clue found one of them, a clue worth its weight in gold.

Dorsey stationed several detectives in the offices of the National Pencil Company. A week after Mary Phagan's murder, on Saturday, May 3, fourteen-year old Monteen Stover went to the factory to collect her pay. She was accompanied by her mother, a divorcee and boardinghouse keeper named Mrs. Homer Edmondson.

Dorsey's sentinel asked the woman what she wanted, and Monteen explained that she had come to the pencil company Saturday a week ago for her money but Mr. Frank wasn't in his office. No one—not Leo Frank, not Lemmie Quinn, not Hattie Hall—had ever mentioned Monteen Stover's appearance.

"What time did you come?" asked the detective.

"A few minutes after twelve," answered Monteen.

The detective rushed her and Mrs. Edmondson not to the police station but to Hugh Dorsey's offices.

Dorsey had the flaw he needed to break down Frank's story. He spent the afternoon patiently helping Monteen and her mother reconstruct her precise actions that last Saturday.

He dispatched Pinkerton detective Harry Scott, the Pinkerton Leo Frank had hired, with Detective John Black to the

Fulton Tower. They went directly to Frank's cell. The wily Scott told his client, "I've insisted to both Chief Beavers and Chief Lanford that you never left the factory that Saturday noon until you went home for dinner."

"That's right," said Frank.

"You were there from noon until you locked up at one o'clock?" asked Black. "You didn't go outside or anything?"

"No, I didn't," answered Frank.

"Think about it and be as positive as you can," said Scott. Frank composed himself and, being sure that he was in the company of an ally, said dogmatically, "I am absolutely certain I didn't leave my office from the time Miss Hall, my stenographer, left until I went up to the fourth floor to tell Arthur White's wife that I was going to lock the building." Leo Frank was a man who always ruled out doubt. Had he been a little flexible he might never have seen the inside of the Fulton Tower in the first place.

Scott and Detective Black rushed back to an exultant Dorsey. Dorsey punched his hand with his fist and said, "I've got him."

He was more than careful with how he got him. He did not let Monteen Stover release the statement she had signed to the press nor did he subpoena her testimony for the inquest. He wanted Leo Frank to have no chance to reconsider his story. He did not want to alert Frank's lawyers to the need for an alibi until Frank's statement was a matter of public record.

Harry Scott, however, couldn't keep quiet. He told reporters on Sunday that he had collected enough evidence to convict the murderer of Mary Phagan. Asked what it was, Scott said it was information supplied by "a girl who has not heretofore figured even in speculation in the case. The new card will not be played until the trial." Among the other opinions he was to offer throughout the case was his judgment that if Leo Frank was not convicted the Pinkertons were through forever in Atlanta.

Dorsey said nothing publicly to confirm Scott's story, though he did confide to an assistant, "I ask for men and they send me clowns."

Once the coroner's inquest held Frank and Newt Lee for grand jury action, Dorsey released the story, explaining that Monteen Stover had worked at the factory for a year. With news of the murder Monteen quit and she had her last week's pay coming to her.

Monteen Stover said, "I went to the pencil factory that Saturday to draw my pay. The front door and the door leading to the second floor were unlocked. The whole place was awfully quiet and kinder scary as I went up the steps."

"The minute I got to the office I looked at the clock to see if it was time to draw my pay. I would have looked at it anyhow, I suppose, as it was always customary for me to punch it the first thing upon entering the place to go to work.

"It was five minutes after twelve. I was sure Mr. Frank would be in his office so I stepped into the inner one. He wasn't there either. I thought he might have been somewhere around the building so I waited. When he didn't show up in a few minutes I went to the door and tried to see if he was in the shop. I couldn't see him there.

"I stayed until the clock hand was pointing exactly to ten minutes after twelve. Then I went downstairs. The building was quiet, and I couldn't hear a sound. I didn't see anybody. As I walked from the building out to the street I saw four young boys standing close to the entrance. When I first came into the place, they were standing on the corner of Forsyth and Hunter Streets. They were only young boys."

Monteen's mother, Mrs. Edmondson, elaborated on the story. She confided to a group of newsmen that it was unfortunate they had found out about her little Monteen. "The Solicitor General is anxious about my girl. He wants her testimony a secret."

Parenthetically, Monteen added that Mr. Frank was popular with his employees, and that she herself thought he was personally kind.

This statement, of course, was the worst news Frank and his defense attorneys could hear. They knew by now that Dorsey was quickly impaneling a grand jury, and the prospect frightened them. At this point they were hopeful that the grand jury would indict Newt Lee, for they were positive of Frank's innocence. If Frank and his defense attorneys, Luther Rosser, Reuben Arnold, and Herbert and Leonard Haas had but guessed how unassailable Monteen Stover's story was ultimately to prove, they would have been even more frightened than they were.

When Solicitor Dorsey notified all the pencil company employees that they would be sworn for testimony for the coroner's inquest that Thursday, May 1, the net finally fished up Jim Conley.

Conley was a chunky, ginger-colored Negro, twenty-seven years old, who worked as a sweeper at the factory. He was occasionally a mean drunk. Police, checking later, discovered he had served time on the road gang and had been arrested often for drunkenness and disorderly conduct.

An anonymous employee, coming up from the factory's cellar on May 1, saw Conley washing his shirt at the solitary faucet.

The machinist wondered if that was blood Conley was washing out and confided his suspicions to the police by telephone. It was near one o'clock, when Black and Scott arrived and found Conley with the shirt still damp on his back.

"You're coming with us," said Black.

"Boss, I haven't done anything," said Conley.

"You were just seen washing Mary Phagan's blood off your shirt."

"That wasn't blood. That was dirt."

"Why were you washing it off this time of day?"

"They done called me for a witness at the court, and I didn't want to go around all those white people in a dirty shirt." It was the last reasonable alibi Jim Conley was to invent.

The stains in Conley's shirt were rust. The police followed the usual procedure they followed with all the suspects in the case: they asked him for a specimen of his handwriting.

"Boss," Conley laughed, "I can't write."

"Can you read?"

"No sir."

Then, of course, he couldn't have written the murder notes. Rather than let him go, the police kept him in his cell, just as they kept Newt Lee in a cell until the day Leo Frank was convicted. Southern policemen kept Negroes under lock and key as long as they chose.

In fact, the Atlanta police literally forgot they had Jim Conley in custody. There was no reason to be concerned about him because he hadn't been around the factory that April 26th. He'd been drunk, he said. No one bothered to check out the story; it wasn't that they believed Conley, it was just that it was embarrassing to invade the Negro saloons. Atlanta was a dry city in 1913. Prohibition had come through the local option law some ten years before. It was no secret, however, that saloons proliferated throughout the Negro ghettoes, and that all the saloon keepers bribed the police for sufferance.

But the police should have checked his story, for several employees of the factory had already suggested that Jim Conley was mixed up in this crime.

Mary Pirk, a factory girl, accused Jim Conley of Mary's murder on the Monday after it happened, and told the grand jury this when Frank's lawyers called her. She was followed by Mrs. E. M. Carson who swore she had told Conley he was lucky he wasn't yet in jail. And when she insisted she knew Leo Frank had never committed such a crime, Conley agreed that Mr. Frank was innocent.

Iora Small, another defense witness, recounted that her suspicions were aroused when Conley declared that he *knew* Mr. Frank was innocent while trying to borrow money from her to buy newspapers.

None of these, however, told the police Conley was a bad actor, generally disliked, sometimes feared. The only one who told the police anything about Jim Conley was Leo Frank. Leo Frank told them Conley could indeed write.

When Leo Gottheimer, a salesman for Montag Brothers and the pencil company visited him in the Tower with the news one morning that Conley denied he was literate, Frank said: "But I know he can write. I have received notes from him asking me to lend him money. In the drawer in my safe, you will find the card of a jeweler from whom Conley bought a watch on the installment plan and you will find Conley's signed receipt. He can write."

The police did find this evidence. It bemused them, for by this time everybody in Atlanta was playing a role. The play-acting blinded justice. Edgar Sentell, accusing the innocent Arthur Mullinax, was playing a role, and so was Monteen Stover, pirouetting before the reporters in a beautiful flash of publicity. Hugh Dorsey, the police officials, the editors, each was enacting his role. Even Leo Frank, whom the papers were beginning to call "The Silent Man of the Tower," was playing a role. But no one played so dramatic a role and played it so self-consciously and successfully as Jim Conley, semiliterate Negro though he was. As one of Hugh Dorsey's staff remarked, "Conley was as sophisticated as Satan himself."

CHAPTER EIGHT

EVERY DAY one hundred and more Georgians went to the Fulton Tower and asked admission to see "the strangler, Frank." The guards told them no. The visitors asked: How did Frank look? Did he rage in the afternoon? Did he cry out confessions? Could they bribe their way upstairs for a quick look?

When the guards turned them away, these Georgians milled about the Tower, seeking some vantage point from which they could catch a brief glimpse of Leo Frank, the monster.

Frank was jailed in the Tower itself, in Cell 2 in the south corridor. His cell was equipped with a cot suspended by chains from the wall, a long wooden table which also served as a bench, and a slop bucket.

The guards woke the prisoners at seven. Frank left his cell and emptied his bucket. He wore the business suit in which he had been arrested, although friends saw to it he had a change of shirts and underwear. Daily he refused to give newspaper interviews, and daily he told Solicitor General Dorsey he had no further statements. Dorsey kept asking.

In the morning, a guard gave Frank a razor and stood by while he shaved. Frank was allowed one privilege—home-cooked meals. These he ate punctually, sitting on his cot and spooning the food from the expensive pots Lucile had purchased. One of the things the guards told the curious was that prison life was not affecting Leo Frank's appetite.

Most of the morning Frank spent reading the daily papers, particularly attentive to the developments of his own case. No guard ever remembered hearing Frank make a comment. He took all the news into that reservoir of rigidity and there it stayed. Even Leonard Haas, one of his defense lawyers, said recently, in 1964, that he had heard only one comment escape Frank about his predicament. That was an involuntary gasp before his trial as he asked incredulously, "Do you really think they can pin this crime on an innocent man?"

Just before 9:00 o'clock every morning, Leo Gottheimer arrived. When Frank was arrested, the Montags asked Gottheimer to fill in as the superintendent at the factory. Sheriff Wheeler Mangum let Gottheimer and Frank talk about business for one hour every day.

Gottheimer remembers that Frank worried incessantly about the adverse publicity and how it affected the fortunes of the National Pencil Company. "Has it hurt us much?" "Were there any cancellations yesterday?" He was always crestfallen when he was told that his notoriety, as well as his absence, had indeed hurt business.

Later in the morning the lawyers would come, and until 2:00 P.M. Frank and they would plan strategy. Frank would then eat a large dinner. Sometimes he played chess with friends in the afternoon. Then a light supper at six-thirty. He would read until eleven.

The single electric lamp that burned in the jail corridor did not give much light for reading. Frank had a candle, which he extinguished as soon as he finished the news.

Lucile Frank, who had visited him the first day, did not return to the Tower until May 12. Frank told his lawyers he didn't want her to see him behind bars. He lived with the false hope that somehow this mistake would be cleared up in "a couple of days." Finally, when he was faced with the ordeal of being tried for murder, he asked to see Lucile.

Sheriff Mangum let them meet in the consultation room, two

floors below Frank's cell. Lucile was a plain woman, overweight, but vivacious. She embraced and kissed him, and Frank spent the rest of the hour trying to comfort her.

Dorsey later charged that Lucile Frank's not coming to the Tower was an admission that she recognized her husband's guilt.* She loved him—and loved him as only a Jewish girl, circa 1913, could love a husband who was a Cornell graduate and who at age 29 was superintendent of a large factory and president of the Atlanta B'nai B'rith.

Frank was composed as he awaited the grand jury. Perhaps Atlanta might have composed itself if the newspapers and police hadn't exploited the nonsense every crackpot offered.

Robert House, a former policeman for a real estate company, came forward to charge he had shadowed Leo Frank and a young lady into a deserted area some weeks before the murder. Once discovered, Frank promised to leave if not arrested. House swore he had been to the Fulton Tower and positively identified the prisoner.

Two witnesses appeared separately at police headquarters, both claiming to have seen Mary Phagan at different places that April Saturday being abducted by a band of men. Another young woman, who refused to reveal her name, swore that when she passed the factory at four-thirty on April 26, she heard screams coming from the basement. "It was three shrill screams," she said, "that died away as though they had been stifled."

Two Southern ladies dreamed about the murder and distinctly re-created these dreams to the attentive police, each giving a detailed description of Mary's assailant. That neither of these dreams had any common content didn't bother the po-

---

* Hugh Dorsey was taking advantage of every angle. As a prosecutor he must have known better. Most first offenders tell their wives (or mothers) not to come and "see me like this." The author knows of one instance, for example, where the wife disregarded her husband's instructions and visited the jail anyway, and the husband refused to leave his cell and go to the visiting room.

lice. They handed out the news to the reporters, who promptly composed colorful headlines.

The lunatic fringe, of course, is always about its own amusements. Once it gains privilege, however, it can do irreparable damage. Colonel Thomas E. Felder hurt Frank's cause. Felder was an Episcopalian whose rank of colonel was self-conferred. He was a prominent figure in Atlanta, a partner in the law firm of Felder, Anderson, Dillon and Whitman.

The year before, Thomas Felder had trapped Cole Blease, the Governor of South Carolina, into damaging admissions about financial juggling over state contracts. Felder had invited Blease to a hotel room, wired so that listeners in another suite could overhear and record the conversation by dictograph. The scandal was embarrassing, if not politically effective, but it made Felder famous as an undercover man.

Felder thought the Frank case fitted his talents. His attitudes toward Leo Frank were ambivalent; it is doubtful he cared about Frank's predicament one way or another. Felder was motivated by a hunger for publicity, and inept as he was to prove himself, he saw a chance to make some quick money as well. He decided to set himself up as a citizen's committee pledged to clearing up the Mary Phagan mystery.

First he dispatched an emissary to Mary Phagan's stepfather, John W. Coleman. Did Mr. Coleman and the Phagan family want help from Atlanta's famous Colonel Felder? Coleman replied that he didn't, but Felder was persistent. He approached Coleman himself.

"I want you to hire me," he said, "to conduct an investigation to assist the state."

"Hire you?" the astounded Coleman asked.

"It will not cost you one red cent," Felder said. "But I will need your name to give my committee some authority."

Coleman said: "I think the police have the murderer right now. I'd thank you to keep your hands off."

This refusal didn't deter Felder. He could do without Mr.

Coleman easily enough. He needed some compliant citizens, whom he found in Mary Phagan's home community of Bellwood. His committee consisted of two men, both of whom were insignificant: one was G. H. Bradley and the other was A. C. McCall, neither of whom knew what Felder was about nor what they were about in sponsoring him.

The committee formed, Felder made a public announcement on May 2: "Thomas B. Felder has been engaged to assist the Solicitor General in the prosecution of the Phagan murderer. He was retained yesterday by a committee of citizens from Bellwood, the community in which the dead girl lived. The counsel fund has been subscribed by residents. Mr. Felder said last night to a reporter for the *Constitution* that within a day or so he would be abundantly supplied with convincing evidence. He already has started a private investigation, he said, but would not divulge its form. He would not discuss the rumor that the William J. Burns Detective Agency has been employed."

The rumor, so called, was started by Felder himself. William J. Burns enjoyed an international reputation, and hiring him was just the sort of a cause to which some of the Jews of Atlanta would subscribe.

Joseph Hirsch, a former alderman and for many years chairman of the Grady Hospital Board, was the first contributor. Six other anonymous businessmen pledged funds, and their wives promised to raise money. Their "vested interest" was the burden of history—the identification of all Jews with the delinquency of one of their members. Besides, there were many other Jews and non-Jews in Atlanta who though they may not have been convinced of Frank's innocence, wanted him to have every chance to clear himself in a fair trial.

But all Felder succeeded in doing was aggravating the open sore of anti-Semitism. Promising to bring William J. Burns to Atlanta convinced the rednecks that the Jews were trying to buy Frank's freedom. The Atlanta newspapers published rumors that the grand jury would never indict Leo Frank because the

Jews had already bribed all of them. This suspicion that an
organized Jewry was behind Frank persisted all through his
trial, and through his several appeals, and eventually it was to
impugn the honor of Governor John Slaton.

Anti-Semitism wasn't the only nerve Felder exposed. His activities brought him close to the police, and it wasn't long before he was aware of their internal bickering and their wide-
spread corruption. Felder learned that Beavers and Lanford
kept a list in their safe with the names of all the whorehouses
and blind-tiger saloons that paid protection. Promptly he be-
took himself to Mayor James Woodward and confided his suspicions. Mayors are perennially worried about vice and fearful
that a vice scandal will shake them out of office. Woodward
was no exception. "Get the evidence," he told Felder. "Bring
it to me."

Felder decided to get what he wanted with a bribe. He hired
an unsavory character, one A. S. Colyar, who was later instru-
mental in rounding up witnesses for Hugh Dorsey, and told
him to offer G. S. February, Lanford's male secretary, one
thousand dollars for the files from the police safe.

February said he was interested. Felder personally repeated
the offer in Room 31 of the Williams House on North Forsyth
Street. In the next room was a stenographer transcribing the
conversation through earphones. Beside the stenographer were
Beavers and Lanford, trapping Felder precisely the way Felder
had trapped Governor Cole Blease of South Carolina. A. S.
Colyar was their man, not Felder's.

Not only did Mr. February come to Room 31, but Mayor
Woodward and other elected officials of his administration, all
eager to promise February immunity.

Assured of success, Felder thought he would clean his own
skirts. Along with the whorehouse file, he asked February to
steal the deposition J. W. Coleman had given to the police
swearing he had never hired Felder.

This was a natural for Beavers and Lanford. Any development in the Frank case was news. They released the entire transcript to the Atlanta *Journal* charging that Felder was trying to free Frank by bribery.

Felder had been booby trapped. He responded with a cry of outrage. In turn, he charged the police with shielding Frank. To preserve his damaged reputation, Felder began making anti-Frank speeches. The issue of police corruption had been forgotten, happily for Lanford and Beavers. They were even rid of the William J. Burns agent, C. W. Tobie, who went back to New York after stating that this "was a hell of a family row and no place for a stranger." At the grand jury hearings, Felder and Lanford were to come to near blows in the court. So irresponsible were the conflicting charges they hurled at each other that a subsequent grand jury indicted them both for criminal libel.

What hurt Leo Frank was that the police, to rebut the charge they were shielding Frank, started to fabricate stories about his guilt.

Chiefs Lanford and Beavers were under pressure. They had to deal with the charges made by a charlatan—always hard charges to rebut since charlatans can neither be humored nor ridiculed. Hugh Dorsey had also invaded their domain. He was sharper than either Lanford or Beavers, with a better flair for personal publicity. Beavers and Lanford knew they were supposed to solve Atlanta's mystery of the decade, the murder of Mary Phagan, and the public was beginning to suspect they couldn't. So they set out to prove how smart they really were.

They drafted a whorehouse madam and had her make a statement that Leo Frank sought refuge in her brothel that April 26.

Her name was Nina Formby, or Mima Faby, or Nina Fomby. Like many whores she had a constitutional incapacity for telling

the truth even about her own name. The papers never quite
reached any consistent spelling. She was fat and tasteless and
probably mindless.

Beavers and Lanford produced her statement on Friday,
May 23, claiming she had given it to them two weeks before.

Her affidavit alleged that while she was playing bridge with
friends on the afternoon of Saturday, April 26, she received the
first of many telephone calls from Leo Frank. He said he wanted
to rent a room for himself and a girl. Mrs. Formby refused.
Frank persisted.

"He said he was forced to obtain a room for him and the
girl," Mrs. Formby's affidavit went on. "He said he didn't want
to go elsewhere because he put such implicit trust in me."

She said he called back shortly pleading this was a case of
life and death—the girl was unconscious and he needed a place
where he could revive her; and that he called her at least half a
dozen times until 10:30 P.M., when she went "automobiling"
with friends.

When she talked to the reporters she embroidered on this
story telling them that Frank had been a frequent customer of
hers when she had lived at 87 Armstrong Street; that a great
deal of money had been offered her to leave Atlanta until the
Frank case was through the courts; that she had visited Frank
in the Tower shortly after his arrest.

The wonder is that the public listened to her at all. Her
statement was desperately suspicious. What whore would dare
tell a policeman she was playing bridge on a Saturday afternoon? Moreover, there had been several guests at the Selig's
home that Saturday night who immediately came forward to
say Frank made no telephone calls that evening. (This was
much later in the evening of course—after Frank had called
Newt Lee.)

When some of the reporters began probing, Lanford tried
reinforcing Mrs. Formby's already incredible charge. "The intent," said Lanford, "was to carry the girl to Mrs. Formby's

apartment so that she could be restored to consciousness in surroundings which would not excite suspicion. The assault attempt had already been made, and Mary Phagan had been rendered insensible by the blow she'd received from the fall against the lathing machine. I believe that all the while Mrs. Formby was being telephoned, the unconscious girl was lying hidden in some part of the pencil factory, oblivious to everything, awaiting the terrible death which befell her. Mrs. Formby's statement is to the effect that Frank persisted desperately in an attempt to obtain a room and even went so far as to say it was a matter of life and death. When it was seen that the woman would not rent him a room in her apartment and the girl could not be removed to a place where she could be revived without creating suspicion, it was absolutely necessary to dispose of her. 'Dead folks tell no tales . . . !' "

To a reporter who asked why in the world Frank would want to carry a dead girl through Atlanta's streets, Lanford replied that Frank didn't know the girl was dead yet.

If the prosecution had had to depend upon the Formby story, very probably the defense would have shredded it. Leo Frank was an able-bodied male and if he knew one whorehouse, he knew others. But the police never bothered to check with the other madams; or if they did check, they found nothing to substantiate Mrs. Formby's story.

Mrs. Formby probably owed the police a favor. Very probably she had little choice when the police told her what they wanted her to do. Since all madams despise public attention, there is little likelihood that she volunteered the story.

But the story that Lanford and Beavers released in the *Constitution* was, in one respect, irretractable. Among the other charges Mrs. Formby leveled at Frank was the charge that he was a pervert. She did not enlarge on this, but that is why so many hundreds of Georgians came to the Tower. Mrs. Formby's allegation—"pervert" was precisely the charge the rednecks wanted to hear about the monster in the Tower. "Lascivious

Sodomite," Tom Watson was to call him, and many of his readers wallowed in their sexual phantasies. For the next two years that story took precedence over all the other charges against Frank. The labels "Yankee," "exploiter," "capitalist," "Jew," were joined by "pervert."

In the end, of course, the prosecution didn't need Mrs. Formby, who even before preparation for the trial got under way, had already publicly repudiated her affidavit. The police were happy to drop her. But she had put an incipient idea into the mind of Hugh Dorsey. Dorsey didn't bring that idea to fruition right away, because on the day that Chief Newport Lanford released Mrs. Formby's story, everybody learned Jim Conley could write.

CHAPTER NINE

THE POLICE finally took a statement from Jim Conley on May 19. "My full name is James Conley," he said. "Reside 72 Rhodes Street with Lorine Jones. This woman is not my wife." He went on to describe how long he had worked at the National Pencil Company and what his duties there were. "On Saturday, April 26, at 10:30 A.M. left my house and visited a number of saloons between Fair and Peters and Haynes and Peters Street. I arrived home at 2:30 P.M. and found L. Jones there. She asked me if I had any money. Gave her $3.50. I remained home all Saturday night, at noon Sunday, walked up Mitchell Street and got a cigarette. And returned home, remaining until 6:30 P.M. when I went to my mother's house and then returned home and remained at home until Monday. On April 28 reported for work at the pencil factory at 7:05 A.M."

On May 23, Detectives Starnes, Black, and Harry Scott went to Conley's cell and showed him the IOU's and requests for loans he had written.

"White folks," said Conley, "I'm a liar."

"Why did you lie?"

"I wasn't near that factory once that whole Saturday. But I thought if I told you I could write, you'd put that murder on me. I told you where I was. You ask that man didn't I buy a pint of whiskey from him."

Starnes took a sample of Conley's handwriting, making him

copy out the text of the murder note. Even to his untrained eye
there was a clear similarity. The detectives grilled him, taking
turns in asking questions and beating him, but he stuck to his
story. Sometime Saturday, May 24, he broke. "Mr. Detective,"
Conley said to Black, "I did write those notes. This is the truth.
I wrote those notes because Mr. Frank asked me to."

Elated, Black called for a police stenographer. "Go ahead,
go ahead," he said to Conley.

"Friday, about three o'clock   . . ."

"You mean Saturday," interrupted Black.

"No," said Conley, "Friday. Friday was the day."

Black acquiesced. Conley dictated the following statement
which he signed on May 24:

"On Friday evening before the holiday, about four minutes to one o'clock, Mr. Frank come up the aisle and asked
me to come to his office. That was the aisle on the fourth
floor where I was working and when I went down to the
office he asked me could I write and I told him yes I could
write a little. He gave me a scratch pad and told me what
to put on it, and told me to put on there, 'dear mother,
a long tall black Negro did this by himself.' And he told
me to write it two or three times. I wrote it on a white
scratch pad, single ruled. He went to his desk and pulled
out another scratch pad, a brown looking scratch pad and
looked at my writing and wrote on that himself. . . . He
pulled out a box of cigarettes that cost 15¢ and in that
box he had $2.50 . . . and he said that was all right, I was
welcome to [them] for I was a good working Negro around
there. And he asked me if I knew the night watchman and
I said no sir, I didn't know him and he asked me if I ever
saw him in the basement and I told him no sir, I never did
see him down there. . . . When I asked him not to take
out any money for the watch [sales] man he said you ought
not to buy any watch, for that big fat wife of mine wants

me to buy her an automobile but he wouldn't do it. I never did see his wife. . . ."

Beavers and Lanford could not contain themselves. They tumbled into a police car and went over to Dorsey's office. They were both sure now they had the upper hand on the solicitor general, for Dorsey was terribly worried about convincing a jury Leo Frank had written the murder notes. Beavers and Lanford thought they had solved the case.

Hugh Dorsey was a man of iron control and absolute dedication, never a man to lose his temper. As he read Conley's statement and looked into the faces of these two unthinking policemen, his fists must have shaken and his voice cracked.

"You fools! You silly fools!"

"What's the matter?" asked the incredulous Lanford.

"I am going to have to prove to a jury," explained Dorsey, "that Leo Frank wrote those murder notes when he killed Mary Phagan after an unsuccessful sexual assault. You come over here with a statement that he dictated the notes on Friday. No one in this town will ever believe this was a premeditated murder. He premeditated *the rape*. When the girl struggled, he killed her."

"Oh," said Beavers.

"Not only do you cook up this foolish statement," shouted Dorsey, "but you cook it up when you have that Formby whore out on the streets telling everybody Frank wanted to trundle Mary Phagan up to her crib. Between the Formby woman and Jim Conley, one's got to be lying. They just don't fit together. You tell me how a grand jury will indict Frank this afternoon if they get wind of this statement."

"We better keep it quiet then?" asked the crestfallen Beavers.

"That's right, you better keep it quiet," said Hugh Dorsey. They knew he meant it.

Dorsey had spent that very morning trying to persuade the grand jury to hand down an indictment for murder against Leo

Frank. The grand jury started hearing testimony on Friday and adjourned after Dr. Hurt, several policemen, and the *Constitution*'s reporter, Britt Craig, testified. This Saturday morning, May 24, Monteen Stover had offered her testimony, John Gantt his, and police officers theirs that Frank was exceedingly nervous all day Saturday and Sunday.

By two o'clock Dorsey had the indictment. It had almost eluded him. The police in their clumsy way let the reporters in on the Conley affidavit. Frank was indicted before the news raced all over Atlanta. The grand jury returned a bill against him but took no action on Newt Lee, who remained a prisoner in the Tower. (Under Georgia Law, it took two "no true bills" to free a suspect.)

Conley's "confession" caused a sensation. Dorsey's attempt to keep that confession quiet compounded it. The solicitor general was uncomfortably pressed by subsequent grand juries as he tried to keep Jim Conley off the stand.

"We have Jim Conley locked up," he told one jury. "He has no more chance of escaping now than he would have if charged with murder. No bond is big enough to get him out of jail. Frank is already indicted, and I am firm in my conviction that he is guilty of the crime. If I am wrong a jury of twelve men will not convict him. Then there will be plenty of time to talk about indicting Jim Conley."

Several of the grand jurors were determined, however. Dorsey had to continue his protests against their demands that he produce Conley. "I am absolutely certain that an indictment of Conley can do no good, and it may cause a miscarriage of justice. In addition, I promise you this: if I remain solicitor general, Frank will go to trial before Conley."

He held his breath while the grand jury secretly took a vote on the advisability of demanding that evidence against Conley be brought before them. Dorsey knew he could never manipulate an indictment against Frank if the ill-behaved Conley were indicted. Somehow he could manage Conley's testimony as a state's witness, but he could manage nothing if he had to prosecute him. Moreover, Dorsey knew that the testimony of an accomplice to a murder demanded corroboration; he wanted Conley as a state's witness, not as an accomplice.

The grand jury obeyed him, but not with universal enthusiasm. One member immediately went before the Superior Court and resigned, charging the jury had been prejudiced. In fact, before Frank came to trial, another grand jury, led by its foreman, W. D. Beattie, called a meeting to consider the Conley affidavits. Dorsey had another fight and again, unfortunately for Frank, he won.

Managing Conley's story was not so easy as Dorsey anticipated. To all appearances, James Conley was simply a semiliterate Negro roustabout. But he was more, much more. Conley was alert, canny, filled with guile, a complex entity. He also possessed the finely developed defenses Negroes must have to cope with the hostile white society, defenses few white men understand and fewer penetrate. Conley was a Negro living in Atlanta, Georgia, in 1913, and he knew precisely with whom he was dealing, and he knew precisely what they wanted to hear.

Dorsey kept after the police to get a more reasonable statement from Jim Conley.

The police made Conley's second statement public on May 28. "I make this statement, my second statement, in regard to the murder of Mary Phagan. I made the statement that I went to the pencil factory on Friday, April 25, and went to Frank's office at four minutes to one, which is a mistake. I made this statement in order that I might not be accused of knowing anything about this murder, for I thought if I put myself there on Saturday, they might accuse me of having a hand in it."

He delivered himself of a closely detailed five-thousand-word summation of what he had done that Saturday. On his way to the Butt-In Saloon, Conley said, he met Leo Frank, who was going to the Montags. Frank asked him to come back to the factory and there had asked him to hide beneath the front steps.

He was to stay there until Frank whistled from the second floor.*
He described the workmen and factory girls who passed in and out. Finally, Frank whistled. Conley found him at the top of the stairs.

> "Mr. Frank grabbed me by my arm so tight his hand was trembling. He carried me into his private office, then he saw two ladies coming and he said to me, 'Gee, here comes Mrs. Emma Clarke Freeman and Miss Corinthia Hall,' and he come back in there to me; he was walking fast and seemed to be excited, and he said to me, 'Come right in here, Jim.' Mr. Frank grabbed me and gave me a shove and put me in the wardrobe and he shut the doors and told me to stay there until after they had gone. . . . I stayed in the wardrobe a pretty good while, for the whiskey and the beer I had drunk got me to sweating. He said, 'Jim, can you write?' I said, 'Yes, sir, I can write a little bit,' and then he give me a pencil that he got off the top of his desk, and told me to put on there 'dear mother, a long tall black Negro did this by hisself. . . .' Then Mr. Frank looked around at me and held up his head to the top of the house and said, 'Why should I hang, I have wealthy people in Brooklyn.' I didn't know what he was talking about, I didn't have any idea in the world what he was talking about."

Conley knew. If any single statement guaranteed Leo Frank's lynching it was, "Why should I hang? I have wealthy people in Brooklyn." In the course of his affidavit, Conley repeated these sentences three times, repeated them because he had divined the poor whites in Atlanta hated the employer, and particularly

---

* Neither Conley nor the police nor Dorsey were curious as to what Frank's motive could possibly have been for the whistle. By the time of the trial, Dorsey devised a logical motive.

hated the Jewish employer who would buy his way out of a sex crime against a Southern white female.

The obvious touches the police provided are those describing Frank's nervousness. Yet, the statement still absolved Conley from participation in the murder.

"This will not wash," Dorsey told the detectives. "There must be more to it than this. How did the girl and the notes get into the basement?"

That night the police found out. Conley gave them his third story (he was to tell a fourth at the trial) .

This last story was released to the papers the next day, May 29.

"On Saturday, April 26, 1913, when I came back to the pencil factory with Mr. Frank I waited for him downstairs like he told me. And when he whistled for me I went upstairs and he asked me if I wanted to make some money right quick, and I told him yes and he told me he had picked up a girl back there and had let her fall and that her head had hit against something—he didn't know what it was—and for me to move her and I hollered and told him the girl was dead. And he told me to pick her up and bring her in the elevator and I told him I didn't have nothing to pick her up with and he told me to go look by the cotton box and get a piece of cloth. I taken her and brought her up there to a little dressing room. She got too heavy for me and she slipped off my shoulder and fell on the floor. I hollered for Mr. Frank to come there and help me . . . and he run down there to me and he was excited, and he picked her up by the feet. Then we brought her to the elevator, Mr. Frank carrying her by the feet and me by the shoulder. And then Mr. Frank says, 'Wait, let me get the key,' and he went into the office and come back and unlocked the elevator door and started the elevator down.

"Mr. Frank turned it on himself and we went on down

to the basement and Mr. Frank helped me take it off the elevator and he told me to take it back there to the sawdust pile. Mr. Frank he went up the ladder and watched the trapdoor to see if anybody was coming and I taken her back there and taken the cloth from around her and taken her hat and shoes which I picked up upstairs right where her body was lying and brought them down and untied the cloth and throwed them on the trash pile in front of the furnace.

"He didn't tell me where to put the thing. I laid her body down with her head toward the elevator. Mr. Frank joined me back of the elevator and he said, 'Gee, that was a tiresome job.'

"And Mr. Frank, he couldn't hardly keep still. He was all the time moving about from one office to another. (Conley here repeated the story about the arrival of Corinthia Hall and Emma Clarke Freeman.) . . . Mr. Frank then asked me to write a few lines on that paper, a white scratch pad he had there and he told me what to put on there and I asked him what he was going to do with it and he told me to just go ahead and write, and then after I got through writing Mr. Frank looked at it and said it was all right and Mr. Frank looked at the top of the house and said, 'Why should I hang? I have wealthy people in Brooklyn,' and I asked him what about me and he told me that was all right about me, for me to keep my mouth shut and he would make everything all right.

"And then I asked him where was the money he was going to give me and Mr. Frank said, 'Here is $200,' and he handed me a big roll of greenback money and I didn't count it. The reason I have not told you this before is I thought Mr. Frank would get out and help me out, but it seems that he is not going to get out, and I have decided to tell the whole truth about the matter.

"When I was looking at the money in my hand, Mr.

Frank said, 'Let me have that and I will make it all right with you Monday if I live and nothing happens, and he took the money back and I asked him if that was the way he done, and he said he would give it back Monday."

The next day, May 30, was Friday, and Chief Beavers drove Conley and a squad of detectives to the factory for a re-enactment. Handcuffed to Beavers, Conley was pushed past the curious workers herded downstairs during their noon hour.

Conley proceeded on the grim drama while Detective Coker put down every word. The Negro never hesitated, nor was he ever at a loss for words. He lay down in the rear of the metal room, where Mary Phagan was supposedly murdered, to illustrate the posture of the corpse when he first saw it; he lay down again in the basement and simulated her position when he left. The dozen men in the police party stood mesmerized as Conley said: "Here we dropped the body like a sack of salt," and "The cord was laying right there. It was right by the body, but I didn't notice it was around her neck."

That afternoon, the police called in the reporters and they crowded before Conley's cell. Calmly Conley said: "I was intending not to tell the whole business. I was fixin' to take care of Mr. Frank like he told me. I was going to keep my mouth shut and say nothing until some of those folks down at the pencil factory open up and begins trying to make out I killed the little girl and that I'm trying to save my own neck by fixin' it on Mr. Frank.

"That made me mad. Finally the thing got working in my head so much that I just couldn't hold it any longer. I just decided it was time to come out with it and I did. The detectives and Mr. Lanford treated me mighty fair and I felt a whole lot better when I went up before them and told the truth."

Newport Lanford also expatiated. "I feel like a mountain has been lifted from my shoulders," he said. "I feel more relieved at present than I have in my whole career. The affidavit is worth its weight in gold, and more, too. I wouldn't take a million for it." He managed to avoid telling the reporters that it was Leo Frank who had informed him Conley could write.

Hugh Dorsey also had a statement. He was going to move to indict Jim Conley as an accessory.

Harry Scott, the ubiquitous Pinkerton, said in awed tones, "You can't help but believe Conley."

And Leo Frank, the "Silent Man of the Tower," said nothing. He refused Lanford's offer of a confrontation with Conley, another instance of his foolish inflexibility.

CHAPTER TEN

THERE WAS NOTHING episodic about the Frank case; every new event was a climax promising revelation, but each ultimately beclouded the truth.

These climaxes kept exploding because Hugh Dorsey kept looking for them. Just before the trial, he had another blow to strike.

Albert McKnight, a colored handyman who worked for the Seligs, came to him with a jumbled story. Albert himself dreamed of the reward, and he thought his wife Minola, who was the Selig maid and cook, would back him up. He was wrong. During the trial, Minola testified for the defense and Albert for the prosecution, but this does not mean they canceled each other out. Conflicting testimonies always bear unequal weights with a juror.

On June 2, Dorsey sent Detectives Starnes, Pickett, and Campbell to the Selig residence and brought the bewildered Minola McKnight to his office, where she found her husband Albert beside a stenographer, incoherently spelling out a story he had manufactured. Minola kept shaking her head. She said no such thing was true.

But Dorsey wanted that story. He knew how to get a story out of a Negro woman. He terrorized her. He sent her to jail, where relays of detectives kept after her, threatening her with imprisonment, badgering her through the night. By the next noon, her morale was shattered. Hysterical and tearful, she signed a statement damning Frank.

Minola McKnight alleged that on Saturday, April 26, her husband Albert arrived at the Selig residence at a quarter to one, was there when Leo Frank arrived which was half-past one.

"Mr. Frank did not eat any dinner, and he left in about ten minutes after he got there." She went on to describe the activities of the Selig household the Sunday morning Leo Frank accompanied the detectives to the morgue. "I didn't hear them say anything at the breakfast table, but after dinner I understood them to say that a girl and Mr. Frank were caught at the office Saturday.

"I don't know who said it, but Miss Lucile and Mr. and Mrs. Selig and Mr. Frank was standing there talking after dinner. I understood them to say it was a Jew girl, and I asked Miss Lucile and she said it was a Gentile. . . .

"Sunday Miss Lucile said to Mrs. Selig that Mr. Frank didn't sleep so good Saturday night. She said he was drunk and wouldn't let her sleep with him and she said she slept on the floor on the rug by the bed because he was drinking. Miss Lucile said Sunday that Mr. Frank told her Saturday night that he was in trouble, that he didn't know the reason why he would murder, and he told his wife to get his pistol and let him kill himself. I heard Miss Lucile say that to Mrs. Selig. It got away with Mrs. Selig mighty bad, but she didn't know what to think. I haven't heard Miss Lucile say whether she believed it or not. I don't know why Mrs. Frank didn't come to see her husband, but it was a pretty good while before she come to see him, maybe two weeks. She would tell me, 'Wasn't it mighty bad he was locked up,' and she said, 'Minola, I don't know what I am going to do.'

"When I left home to go to the Solicitor General's office they told me to mind what I said. They paid me $3.50 a week but last week she paid me $4 and one week she paid

me $6.50. But at the time of this murder I was getting
$3.50 a week and the week after the murder I don't know
how much they paid me. The next week $4 and the next
$4. One week Mrs. Selig gave me $5, but it was not for my
work, and they didn't tell me what it was for. They just
said, 'Here is $5, Minola,' but of course I understood what
they meant, but they didn't tell me anything at the time.
I understood it was a tip for me to keep quiet. They would
tell me to mind how I talked and Miss Lucile would give
me a hat."

"Was the reason you didn't tell the Solicitor yesterday all
about this was that Miss Lucile and others had told you not
to say anything about what happened out there?" asked Detective Starnes.

"Yes sir."

"Is that true?"

"Yes sir."

"And that is the reason why you would rather have been
locked up last night than tell this?"

"Yes sir."

"Has Mr. Pickett or Mr. Campbell or me influenced you in
any way or threatened you in any way to make this statement?"

"No sir."

"You make it of your own free will and accord in their
presence and in the presence of Mr. Gordon, your attorney?"

"Yes sir."

As soon as she had signed, the police released her.

To convict Leo Frank, Dorsey knew he would have to prove
the superintendent was in the factory at least ten minutes longer
than he swore he was. Frank said he left at one, and Dorsey was
going to insist he left at one ten. Minola McKnight's story substantiated the state's case.

More than this, Dorsey had wounded Frank where Frank
thought he was invulnerable. Frank had begged his wife to stay

at home while he was in the Tower. Dorsey had turned this
against him. Minola McKnight, obviously under Dorsey's careful prodding, had convinced Atlanta that Lucile Frank wouldn't
see her husband because she knew he was guilty.

While Frank and his defenders had never held the initiative,
they had lost more ground than ever.

Two days later, Lucile Frank made her first public statement.
She accused the police of torturing Minola McKnight and falsi-
fying her statement. In a signed letter to the newspapers, prepared by Rosser, Lucile Frank said:

> "It is not surprising that my cook should sign an affidavit
> to relieve herself from the torture that had been applied to
> her for four hours. It would be surprising if she would not,
> under such circumstances, give an affidavit. That the Solici-
> tor, sworn to maintain the law, should thus falsely arrest
> one against whom he has no charges and whom he does
> not even suspect, and torture her contrary to law, to force
> her to give evidence tending to swear away the life of an
> innocent man is beyond belief. Where will this end? My
> husband and my family and myself are the innocent suffer-
> ers now, but who will be the next to suffer?"

This was child's play to Dorsey. He sighed and told the reporters that in his experience it was always the wives and families of murderers who suffered most.

On that same June 5, however, Minola McKnight repudiated her affidavit. She did it before reporters with her husband
Albert beside her in her home at 351 Pulliam Street, no member of the Frank family present. When a reporter asked why,
if her lawyer, Gordon, was present she had signed the statement,
Minola replied, "Ain't got no lawyer 'cept God. He's my lawyer.
I never had pen or pencil in my hand." She was unable to read
or write.

This repudiation might have left some of the reporters wondering, but not the mass of Atlantans. Her statement was intro-

duced as testimony at the trial, and Albert supported it. In a deposition for Frank's appeal, Albert repudiated that support then later reaffirmed it. Both Minola and Albert during Frank's appeals, when their depositions were introduced, were the victims of savage beatings from persons unknown. Both survived. Albert never collected the reward.

Lucile Frank might again make a public statement condemning the solicitor general for his readiness to accept evidence from any source, as indeed she did on June 7, but Dorsey knew that though Minola McKnight's statement was not a trump card, it strengthened his long suit. He could read the papers, too, and he knew that nobody in Georgia wanted him to give up anything he had. And he wasn't going to.

CHAPTER ELEVEN

LEO FRANK'S TRIAL was set for June 30. It was postponed because two of his attorneys, Luther Rosser and Reuben Arnold, were defending the rights of a certain Mrs. Crawford who was involved in litigation over an estate totalling more than $250,-000. The principals in this civil case had precedence over the criminal proceedings. By the middle of July this litigation had yet to come before the court, and another postponement of Frank's trial seemed imminent. But Arnold prevailed upon Mrs. Crawford to yield her precedence and she agreed. Frank was to go on trial July 28.

But then it appeared that Atlanta's weather would force another postponement. The heat was intolerable. The week before the trial, the temperature soared over 100° every day. The trial judge told both prosecution and defense that if it continued this hot he would entertain a motion for a postponement.

July 28, however, dawned partly cloudy and muggy. The temperature went to 90° that day and to 90° or above every day during the month-long trial.

The trial judge was the Honorable Leonard Strickland Roan, then sixty-four years old and in failing health. (He died in 1915.) He had served as the presiding judge in almost all of the murder trials since his appointment to the Superior Court of Fulton County in the Stone Mountain Circuit thirteen years before. He was eminently fair, held in high esteem by the members of the bar for his knowledge of criminal law and procedure. Hugh Mason Dorsey, who headed the prosecution, was assisted by Frank Arthur Hooper, a successful corporation lawyer who had volunteered his services. Hooper was undeniably clever and had been himself the solicitor general of the Southwestern Circuit between 1896 and 1908. The third member of the prosecution was Edward A. Stephens, Assistant Solicitor General.

The Frank defense was handled by seven lawyers. The three lawyers of record were Luther Zeigler Rosser, Reuben Arnold, and Herbert Haas. Attorney Leonard Haas handled the administrative work and the legal research. (Three other lawyers were associated with the several motions for a new trial and the appeals to the Georgia Supreme Court and to the U. S. Supreme Court.)

Rosser had been born in Gordon County, Georgia, in 1859 and had practiced law in Atlanta since 1885, a few years after he was graduated from Emory College. Probably he was the richest lawyer in Atlanta; everyone ceded he was the best.

"Of the attorneys working on the case," [write the Samuelses in *Night Fell on Georgia*,[1]] "Rosser quite properly drew the most attention. Rosser was then fifty-three and at the peak of his quite considerable powers. He liked playing the role of an old country boy who was still a rough diamond despite his long acquaintance with the city and its sophisticated ways. He was stout, wore old-fashioned clothes, a bowler hat, carried a knobby cane, and hated to have his photograph taken. He also had never been seen wearing a tie since the day he graduated from law school—with one exception: the day he got married. Rosser's chief associate in Frank's defense was an equally celebrated criminal lawyer, Reuben Arnold, who had been called in to help a few weeks before the proceedings started. An aristocratic, heavy set man with curly blond hair, Arnold was aptly

---

[1] *Op. cit.*

characterized by Dorsey during the trial as 'the mildest-mannered man who ever cut a throat or scuttled a ship.' "

The only Jew to represent Frank in the courtroom was Herbert Haas, the Montag lawyer. He was the one member of the defense who was not a bone-of-the-bone and blood-of-the-blood Southerner. He had attended Columbia College and Columbia Law School before coming to Atlanta in 1905, a few years before Frank.

These men were about to conduct as inept a defense of an innocent man as was ever offered in an American courtroom. As brilliant and professional as they were, Arnold and Rosser simply refused to believe witnesses would lie and a jury believe. In their defense, it is only fair to say no three American lawyers ever believed a mob could invade a courtroom, but invade the mob did.

In a monograph on the Frank case, written under the sponsorship of the Anti-Defamation League in 1948, DeWitt H. Roberts, a Georgia newspaperman, said:

"The defense of Leo Frank was one of the most ill-conducted in the history of Georgia jurisprudence. The defendant made all possible mistakes in handling himself before his arrest. His attorneys completely misunderstood the nature of the evidence against him.

"The presence of some seven lawyers and several relatives at the defense table prejudiced the jury. The fashionable dress of some of the Frank relatives was in sharp contrast to the simple clothes that Stephens, the real genius of the prosecution, saw that Mary Phagan's mother wore.

"Introduction of a horde of character witnesses by the defense was one of three major mistakes of the actual trial. The local witnesses were compelled, upon cross-examination to admit Frank 'looked into the women's dressing room'—a sure proof in the eyes of a 1913 jury of the charge of perversion. . . . On the other hand, Frank's explanation of his looking into the dressing room is consistent with the savage employer mores of 1913.

"The second major mistake at the trial was the verbose cross-examination of Jim Conley.

"The third major mistake was the parading of a spurious witness, one Mincey, before the jury during the cross-examination of Conley, and the subsequent failure to place him on the stand.

"As for Frank's attorneys, the answer is even simpler. First they were far too numerous. At the actual trial there appear to have been but three attorneys of record, but at least two or three more always occupied space at the defense table, and certainly at least seven or eight individual attorneys always busied themselves with one or another aspect of the defense.

"The leading counsel, Arnold and Rosser, were acknowledged powers as trial attorneys. They handled many important cases. Arnold, a great figure before juries, had a marvelous range of forensic arguments. Rosser excelled on cross-examination. Undoubtedly they underestimated the skill with which Dorsey, guided by the technical genius of Stephens, had prepared the case. (Actually, the pair went into retirement for more than two weeks to map the trial.) Stephens, who dominated the solicitor general's office in Fulton County for more than thirty years under several chiefs was an extraordinary character; he believed the prosecutor's office was supposed to prosecute; he had the tenacity of a Javert; he was the greatest expert on homicide law and the law of evidence in the South; he was wholly incorruptible; he was entirely without feeling or sentiment in the conduct of office. Whether Stephens held any opinion at all about Frank's guilt or innocence could never be determined. Discussing the case almost forty years

later, he said, 'The jury thought him guilty. The evidence
authorized the verdict. When the appeal came down I dismissed it from my mind.'

"In addition, the defense attorneys, especially Rosser, appeared to desire to make this big case a demonstration of
virtuosity. Pulled from the context of the trial, Rosser's
cross-examination of Conley was a marvel of art. But the
Negro had been coached competently. . . . A different line
of cross-examination would have produced acquittal.

"Arnold's injection of the race-religious issue into the
trial was a matter of more calculated risk. With a different
stage setting, it might well have succeeded. His speech was
intense, brilliant, and moving. Considering his tempera-
ment, he could not have made a better one. Had he been
Frank's only attorney, had the defense rested its case wholly
on Frank's unsworn testimony and a different type of cross-
examination, if the ninety-nine character witnesses had not
prejudiced the jury already, had Arnold, Frank, and his
wife been the only occupants of the defense table, the
Arnold speech might well have swept the jury to acquittal."

But there was no reason why these lawyers should have underestimated Dorsey and Stephens, no reason why they shouldn't
have gauged accurately Atlanta's rage, no reason why they
shouldn't have sensed the hostility of the jury. These men,
Rosser, Arnold, and Haas, could feel this. They saw it, suffered
from it. Each morning during the trial, as these dignified, respected lawyers walked to the courthouse and up the steps, the
crowds on the street jeered and spat at them.

"How much the Jews paying you, Rosser?" called the rednecks.

One morning one of these roughs tripped Rosser, who luckily
only stumbled, while the mob applauded and laughed.

Ordinarily, Judge Roan tried criminal cases on the fourth
floor of the Thrower Building. This summer, the heavy miasma

of heat made the Thrower Building impractical. The room had low ceilings, was small, and the building had no elevator. Roan changed the site of the courtroom to the first floor of the City Hall building. Atlanta had not yet completed its new court-house where the Superior Civil Court would locate.

A week before he opened this makeshift court, Judge Roan instructed Deputy Sheriff Plennie Miner to ready the room. Miner put a battalion of janitors to work, lining up extra benches, rails, tables, and electric fans. A new ventilating device, the "ozonator," was installed. Miner threw a rail around the judge's desk to enclose the lawyers, the defendant and his friends, and the stenographers. A large table in the corner was reserved for the press. It was laden with dozens of lawyer's inkstands, for Roan and everybody else anticipated the thousands of words that would be filed.

Roan was holding court in Covington on July 24, so Judge J. T. Pendleton drew the names of 144 veniremen. Under Georgia law, the defense was allowed twenty strikes without a cause, the prosecution ten. Of the 144, fifty-four were excused from jury duty other than by peremptory challenge. Fourteen were excused because they opposed capital punishment; three were excused because they were over sixty years old; thirty-seven because they confessed an opinion about Frank's innocence or guilt. The defense used eighteen of its twenty challenges, the prosecution seven.

Remarkably, the jury was picked on the morning of the first day. Testimony was introduced that afternoon. Even more remarkably, a Negro, Earl Davis, was ruled eligible for duty by Judge Roan, although as the judge said, "There is little prospect he will be drawn."

The twelve good men and true who tried Leo Frank for the murder of Mary Phagan that August of 1913 were: Foreman F. E. Winburn, thirty-nine, married, claims agent for the Atlanta and Westpoint Railroad; C. J. Basshart, twenty-six, single, a pressman; A. H. Henslee, thirty-six, married, salesman for the

Franklin Buggy Co.; J. F. Higdon, forty-two, married, a building contractor; W. M. Jeffries, thirty-three, married, real-estate agent; M. Johenning, forty-six, married, a shipping clerk; W. D. Medcalf, thirty, married, a mailer; J. T. Ozburn, thirty-six, married, an optician; F. van L. Smith, thirty-seven, married, an electrical manufacturer's agent; D. Townsend, twenty-three, married, a bank teller; A. L. Wisbey, forty-three, married, a cashier; M. S. Woodward, thirty-four, married, a cashier at the King Hardware Co.

That very night, two burglars tried to break into the home of Juror F. van L. Smith. The *Constitution,* in a page-one sidebar to the trial, said, "Two big burly Negroes who had evidently taken a decided interest in the Frank trial . . . attempted to enter Smith's home. His wife saw them at the door and called for the police."

Shortly after 6:00 A.M. on July 28, Leo Frank left the Tower and was escorted to the City Hall building. This early departure was Sheriff Wheeler Mangum's idea. He hoped to avoid leading Frank through the crowds of the curious and the hostile he knew would gather.

Plennie Miner came to Frank's cell and asked, "How you feeling, Mr. Frank?"

"I'm hungry," said Frank.

"Commissary ain't open yet."

"Well, my wife will bring me breakfast," said Frank.

Frank, Miner, and Mangum made the trip to the courthouse in the sheriff's car, Frank chatting cheerfully. He wore a natty light gray mohair suit and an expensive gray tie.

Britt Craig, who felt he had a proprietary interest in the case, was already at the courthouse. Frank told him, "I am sure of acquittal. I am glad the trial is about to begin after this long wait. I have no fear. I am not only innocent of this crime, but I am innocent of any knowledge about it."

Frank passed in. Charles Ursenbach, with whom Frank was supposed to have seen the ball game on April 26, arrived with breakfast. He stayed with Frank in the anteroom until court convened at 10:00 A.M.

It was time.

Frank came into the court, looking quickly about him, as though he was unable to take in the whole scene of the crowded room. His appearance incited a general stir. Everyone craned for a look. Frank never lost composure. He walked straight to his place at the defense table.

Several of his friends, sitting inside the rail, crowded around him and clasped his hand. His wife and mother sat beside him, both in white gloves and large black hats.

That morning, one of Dorsey's deputies brought Jim Conley a new suit, and a jailer shaved him. Conley told the reporters he was ready for the witness stand. He would stick to the story he had told.

"If they had just let me face Mr. Frank," he said, "I could have made him tell the truth long before this."

CHAPTER TWELVE

THE NEW RUDIMENTARY air conditioners, the ozonators, did not work. They were useless. Inside the courtroom nearly everyone suffocated. Judge Roan ordered the bailiffs to open all the windows. That brought some relief to jammed benches. The open windows also admitted the Atlanta mob, all of it.

The crowd that had gathered in front of the temporary courthouse blocked the traffic on Pryor and Hunter Streets. The police never tried dispersing them. The trolley cars had to inch their way through this mob which gave way only grudgingly. On another side of the building, a crowd constantly pressed against the open windows, some of them leaning over the sills. Behind the building was a row of storage sheds, all of them an even ten feet high. On top of these sheds, hundreds climbed to get the best view of all. They squatted there for the six to seven hours the court was in session, none of them able to sit because the sun made the tarred roofs beneath them blisteringly hot.

The mob cheered the points Dorsey scored and booed the refutations of the defense. Often their excited comments were noisy enough to drown out the speeches of the opposing counsel, and the tired Judge Roan would ask the bailiffs or the deputy sheriffs to restore order—to no avail.

The subpoenaed witnesses waited in a hallway, a place stuffier than the court. Sometimes to while away the time, they sang hymns, rocking the building with music. One newspaperman reporting the trial said it reminded him of an evangelical tent meeting.

> "Frank's lawyers protested," [C. P. Connolly writes] "but the only relief the court gave was to direct the sheriff *to find out who was making the noise.* When Frank's lawyers in the early stages of the trial called the names of several Jewish ladies as character witnesses for Frank, the crowd jeered and laughed. When, toward the end of the thirty days' trial, they moved the court for a mistrial on the grounds of these various demonstrations of applause and hisses—the clapping of hands, the stamping of feet, and the boisterous sarcastic laughter in the presence of the jury—the crowd jeered more uproariously than before." [1]

The crowd had come to stare at Leo Frank, to watch the state prepare him for hanging. Every time Frank's attorneys tried to spare him the mob shouted, "Hang the Jew, or we'll hang you." The jury heard the mob, they could see it, they could feel its desperate presence.

Rhea Frank, the defendant's mother, who sat wretchedly behind her son throughout, was often brought to the point of hysteria; Lucile Frank, the wife, was steadfastly composed; Leo Frank himself remained curiously unmoved. The anger and the hostility never made Frank lose his poise. It was an ordeal; he knew that. But an innocent man ought to be able to bear an ordeal once in his life, particularly if protected by an American legal proceeding.

Mrs. John W. Coleman, Mary Phagan's mother, was the first witness.

"I last saw her alive on the 26th of April, about a quarter to twelve," she testified. "She was getting ready to go to the pencil factory to get her pay envelope. About eleven-thirty she

---

[1] C. P. Connolly, *The Truth About the Frank Case* (Vail-Ballou, New York, 1915), pp. 21–22.

ate some cabbage and bread. She would have been fourteen years old the first day of June. She was fair complected, heavyset, and was extra large for her age."

"Was she pretty or ugly?" asked Dorsey.

"She was pretty, mighty pretty."

"Did she not have dimples in her cheeks?"

"Yes, a dimple in either cheek."

"Are these her clothes?" asked Dorsey. He held them up and, one by one, he let them fall to the table as exhibits, blue hat, and her lavender dress.

Mrs. Coleman held her fan to her face. Her sobs started in crescendo.

Deputy Sheriff Plennie Miner advanced with a glass of water.

"Your witness," said Dorsey to Defense Attorney Rosser.

Rosser tried to handle Mrs. Coleman as gently as possible. He wanted the admission that Mary Phagan despised George Epps. At this question, Mrs. Coleman broke down again. Again the glass of water and finally the admission that the Epps boy was a neighbor. "He wasn't no special friend of hers."

The *Constitution* reported that night that Leo Frank kept averting his eyes from Mrs. Coleman, "unwilling or unable to view the mother's grief."

Barefooted again, his cap in hand, George Epps, with his close-shaven head, was next. Judge Roan refused to let him testify as to what Mary Phagan had supposedly told him about the attentions of Leo Frank, but Dorsey still elicited the statement, "It was about ten minutes to twelve when I first saw her. I left her about seven minutes after twelve at the corner of Forsyth and Marietta Street. She was going to the pencil factory to draw her money."

Rosser attacked. "How did you know what time it was when Miss Phagan joined you going downtown that morning?"

"I looked at a clock just before I took the car."

"You didn't say anything about a clock when you testified before the coroner's jury."

"No, but I looked at one just the same."

"How did you know what time it was when Miss Mary left you?"

"I estimated it from the time she got on the car, and I told it by the sun. I can tell time by the sun. I live in the country and when I got off I looked at the sun."

Rosser would remind the jury in his summation that April 26 had been a cloudy day.

Newt Lee was the last witness of the day. "When I went upstairs," he said, responding to Dorsey's questions, "I had a sack of bananas and I stood to the left of the desk like I do every Saturday. I says like I always do, 'All right, Mr. Frank,' and he come bustling out of his office. He had never done that before. He always called me when he wanted to tell me anything and said, 'Step here a minute, Newt.' This time he came up rubbing his hands and says, 'Newt, I am sorry I had you come so soon, you could have been home sleeping. I tell you what you do, you go out in town and have a good time.' "

"Had he ever done this before?" asked Dorsey.

"He had never left me off before that."

"Was there any place you could have slept in the factory?"

"I could have laid down there in the shipping room and gone to sleep, and I told him that."

Under Dorsey's prodding, Lee went on: "He took a long time to change my punch slips. He fumbled and was nervous. Mr. Gantt came from across the street from the beer saloon. Mr. Frank come busting out of the door and run into Gantt unexpected and he jumped back frightened."

"Did Mr. Frank do anything else that day unusual?"

"Mr. Frank phoned me that night about an hour after he left, sometime after seven o'clock."

"What did he say at that time?"

"He says, 'How is everything?' "

"And you replied?"

"I says, 'Everything is all right so far as I know.' "

"Is this the first time he called you on a Saturday night?"

"This is the first time he phoned me on a Saturday night or at all."

On cross-examination, Rosser forced Lee to admit that Gantt and Frank had had an argument; that perhaps Frank might have been nervous because Gantt had been drinking.

"Then your first thought at that time," asked Rosser, "was that Frank was afraid of Gantt on account of the difficulty they had had?"

"Yes, sir."

"How big a man is Gantt?"

"I reckon he must be about seven feet tall."

Rosser went on to the murder notes. "When you were in the basement, didn't one of the policemen read a note which said something about a long, tall, black Negro? When he read, 'the night witch' didn't you say, 'Boss, that's me?' "

"No, sir. I said, 'Boss, it looks like they are trying to lay it on me.' "

Rosser concluded his cross-examination on Tuesday. All in all, Lee had been grilled for four hours, yet he was not tired. He told his jailer all he wanted was a chew of tobacco. When one of the reporters asked him which of the questions the lawyers or the detectives asked had bothered him most, Lee replied, "Mr. Rosser certainly is terrible, but I would just as soon have one crowd as another."

Police Sgt. L. S. Dobbs described the condition of the body when the police arrived at the factory. Detective J. S. Starnes testified, "Mr. Frank appeared to be nervous. He was in a trembling condition." W. W. ("Boots") Rogers enlarged on this. "Mrs. Frank opened the door. Mr. Frank stepped into the hall through the curtain. Mr. Frank asked Mr. Black if anything had happened at the factory. I didn't answer. Mr. Frank said, 'Did the night watchman call up and report anything to you?' Mr. Frank seemed to be extremely nervous. His questions were jumpy. He was rubbing his hands when he came through the curtains. He moved about briskly. He seemed excited. He asked questions in rapid succession."

Rosser started by asking Starnes, "Had you ever met Leo Frank before?"

"Not until that morning."

"Did he refuse to accompany the police?"

"No. He went with us."

"Did he go willingly?"

"Yes."

"Right away? As soon as you asked him?"

"Yes, right away."

In the cross-examination, Rosser drew from Starnes a statement on which the defense never capitalized. It was indelicate and offensive testimony, for the papers never reported it, and the Samuelses do not include it in their authoritative work. It was this testimony, corroborated by a subsequent state witness, Police Officer Lassiter, that ultimately convinced Governor John Slaton of Frank's innocence.

Rogers testified, describing the scene in the basement with Frank on Sunday morning: "During that time neither the shoe, the hat, nor the umbrella had been found. In the elevator shaft there was some excrement. When we went down on the elevator, the elevator mashed it. You could smell it all around. It looked like someone had dumped naturally; that was before the elevator had come down. When the elevator came down afterwards, it mashed it and then we smelled it." The excrement was Conley's. He confessed this in his testimony. He had evacuated his bowels Saturday morning. Obviously, Sunday morning was the first time since Conley's deposit that the elevator had been used, since it only came to a stop by hitting the ground in the shaftway.

Dorsey called Detective John Black, heralded as the star police witness. "Mr. Frank stepped from behind a curtain," Black told the jury. "His voice was hoarse and trembling and nervous and excited. He asked if something had happened at the pencil factory and if the night watchman had reported it. Frank made no objections to talking to Newt Lee. He was nervous on Monday."

Black was the star witness because Dorsey wanted him to convince the jury the police knew Frank was guilty when the factory superintendent suddenly availed himself of lawyers.

"Mr. Black," asked Dorsey, "please state when Frank first had counsel?"

"On Monday morning. We reached the station house at eight thirty and in a few minutes Mr. Rosser came in, Herbert Haas following him a moment later."

"Did you hear Haas make a statement in Frank's presence?"

"Yes, Haas demanded that Chief Lanford and the detective search Frank's residence. That was about eleven-thirty."

"Was Frank under arrest at the time?"

"No."

"Was he restrained of his liberty?"

"No. But Haas said he was Frank's attorney and was entitled to demand a search."

Rosser on cross-examination quite literally confounded this star witness.

"Wasn't it eleven o'clock before I got to the station?"

"No. I know that you got there between eight-thirty and nine o'clock."

"Didn't you swear a little while ago that I was there at eleven?"

"I won't answer it."

"Didn't I say, 'Frank what do they have you for?' and he answered, 'They want me to make a statement'? Didn't I say, 'Give it to them'? Didn't Lanford say, 'Come on in here,' like he was snarling at a Negro?"

"Yes, but he wasn't 'released' as you call it."

"You swore so, didn't you?"

No answer.

"And it isn't true that he declined to make a statement?"

No reply.

"You're depending entirely upon your recollection, aren't you?"

"Yes."

"Then why is it you recollect so well some things, and fail so badly in others?"

No answer.

"What time did you get to the Selig home?"

"I don't recollect perfectly."

"Why did you wait to tell Frank of the murder until you had got away from his home?"

"I had talked with Newt Lee and, therefore, wanted to question him."

"Hurry and scurry is an enemy to memory, isn't it?"

"Yes."

"Did Frank and Darley both say the slip was punched wrong?"

"I don't know."

"Frank intimated Gantt had been caught stealing, didn't he?"

"I think so."

"Were you present when Frank revealed his underlinen to me at police headquarters that Monday?"

"I don't recollect that I was."

"Didn't I myself demand Haas go with you?"

"I didn't hear it if you did."

In the words of the Samuelses, Black left the stand sheepishly confessing, "I don't like to admit that I'm crossed up, but you've got me in that kind of a fix and I don't know where I'm at."

The lanky Gantt was the day's last witness. He said he had known Mary Phagan since she was a little girl. He also established that Frank knew her, too. "One Saturday afternoon she came in the office to have her time corrected and after I had gotten through, Mr. Frank came in and said, 'You seem to know Mary pretty well.' I had not told him her name."

According to Gantt, Leo Frank was unusually pale and nervous that Saturday morning.

Throughout, Rosser and Arnold constantly challenged the

introduction of evidence as to Frank's nervousness. They argued
that such testimony was irrelevant and immaterial, that others
were equally as nervous, that they wished to place in evidence
proof of Frank's stability that Saturday. In this they lost. The
judge ruled Frank's nervousness was an issue, but over Dorsey's
objections, the judge also ruled that Frank's financial report,
on which he had worked that Saturday afternoon, could be introduced, an indication of the defendant's stability.

Mrs. Arthur White, whose husband had been repairing the
floor boards on the fourth floor that Saturday, told the jury
that at twelve-thirty she had seen Frank in front of his office,
that he had jumped when she asked him if her husband was
upstairs, and that as she was going down the steps on her way
to the street near one o'clock, she saw a Negro sitting on a box
close to the stairway on the first floor.

Dapper Harry Scott, the two-faced Pinkerton agent, happily
took the oath. He detailed how Frank and Sigmund Montag
had retained him, and repeated the narrative he had taken
from Frank: "He [Frank] returned to the factory about eleven
o'clock and just before twelve o'clock Mrs. White came in and
asked to see her husband. Mary Phagan came to the factory at
twelve-ten to draw her pay. He paid her off inside his office,
and then she asked if the metal had come yet. He replied he
didn't know; at one-ten he left the factory and arrived at the
factory again at three."

This testimony, of course, substantiated the State's claim.
The answer, "I don't know" to the query about the metal created the possibility that Frank lured Mary Phagan to the metal
room at the rear of the second floor. Leaving the factory at one-
ten gave him more time to dispose of the body.

Dorsey asked, "What, if anything, did Frank say in reference
to Gantt?"

"Nothing."

"Your Honor," shouted Dorsey, "I have been misled!"

It was a brilliant, if unethical, legal maneuver. Dorsey had
established that Frank had hired Scott, and though Scott was

called as a prosecution witness, Dorsey was trying to intimate that the Pinkerton operative was withholding evidence to protect Frank. And Dorsey kept bellowing, finally prevailing upon the bench to admit Scott's notes and memoranda as evidence which added little, if anything, to the State's case.

To Rosser's questions, Scott replied, "Mr. Frank told me when the little girl asked if the metal had come back that he said, 'I don't know.' "

"Is that what you swore before the coroner's jury?"

"I think so."

"Here is the testimony. You swore to the coroner that Leo Frank said, 'No.' "

"It may be true," apologized Scott, "that I swore before the coroner that in answer to that question from Mary Phagan that Frank said, 'No,' and it is possible I so reported it to you. If I said, 'No,' I meant, 'I don't know.' "

"You say now that Frank told you that he left the factory about one-ten. But didn't you report to me that Frank said he left about one o'clock?"

"I said one-ten."

"Read your report," demanded Rosser.

"Well, I made an error," said the sullen Scott. "It should have read one-ten."

Before the trial opened, all of the Atlanta newspapers had conjectured on the formidable task awaiting Solicitor General Dorsey. He was up against two of the ablest lawyers in the South, and he was up against them with what seemed at first glance a frail case. But when Monteen Stover took the stand, Dorsey's case took on substance.

Monteen Stover said, "I worked at the National Pencil Company prior to April 26th, 1913. I was at the factory at five minutes after twelve that day. I stayed there five minutes and left at ten minutes after twelve. I went there to get my money. I went in Mr. Frank's office. He was not there. The door to the metal room was closed. I had on tennis shoes, a yellow hat, and a brown coat. I looked at the clock on my way up. It was five minutes after twelve, and it was ten minutes after twelve when I started out. I had never been in his office before."

Rosser could not impeach this testimony. "I didn't look at the clock to see what time it was when I left home or when I got back home," Monteen Stover testified quite simply. "I didn't notice the safe in Mr. Frank's office. I walked right in and walked right out. I went right through into the office and turned around and came out. I didn't notice how many desks were in the outer office. I didn't notice any wardrobe to put clothes in. I don't know how many windows are in the outer office. The factory was still and quiet when I was there. I am fourteen years old, and I worked on the fourth floor of the factory. I knew the paying off time was twelve o'clock on Saturday and that is why I went there. They don't pay off in the office, you have to go up to a little window they open."

She stepped down. Leo Frank looked closely at her. All Rosser had done was prove she was unobservant. But Dorsey had put a substitute Mary Phagan on the stand, a little girl the same age who faced the same hard life and who might have died that Saturday the same hard way. No Southern jury was ever going to believe little Mary Phagan would lie.

"I found the strands of hair on the handle of the lathing machine in the National Pencil Company Monday morning," machinist R. P. Barrett testified. "I also found the blood spots on the second floor by the water cooler at the ladies' dressing room. I know they were blood. The same day I found the spots of blood, I found the pay envelope under the machine at which Mary Phagan worked. The lathe on which I found the hair was about twenty feet away from where I found the pay envelope. The hair was not there Friday, for I worked on the lathe up to five thirty, quitting time. The factory was closed Saturday. The spots were not there Friday."

Later testimony established that of the five spots, only one could be called blood. It was also impossible to determine whether it was human blood or not.

Cross-examining, Rosser asked, "The pay envelope you found had no name or number on it—only this little loop, part of something written in pencil?"
"Yes."
"It is the same sort of envelope they always have used at the factory?"
"Yes."
"There is nothing to identify it unless this little loop be part of a name?"
"Yes, sir, the top of the envelope was torn off. All the writing on it was a loop that looked like the lower part of a 'G.' "
A procession of factory employees followed, all asserting they too had seen the spots. Others like N. V. Darley testified as to how nervous Frank was.

And Albert McKnight, the husband of Minola McKnight, the Selig cook, swore that Frank did not eat dinner that noon but remained at his father-in-law's house only fifteen minutes.

Rosser broke this testimony immediately by making Albert admit he had not entered the dining room at all. McKnight tried to say he had observed Frank through the angles afforded by a buffet mirror, but a diagram produced by the defense invalidated this. There was no possible reason Albert McKnight, husband of the Selig cook, would have kept his eye on Leo Frank that noon of April 26.

Dorsey had one more occasion to complain that a witness entrapped him. E. F. Holloway, a sixty-year-old day watchman at the factory, supervised the freight arrivals. He had signed an affidavit that he locked the elevator power box on Friday and Saturday, but now he recanted. Dorsey was enraged.

Holloway tried to explain: "On May 12, 1913, I told you that the elevator was locked because I forgot to tell you I done some sawing Saturday. I took the key out and left the elevator unlocked and took the key back and put it in the office. The insurance company didn't want it locked anyway."

This was important testimony for Frank because Conley

was to swear that to get Mary Phagan to the basement Frank
had to unlock the power box.

Medical testimony followed. Sworn in were W. H. Gheesling,
the funeral director who first examined Mary Phagan at Bloomfield's mortuary; Dr. Claude Smith, a physician and city bacteriologist; Dr. J. W. Hurt, the county physician; and Dr. F. H.
Harris, who conducted the second autopsy on May 5.

Gheesling described the cord that was embedded in the
girl's neck and the rag around her hair and over her face. He
thought she had been dead ten or fifteen hours. There were
dry blood splotches on her clothes, and the right leg of her
drawers had been split with a knife. He thought the swelling
about her eye had been induced before death, as had the two-
and-a-half-inch wound on the back of her head, for it had bled
a great deal. The scalp was broken, but the skull was not
crushed.

On cross-examination, Gheesling was the first to tell the jury
that the girl had not been mutilated sexually. He judged she
died of strangulation because the rope was tight enough to
choke and her tongue protruded an inch and a quarter.

Dr. Claude Smith testified that he found some blood corpuscles on one of the chips the detectives had scraped from
the factory floor but refused to commit himself on whether
it was human blood or not.

Dr. Harris was the prosecution's medical expert. He outlined
Mary Phagan's injury, but speculated there was some violence
done the vagina. His importance to the State's case was his
analysis of how long the cabbage had been in Mary Phagan's
stomach before she died.

"I examined the contents of the stomach, finding one hundred sixty cubic centimeters of cabbage and biscuit or wheaten
bread. It had progressed very slightly towards digestion. It is
impossible for one to say how long this cabbage had been in
the stomach, but I feel confident she was either killed or received the blow on the back of the head within a half-hour

after she finished her meal. From my own experience, I find that the behaviour of the stomach after taking a small meal of cabbage and bread is practically the same as taking some biscuit and water alone. I examined Mary Phagan's stomach. It was normal in size, normal in position, and normal in every particular. I made a microscopic examination of the contents. It showed plainly that it had not begun to dissolve, or only to a very slight degree, and indicated that the process of digestion had not gone on to any extent at the time this girl was rendered unconscious."

Defense Attorney Arnold, an expert in forensic medicine, conducted the cross-examination. All he got Dr. Harris to admit was that the science of digestion was a rather modern discipline.

The county physician, Dr. Hurt, saw the body of Mary Phagan on Sunday morning, April 27th. He also detailed the wounds and contusion for the jury. The scalp wound, in his opinion, was inflicted before death, calculated to produce unconsciousness.

"The black eye," he said, "appeared to have been made by some soft instrument in that the skin was not broken. I examined the hymen. It was not intact. There was blood on the drawers. I don't know whether it was fresh blood or menstrual blood. The vagina was a little larger than the normal size of a girl that age. It is my opinion that this enlargement of the vagina could have been produced by penetration immediately preceding death. She was not pregnant."

This time Arnold was more successful in his cross-examination. He made Dr. Hurt admit that the hymen was not intact and that the doctor could see no indication of an injury to the hymen.

"Was the blood menstrual blood?" asked Arnold.

"It was characteristic of the menstrual flow," answered Hurt.

"Was there any laceration of the girl's vagina?"

"There was no laceration of the vagina and no mutilation on the girl's body except those wounds I've described."

"Ordinarily," asked Rosser, "what would the size of a vagina indicate?"

"The size of a vagina is no indication of anything except the anatomy and the natural build of the person. It is no indication of rape. I found no outward signs of rape."

Arnold had made a State's witness admit there had been no rape. He now proceeded to make this State witness impugn the testimony of another State witness.

"Doctor," asked Arnold, "it depends on the individual just how soon cabbage is digested, doesn't it?"

"Yes; some digest it sooner than others."

"Isn't each man a law unto himself?"

"Yes, more or less."

"Cabbage is one of the hardest things in the world to digest, isn't it?"

"Yes, it is generally regarded as hard."

"Doesn't it take from three to four hours to thoroughly digest it?"

"It depends a great deal on how well it was chewed," answered the doctor.

"Suppose a little girl in a hurry to catch a car ate some cabbage and allowed it to go down unchewed. Wouldn't it take much longer to digest the unchewed part?"

"Yes."

During this questioning, Judge Roan inadvertently held up the latest extra of the *Georgian* with the red headline, "State Adding Links to Chain" clearly visible to everyone.

Arnold immediately broke off, and he and Rosser went into a five-minute conference behind the rail. They were certain the jury had read the headline. They told this to Dorsey and asked if he would consent to a new trial. Dorsey refused.

Rosser addressed the Court and asked Roan to withdraw the jury. The judge complied.

"Your Honor," said Rosser, "you inadvertently displayed a newspaper just now. One side was turned up with large red

letters reading 'State Adding Links to Chain.' Every member of
the jury read it. I saw them leaning forward to see it. We don't
want to make a motion for a new trial, but we want this jury
called back and such explanation made by Your Honor as will
eliminate any harm that might have been done by the jury seeing this paper."

Dorsey objected, arguing the jury might have seen newspapers to and from the courtroom and insisting the judge instruct the jurors that this objection was initiated by the defense.

Roan said heatedly, "Call the jury, and I will instruct it as
I see fit."

When the jurors returned, Roan said, "Gentlemen, this is an
important case. You will have to be extremely cautious and
extremely careful. You are to try this case from the evidence
and from nothing else. It has been suggested that you have
been able to see some headlines or some writings which may
have influenced you in your judgment. I desire to tell you—you
are the ones trying this case. And I desire to warn you again
that nothing you see in the newspapers or on the streets or in
the courtroom should have any influence on you either in respect to the case of the State or the defense."

This ended the first week of the trial. The State had set forth:

—that Frank displayed unusual signs of nervousness following the murder of Mary Phagan;

—that Frank was not in his office between twelve-five and
twelve-ten;

—that Conley was eliminated as a possible slayer since Mrs.
White saw him at the foot of the stairs at one;

—that Frank had engaged counsel before he had been placed
under arrest.

The defense had contended:

—that Frank's nervousness was only natural;

—that Monteen Stover did not enter Frank's office, and that
he may have been there without her seeing him;

—that it is impossible to determine the time it takes an ordinary human being to digest cabbage;

—that Conley had greater opportunity to commit the crime than Frank, and a better motive—robbery;

—that Conley, when Mrs. White saw him, had already killed Mary Phagan and thrown her body down the elevator shaft;

—that Frank was under arrest when he engaged counsel.

If the jury wondered that weekend in the Kimball House about the evidence it had heard and was expected to sift, it must certainly have occurred to some of the members to question why, if Frank hadn't raped the girl, he should have had to kill her.

Rosser and Arnold must have wondered, too, why Dorsey admitted the testimony that Mary Phagan hadn't been ravished.

But Jim Conley had prepared an answer for the jury. Jim Conley this next week would point his finger at Leo Frank and call him a sexual pervert. And that jury would believe that sexual monsters murder.

CHAPTER THIRTEEN

THE ACCUSATION Conley was about to level against Leo Frank, the charge of perversion, would outrage any populace of 1913, but particularly the Southern populace. It would outrage large sections of Americans everywhere today. And today, we are far more sophisticated than we were in 1913. In 1913, no Southerner charged another man with sexual deviation unless he was ready to die for making that charge or have the man against whom he made it forever ostracized. As recently as 1964 a judge in the comparatively liberal state of North Carolina sentenced two consenting adults, convicted of homosexuality, to thirty years in prison.

In her original affidavit, Mrs. Formby, the whorehouse madam, had charged Leo Frank with perversion. She had not elaborated. Before the trial, she had repudiated all her charges, claiming she had been browbeaten by the police and plied with liquor. That repudiation, however, received none of the publicity nor did it assume the importance her original charges did. Atlanta didn't care that the first Formby affidavit was a fake, that Hugh Dorsey wouldn't dare call her. She had done her damage.

Despite the most exhaustive search into Frank's past—into the life he had spent in Brooklyn, at Cornell, in Massachusetts, and in Atlanta—and a query addressed to no less than eleven of his classmates and former fellow employees, there was never a hint of any sexual deviation in Frank.

That made no difference. The charge made by Mrs. Formby,

which the fired-up mob believed, now could be repeated by Jim Conley. Frank and his lawyers were unaware of these subtle menaces day by day binding and destroying them.

In his concern with sex, the Southerner is like everybody else —with this difference: the Southerner has a running head start. The Southerner's running head start owes its inspiration to the sexual fear of the black man. Once the Southerner had created the menace of the oversexed Negro, it followed that the Southern woman was everlastingly in peril.

Throughout the South, to this day, any sexual deviation is called, legally, a "crime against nature." A woman who murders her husband and charges he made her submit to such practices usually gets off with a minimum sentence or wins an acquittal— and wins it even though she has been married to the same man for twenty-two years, as happened in a case less than fifteen years ago.

Literally, there have been moments in the life of the Southerner when sexual fantasies have overwhelmed him. In nearly half the cases of lynching, since Tuskegee Institute established the first records, the Negro was castrated *before* he was hanged or burned alive. In some of these cases, his genitals were mutilated even though the crime alleged against him had nothing to do with sex.

No one expressed this obsession as well as Nat Harris, the Georgia governor who succeeded John M. Slaton. Harris laid bare this obsession when he tried to explain Frank's lynching to a *New York Times* correspondent. This remarkable interview was published in the *Times* on August 20, 1915, four days after Frank was hanged. Harris was an old Confederate soldier, a man with a gentle voice, a thick mane of white hair, and full and expressive blue eyes.

He told the *Times:*

"This awful lynching hurts the state. But I don't think the North has had the right idea about this feeling against this dead man, Frank. It was not for the reasons given for it. It was not because he was a Jew; there has never been any anti-Jewish feeling in Georgia until now. It was because, in the first place, there is something that unbalances men here in the South where women are concerned. I won't call it chivalry, or call it anything; it is, if you like, something that destroys a man's ability and even willingness to do cold and exact justice. That is the way it is in the South; it cannot be argued against, and must be accepted as a fact. If a woman is the victim of a crime, a fury seizes our men."

This old Confederate, Governor Nat Harris, understood and clearly articulated the sexual obsession of the South. All the great Southern writers from W. J. Cash through Lillian Smith through William Faulkner have corroborated his insight.

The Southern white woman was a fantasy-virgin, dwelling in a fairyland Southern men imagined filled with grotesque dangers. When the fairy tale played itself out, when indeed the virgin succumbed to the assaults of the foreign dragon, Southern men became desperate, but they exercised their desperation in the entire world around them, and exercised it all too often against real innocents.

CHAPTER FOURTEEN

"CALL JAMES CONLEY."

On Monday, August 4, Conley entered the courtroom looking a different man than the one arrested two months before. He wore a new suit, neatly pressed, and a blue shirt, newly laundered, though ill fitting. He had new shoes and socks. He took the oath and mounted the witness chair, perfectly at ease, resting his elbows easily.

Dorsey began his examination.

"What is your name?"

"James Conley."

"Do you know Leo Frank?"

"Yes."

"Point him out."

Conley pointed.

"Did you have any conversation with him on Friday afternoon before the murder of Mary Phagan?"

"I had a little conversation with him on Friday afternoon, the 25th of April. He wanted me to come to the pencil factory that Saturday morning."

Judge Roan interrupted, instructing Conley to speak up. The jurors bending forward in their chairs, some of them grasping the rail with whitened knuckles, couldn't hear him.

"I will talk louder," said Conley. Thereafter, he spoke clearly and rapidly, and though his vocabulary was small, as one of the newspapermen remarked, he knew all the words.

"Friday evening about three o'clock," Conley continued, "Mr. Frank came to the fourth floor where I was working and said he wanted me to come to the pencil factory on Saturday morning at eight thirty, that he had some work to do on the second floor."

"Who got there first, you or Mr. Frank?"

"We met at the front door."

"What did you do this Saturday?"

"I always stayed on the first floor like I stayed the 26th of April and watched for Mr. Frank while he and a young lady would be on the second floor chatting, I don't know what they were doing. He only told me they wanted to chat."

"When you reached the factory, what happened?"

"He opened the door and showed me how to lock it. He said that he was going to have a young lady up there. He said that he would stamp his foot and that would be a signal for me to come up."

"Have you ever watched for him before?"

"I couldn't exactly tell how many times I have watched the door for him previous to April 26th, it has been several times. I don't know who would be there when I watched for him, but there would be another young man, another young lady during the time I was at the door."

"There would be two ladies?"

"A lady for the man and a lady for Mr. Frank."

"Were there always two couples?"

"Mr. Frank was alone there once, that was Thanksgiving Day. I watched for him. A woman came there, she was a tall, heavy-built lady. I stayed down there and watched the door just as he told me the last time, April 26th."

"Just what did he tell you?"

"He told me when a lady came he would stamp and let me know that was the one and for me to lock the door. Well, after the lady came he stomped for me. I went and locked the door as he said. He told me when he got through with the lady he would whistle for me then to go and unlock the door."

Conley proceeded to describe how he spent Saturday morning. He went to the Capital City Laundry to visit his mother and met Frank who was on his way to the Montags. He even recalled how Frank had bumped into a grocery clerk outside of the Albertson Brothers Store.

"Mr. Frank stopped at Curtis's Drug Store, corner Mitchell and Forsyth Streets, went into the soda fountain. He came out and went straight on to the factory, me right behind him."

"What did Mr. Frank say then?"

"Mr. Frank stops me at the door and says, 'You see you turn the knob like this and there can't nobody come in from the outside. And I says, 'All right,' and I walked back to a little box by the trash barrel and sit on it and he says,' Now there will be a young lady up here after a while and me and her are going to chat a little.' And he says, 'When I whistle I will be through so you can go and unlock the door and you come upstairs to my office then like you were going to borrow some money from me and that will give the young lady time to get out.' "

Conley went on to list the entrances and exits of the factory personnel. Mr. Darley came in, Mr. Holloway, and a Negro drayman.

"Who was the next person you saw?" asked Dorsey.

"The next person I saw was Miss Mary Perkins, that's what I call her, this lady that is dead, I don't know her name.* After she went upstairs I heard her footsteps going toward the office, and after she went into the office, I heard two people walking out and going like they were coming down the steps, but they didn't come down, they went back towards the metal department."

---

* Curiously, that made two people in Atlanta who professed not to know the name of Mary Phagan: Leo Frank and Jim Conley.

"Then what did you hear?"

"After they went back there, I heard a lady scream. Then I didn't hear no more."

"Did you see anyone else?"

"The next person I seen come in there was Miss Monteen Stover. She had on a pair of tennis shoes and a rain coat. She stayed there a pretty good time, it wasn't so very long either."

"During this time, did you hear anything else?"

"I heard somebody from the metal department come running back there on their tiptoes, then I heard somebody tiptoeing back towards the metal department. After that I kind of dozed off and went to sleep."

"What was the next thing you heard?"

"Mr. Frank stamping on the floor three times. Then he called me. Then I went and locked the door and sat on the box a little while, and the next thing I heard was Mr. Frank whistling. Mr. Frank was standing there at the top of the steps and shivering and trembling and rubbing his hands like this."

"Did he have anything in his hands?"

"He had a little rope in his hands—a long wide piece of cloth."

"And how did he look?"

"His eyes were large. They looked right funny, like diamonds. His face was red."

"Did the cord look like this cord?" asked Dorsey, showing him the cord that strangled Mary Phagan.

Conley handled it. "Yes, he had a cord just like this here cord."

"What did he say to you?"

"He asked, 'Did you see that little girl who passed here a while ago?' I told him I saw one come along there and she has not come down and he says, 'Well, that one you say didn't come back down, she came into my office a little while ago and I wanted to be with the little girl and she refused me, and I struck her and I guess I struck her too hard and she fell and hit her head against something and I don't know how bad she got hurt.' "

Neither Dorsey nor Conley had surprised either the jury or the defense at this point. The narrative Conley related did not follow precisely the last affidavit, but neither did his testimony make radical departure. He had been well coached; he did not testify, for example, that he heard *Leo Frank* running to the metal room, which would have been legally challenged. He was, at this point, a little more effective than either Rosser or Arnold had suspected: he was able to recite a wealth of detail, and he was able to localize every one of his actions.

What neither the defense nor the spectators realized was that Hugh Dorsey was going to touch all the bases. Dorsey was going to relieve Conley of having to remember all those details on cross-examination.

He asked Conley, "What else did Frank say?"

"After he said about how she got hurt, he said, 'You know I ain't built like other men.' The reason he said that was that I had seen him in a position I haven't seen any other man that has got children.* I have seen him in the office two or three times before Thanksgiving and a lady was in his office and she was sitting down in a chair and she had her clothes up to here (Conley demonstrated whipping back an imaginary skirt) and he was down on his knees and she had her hands on Mr. Frank."

"You say you saw this two or three times?"

"I have seen him another time there in the packing room with a young lady lying on the table. She was on the edge of the table when I saw her."

Sexual abnormalities are as old as civilization itself. The Bible describes cunnilingus, rape, incest, sodomy—these activities are no secret to anyone, not even to school boys. But collectively a jury entertains a higher moral standard than the individuals who compose society.

---

* Remember, the Franks were childless. They had been married for less than two years.

Frank had turned in amazement to his attorneys. Rhea Frank, his mother, buried her head in a handkerchief. Lucile Frank, after a brief moment of discomposure, put her hand on her husband's shoulder.

"What did Frank do next?" Dorsey continued.

"He asked me if I wouldn't go back there and bring her up so that he could put her somewhere, and he said to hurry, that there would be money for me. When I came back there, I found the lady laying flat on her back with a rope around her neck."

"How was it tied?"

"The cloth was tied around her neck and part of it was under her head to catch the blood. I noticed the clock after I went back there and found the lady was dead and came back and told him."

"What time was it?"

"The clock was four minutes to one."

Conley told the jury how Frank ordered him to find a piece of cloth in which to wrap the body, and after he had rolled the corpse into some bagging, he looked back and saw her hat and a piece of ribbon and her slippers, which he stuffed into the roll.

"How was this cloth tied?"

"The cloth was tied just like a person that was going to give out clothes on Monday. But the bundle was too heavy for me to carry alone.

"So what did you do then?"

"I let her fall, and I was scared and I kind of jumped and said, 'Mr. Frank, you will have to help me with this girl, she is heavy.'"

Frank thereupon took her feet and Conley her shoulders, and they struggled with the body to the elevator, where Conley said Frank left him to get the key to unlock the power box.

"Then you took the elevator to the basement?"

"We went down to the basement and we carried her out and I opened the cloth and rolled her out there on the floor and

Mr. Frank turned around and went on up the ladder and I noticed her hat and slippers and a piece of ribbon and I said, 'Mr. Frank, what am I going to do with these things?' and he said, 'Just leave them there,' and I taken the things and pitches them over in front of the boiler."

Conley started the elevator.

"You picked up Frank there?"

"He didn't give me time to stop the elevator he was so nervous and trembly, and before the elevator got to the top of the first floor, Mr. Frank made the first step onto it and the elevator being a little down like that, he stepped down and hit me quite a blow right over about my chest. And that jammed me up against the elevator and when we got near the second floor he tried to step off before it got to the floor and his foot caught as he was stepping off and that made him stumble."

In Frank's office, according to Conley, the arrival of Emma Clarke Freeman and Corinthia Hall interrupted them.

"Did those women see you?"

"He put me in a wardrobe and I stayed there a good while and they come in there and I heard them go out and Mr. Frank come there and said, 'You are in a tight place,' and I said, 'Yes,' and he said, 'You done very well. . . .' "

"Did you and Frank then have any further discussion?"

"He said, 'Gee, that was a tiresome job,' and we sat down and he takes a cigarette and a match and hands me the box of cigarettes and then he said, 'Can you write?' and I said, 'Yes, sir, a little bit.' And he takes his pencil to fix up some notes. I was willing to do anything to help Mr. Frank because he was a white man and my superintendent and Mr. Frank dictated those notes to me. Whatever it was it didn't suit him and he told me to turn over and write again and when I done that and I turned the paper and write again."

"Did he take the notes then?"

"He reached over and got another piece of paper, a green piece and told me what to write. He took it and laid it on his desk smiling and rubbing his hands and then he pulled out a nice little roll of greenbacks and he said, 'Here is $200' and I taken the money. After a while, Mr. Frank looked at me and said, 'You go down there in the basement and you take a lot of trash and burn that package that's in front of the furnace,' and I told him, 'All right.' "

"If you were supposed to burn Mary Phagan's body, why didn't you?"

"I was afraid to go down there by myself and Mr. Frank wouldn't go with me. He said, 'There's no need of my going down there.' And I said, 'Mr. Frank, you are a white man and you done it and I am not going down there and burn that myself.' He looked at me then, kind of frightened, and he said, 'Let me see that money,' and he took the money back and put it back in his pocket."

"What did he say next?"

"He turned around in his chair and looked at the money and he looked back at me and folded his hands and looked up at the ceiling and said, 'Why should I hang? I have wealthy people in Brooklyn.' "

"Go on, Jim."

"I said, 'Mr. Frank, what about me?' and he said, 'That's all right, don't you worry about this thing, you just come back to work Monday like you don't know anything, and keep your mouth shut. If you get caught, I will get you out on bond and send you away,' and he said, 'Can you come back this evening and do it?' "

Conley testified he went from the factory to the beer saloon, after finding two dollars and two quarters in the pack of cigarettes Frank had given him. He went home after buying five cents worth of pan sausage and ten cents worth of fire wood. After his dinner, he lay down and fell asleep.

"When did you next see Frank?" asked the prosecutor.

"I saw him next time on Tuesday on the fourth floor when I was sweeping."

"What did he say to you?"

"He walked right up and said, 'Now remember, keep your mouth shut,' and I said, 'All right,' and he said, 'If you'd come back on Saturday and done what I told you to do down there, there wouldn't have been no trouble.' "

Dorsey concluded his examination by rephrasing his earlier questions about the women who had visited the factory.

"The lady I saw in Mr. Frank's office Thanksgiving Day was a tall built lady, heavy weight. She was nice looking and she had on a blue dress with white dots on it and a grayish looking coat with kind of tails to it."

"What did you tell the police when you were first arrested?"

"I refused to write for the police the first time. I told them I couldn't write."

"Your witness," said Dorsey to Rosser.

Conley had told his story in less than four hours.

Rosser would keep him on the stand three days. To save Leo Frank's life, this was the man they had to break. Rosser thought it would be child's play.

CHAPTER FIFTEEN

TWO YEARS before the Frank case, Max D. Steuer had defended Max Blank and Isaac Harris in the Triangle Fire Case. Blank and Harris were on trial specifically for the death of Margaret Schwartz, one of the 146 girls who perished in a shirtwaist factory fire. The State alleged criminal negligence. There was evidence that all the exits but one were locked to prevent pilfering and that the defendants had consistently neglected the warnings of the fire inspectors about defective hoses, and had failed to institute safety precautions, especially in the use of inflammable dyes and chemicals.

Steuer won his clients' acquittal by impugning the State's main witness, Katie Alterman. In his cross-examination Steuer asked Miss Alterman to repeat her testimony several times, which she did in an amazing word-for-word recital. Steuer convinced the jury the prosecution's leading witness had been coached, since she could never vary her testimony by a single phrase. The jury was forced to the reluctant conclusion that the district attorney had carefully rehearsed the testimony.

This was the strategy Rosser elected to follow in cross-examining Jim Conley. He was pretty sure Conley would confuse the details about which the Negro had been so specific under Dorsey's questioning.

Rosser also wanted to show how Conley's affidavits differed, one from the other, and each in turn, from the trial testimony. He hoped these differences would prove Conley a congenital liar.

The weakest part of Conley's testimony was that Frank had dictated the notes and that he and Conley had managed within twenty minutes to carry the dead girl to the basement, come back up to the second floor, write four notes, and hold a con-versation.

Rosser began gently, asking Conley for a history of his employment at the National Pencil Company, sympathizing when Conley complained he made less money than the other Negroes. Conley began smiling at his cross-examiner. Rosser was winning him over.

"At which point," write the Samuelses in *Night Fell on Georgia,* "Hugh Dorsey got quite nervous. He betrayed it by shuffling papers . . . getting up every few moments to move restlessly around the counsel table." Dorsey knew what was coming.

"When was the first time you watched for Mr. Frank?" asked Rosser, in the same soft voice. "Who was with him?"

"That lady that was with Mr. Frank the time I watched for him some time last July was Miss Daisy Hopkins."

"Tell us about it, Jim. When was it?"

"It would always be somewhere between three and three-thirty. I was sweeping on the second floor. Mr. Frank called me in his office. There was a lady there with him. That was Miss Daisy Hopkins. She was present when he talked to me. He said, 'You go down there and see nobody don't come up and you will have a chance to make some money.' "

Conley related that another man named Dalton and another woman were also present and that Dalton had rewarded him with a quarter for his chore.

"Tell us the next time you watched."

"The next Saturday I watched was right near the same thing. It was about the last of July or the first of August. The next

Saturday I watched for him about twelve o'clock, he said, 'You know what you done for me last Saturday? I want to put you wise for this Saturday.' "

When Conley tried describing the ladies Frank entertained, his memory was faulty. He would fumble with descriptions of their clothes and add, "She had hair like Mr. Hooper's," pointing to F. A. Hooper, one of the prosecution lawyers, but he could not remember their names although he had testified they worked in the factory.

"The next time I watched was Thanksgiving Day in Mr. Frank's office. I don't know that lady. She didn't work at the factory. She was nice looking. I think she had on black clothes. She was a very tall, heavy built lady. She went upstairs towards Mr. Frank's office. Mr. Frank said, 'I'll stamp after this lady comes and you go close the door and turn the night latch.' That's the first he told me about the night lock."

Harshly now, Rosser asked, "What did you do the Saturday before Thanksgiving?"

"I don't remember what I did that Saturday."

"What did you do the Saturday after Thanksgiving?"

"I don't remember."

"What did you do on the Saturdays you did watch?"

"I don't remember."

"Can you remember any of the dates on which you watched?"

"No, I don't remember any of the dates. Couldn't tell you to save my life what time I left home the first time I watched."

"Did you draw money that Saturday you watched?"

"I don't know whether I drew my money on the first Saturday I watched."

"How about the second Saturday?"

"I disremember whether I drew my money or whether anyone else did."

That Conley had a poor memory was patent. It seemed he could only remember the crime and Frank's "perversion." As he continued, Rosser made Conley admit he was a liar.

"Did you tell Detective Scott you got up at nine o'clock on the morning of the murder?"

"Yes. That wasn't true. I ate breakfast around seven and left my house between seven and seven-thirty."

"Your affidavit wasn't true then?"

"Yes. There are some things in my last affidavit that are true. I sent for Mr. Scott to come down when I made my first statement."

Rosser made Conley detail his actions on the day of the murder. When had he bought beer? When had he seen his mother? How much money had he?

"Do you remember telling Detective Black you went to the Butt-In Saloon between three thirty and four o'clock?"

"No, I don't remember. The detectives talked to me nearly every day after I made my first statement."

"Yet you looked them in the face and lied?"

Cheerfully Conley admitted he had. For Rosser's and the jury's benefit he demonstrated how he had hung his head in shame when he knew he was lying. This did not make him an unreliable witness to a Southern jury. On the contrary, his admissions of lying gave his story a ring of truth. In the Southern tradition of 1913 the Negro was a born liar. Dorsey had reminded the press some weeks before, as he would remind the jury in his summation, that everyone knew Negroes lied and lied and lied until they told the truth. It was the Negro characteristic, said the solicitor general. One had to wait them out.

What Frank's jury did not realize in subscribing to this myth was that Negroes were perfectly well aware of this reputation. Negroes walked among the enemy. To survive they had constantly to be alert. They knew more about the white man and what he believed than he ever guessed about Negroes. Jim Conley saw daylight and knew these white men didn't know he saw it. The jurors kept nodding at his admissions of deceit as though assenting to a natural process.

Having established Conley's unreliability, Rosser tried to elicit the truth that the testimony had been dictated by the detectives and the solicitor general.

"I sent for Detective Black," said Conley, "on May 24th when my statement came out in the papers."

"I thought you said you couldn't read the papers, Jim."

"I heard the boys across the street hollering extras. Mr. Black came down after I sent for him and I told him it's awful hot in here and I told him I was going to tell him something but I wasn't going to tell him all of it now. Mr. Black talked to me right smart and Mr. Lanford talked a little."

"Did they talk to you the whole day?"

"No, they never talked to me the whole day."

Rosser kept hammering at the number of interviews to which Conley had submitted. Rosser proved that most of the Atlanta Police Department had concentrated its energies on developing Conley's story over several weeks. All the details about which Conley had been positive had been added to his original story by the police. Rosser worked this vein for a full day. When Assistant Prosecutor Hooper objected to the method, Rosser snapped that Jim Conley had rendered a parrot-like statement on examination, a statement he would not be able to remember on cross-examination.

But Rosser was wrong: Conley did remember.

"Yes, I told the detectives that the first party I saw going up the factory after I got back from Montag's was Mattie Smith. That was a mistake. I didn't see Mr. Darley go up either. No, I didn't say yesterday that I saw him go up after I got back from Montag's."

The Court record proved Conley was right. In the main, he could remember, although now everyone in the courtroom sensed Conley was afraid of Rosser. Pushed and bullied, Conley's composure was shaky. But he could still play his role.

"The most revealing comment," write the Samuelses, "was made by William Smith, Conley's lawyer, who told reporters

that the State's star witness, on getting off the stand, had said to
him, 'Boss, I wonder what that jury's gonna do with me?' When
Smith told him he was just a witness, Conley appeared startled
and muttered, 'Oh, I ain't on trial?' "

Conley well knew who was on trial—Leo Frank, the boss man.
Conley well knew he was fencing for his life against a man who
was fencing for Leo Frank's. Even Arnold and Rosser knew now
that they had encountered as wily a perjurer as would ever oc-
cupy a witness stand: a Negro, defenseless, barely literate, yet
more adept at saving himself than a Cornell graduate.

James B. Nevin, a reporter for the *Georgian,* headlined his
story, "Jim Conley, the Ebony Chevalier of Crime, is Dark-
town's Own Hero." He recorded interviews with several Negroes
along Decatur Street and summed up that all of them were
positive Jim was putting one over on a smart white man. If the
people of the Negro slum knew who was on trial, so did Conley.

Defense Attorneys Rosser and Arnold must have realized they
might not succeed in discrediting Conley. In the midst of this
cross-examination, Arnold rose and asked Judge Roan to send
out the jury so that the defense might argue about admissibility
of Conley's testimony.

Judge Roan complied.

Arnold began arguing that the court strike the testimony concerning Frank's alleged sexual perversion. The evidence was inadmissible because cunnilingus and sodomy were capital crimes,
crimes for which Frank was not on trial. This testimony, he
said, was a violation of a general principle in criminal law that
because a defendant had allegedly committed a crime, even a
similar crime, in the past, it cannot be introduced at his trial
for a crime he is alleged to have committed at a later time.
Frank was on trial for murder. No other crime or crimes bore
on that.

For the State, Hooper argued that the defense had no right
to make this motion since they had not objected until realizing
they would get no retractions from Conley. Having cross-ex-

amined the witness, Hooper said, Conley's testimony was admissible no matter when challenge was brought to it.

Arnold was prepared for this gambit. He cited cases and decisions in which testimony was stricken, at the instance of the defense, even after the cross-examination had been completed.

Judge Roan told the two lawyers, "There is doubt in my mind that this evidence, as an original proposition, is inadmissible, but I shall have to take the objection to it under advisement."

A day later he ruled: "I have serious doubts about the admissibility of this evidence. But it is already admitted, and so you may expunge it from the records, but you can't erase it from the minds of the jurors. I rule that it is admissible. What the little Phagan girl said to Epps is not admissible, but this is."

With that, the spectators in the courtroom applauded. Wild cheering echoed from the streets. When the din subsided, Arnold made an impassioned plea for a mistrial. Roan denied him. "The jury was not present," he said. But the jury was outside the door. The jury heard. The jury knew what that mob was cheering so wildly.

Conley returned to the stand. Rosser tried to break his story about the details of the crime.

"When did you tell the officers you heard the scream?"

"I said I heard the scream before I went to sleep. Monteen Stover came up and went down before I went to sleep."

"And when did you wake?"

"He woke me stamping, then I locked the door. It was about ten or fifteen minutes after he stamped that I heard him whistle."

"What time was that?"

"I went back there and found the cord around her neck. When I looked at the clock it was four minutes to one. That was after I went and seen the girl was dead."

Again the witness and the defense lawyer went over these details.

"How many notes did you tell Black and Scott you wrote?"

"The reason I didn't tell Black and Scott I wrote four notes instead of two is they didn't ask me. Another reason why is because Mr. Frank taken that and folded it up like he wasn't going to use it."

"Which note was that?"

"I wrote three notes on white paper and one on green. The green one is the one folded up like he wasn't going to use."

"What time did you leave the factory?"

"About one-thirty."

"How long did it take you to write those notes?"

"I don't know how long it took me to write those notes, it took me somewhere about two minutes and a half." *

Rosser knew that Conley's excrement, which had been discovered in the basement shaft, had an important bearing on the case. It is probable he was not able fully to exploit just what this excrement portended because the courtroom was filled with women and ringed by a mob outside. If this evidence was going to mean anything, Rosser had to make it mean something by implication.

"What about that dung in the elevator shaft? Wasn't that yours?"

"As to how that dung came to be in the elevator shaft, when Mr. Frank had explained to me where he wanted to meet me and just as I started out of the place that Negro drayman came in there with a sack of hay. I gave him a drink of whiskey I bought at Earley's Saloon on Peters Street that morning and he suggested that I go down in the basement and do it, there's a

---

* Why Rosser did not make him duplicate this feat is anyone's guess. Jim Conley was not literate enough to write those notes that quickly. And if Frank was dictating them, some time had to be allowed for composition. It is possible Rosser suspected the prosecutor had trained Conley over and over in writing those 128 words. A subsequent chapter will investigate what no one else in an official capacity investigated save Governor John Slaton— the content of these murder notes; *and* the meaning, rather than the motive, of their content.

light down there, and I went down the ladder and stopped by the side of the elevator, somewhere around the edges of it."

Then Rosser made a crucial error: he brought up the name of William Mincey.

Two days before, Rosser and Arnold, in an ill-conceived press interview, revealed they had a witness, one Mincey, who would prove Jim Conley had killed Mary Phagan.

Among the affidavits these two defense lawyers had secured was one from William Mincey, a sometime schoolteacher and insurance solicitor. A small man with piercing eyes and a gray mustache, who affected a black felt hat and a black suit, Mincey had sworn that on late Saturday afternoon, April 26, he had met Conley, a Negro whom he knew slightly. Conley had confessed to him he'd killed a girl that day and didn't want to kill anyone else.

While Conley's cross-examination went on, Mincey appeared every day outside the courthouse and posed merrily for the newspaper photographers although declaring to the reporters he deplored publicity. Mincey was obviously a fraud. Prosecutor Dorsey had already summoned as a witness—but released— J. T. Boozer, a collector for Patrick and Thompson Jewelers, who could swear he had met Conley on the corner of Peters Street at the same moment Mincey swore he met Conley at Carter and Electric.

"Did you not meet a man by the name of Mincey that day?"

"No, I didn't see a man by the name of Mincey."

"Didn't you tell him you had killed a girl?"

"I didn't tell him I had killed a girl that day."

"Didn't you say you had killed one and didn't want to kill again?"

"I didn't say I killed one and didn't want to kill another."

What Rosser wanted was to end his cross-examination with a crashing accusation that Conley had committed the murder. Mincey was a poor vehicle for this attack, so poor that Rosser never bothered to call him. A day or two later, Mincey stopped coming to the courthouse.

Rosser finished by pursuing this assumption of Conley's guilt. Conley replied to these questions, "I did not tell Harlee Branch that day that Mary Phagan was murdered in the toilet room of the second floor or that the body was stiff when I got back there or that it took thirty minutes to get the body downstairs and to write the notes."

"I don't remember telling Miss Carson on May 1 Frank was innocent. I didn't have any conversation with Miss Mary Pirk and she didn't say I committed the crime. I didn't shoot out of the room immediately she said that.

"I didn't ask Miss Fuss on Wednesday for an extra newspaper. I didn't tell her Mr. Frank was as innocent as the angels in heaven."

Rosser sighed. "That's all."

If Rosser had planned a decisive finale for his cross-examination, so, too, had Hugh Dorsey. Dorsey wanted Conley to leave the stand still the star witness, not the possible murderer, and the solicitor general had saved a trump which he played on redirect examination:

"Did you ever see the murdered girl's bag?" asked Dorsey.

"Yes, sir, I see it."

"Where was it?"

"It was right on Mr. Frank's desk when I went in there to write the notes."

"Did you see what became of it?"

"Yes, sir, Mr. Frank went and put it in the safe."

"Did Mr. Frank know you could write?"

"Mr. Frank knew for a whole year I could write. On the pencil boxes I used to write the word 'Luxury,' 'George Washington,' 'Magnolia,' 'Uncle Remus,' 'Thomas Jefferson.' That's the names of the pencils."

"How do you spell 'Uncle Remus'?"

"O-n-e R-i-n-e-s."

"Luxury?"

"I spell luxury, l-u-s-t-r-i-s."

"Thomas Jefferson?"

"I spell 'Thomas Jefferson' 'T-o-m J-e-f-f-' or 'J-e-i-s-s.' When I wrote the words 'Luxury' and 'Thomas Jefferson,' I don't have anything to copy from. I was writing it down for Mr. Frank."

Now the State's star witness stepped down, his story unshaken. Sheriff Mangum led him to the anteroom where a reporter offered him a cigarette. "How did you like it?" the reporter asked.

"I liked it all right," answered Conley, grinning.

Mangum interrupted, telling the reporters Judge Roan had ordered that no one speak to Conley. Conley picked up a newspaper and began reading about his own testimony. This twenty-seven-year-old semiliterate Negro had accomplished the incredible. He had made the jury believe a fantastic story, a story in which the computation of time was unbelievable, let alone the motivation of the two principals and their actions that occupied this time.

Conley's general bad character was attested to by a score of defense witnesses, members of his own race who had known him all of his life. The State, with all the power at its command, the police with their intricate associations—none were able to find one witness who would say a kind word for Conley's credibility.

Conley had done more, however, than help convict an innocent man. L. F. Woodruff, a reporter for the *Georgian* sensed these dimensions. Woodruff wrote:

"Sinister as a cloud, as raven as a night unaided by moon, planet, or satellite, Jim Conley is today the most talked-of man in Georgia.

"His black skin has not been whitened by the Emancipation Proclamation. The record of his race for regarding an oath as it regards a drink of gin, something to be swallowed, remains unattacked.

"But Georgia is today listening to the words of Jim Conley with breathless interest. Jim Conley has upset the traditions of the South, even as the Phagan case has upset traditions that have lived for years.

"A white man is on trial. His life hangs on the word of a Negro. And the South listens to the Negro's word.

"Had Jim Conley happened to be a Negro of the new type, now so frequently seen in Dixie, a Negro with education enough to halt his racial tendency to lying under oath; had he happened to be a Negro of the old type, the type the South both loves and venerates, the old slave that is faithful to the family, tradition would still exist.

"But Conley has wrecked tradition. He is a Negro of the type that the South has been trying since reconstruction to destroy, the meagerly educated, shiftless, gin-guzzling, half-anthropoid black that any nation could well be rid of.

"But they are listening to Jim Conley."

Reporter Woodruff could not be expected to get the main point: The reason the South so readily believed the Negro in the Frank case was because the Negro was not testifying against a Southerner; the Negro *belonged* to the Southerners. He was really one of their own testifying against an "outsider." For in truth, the Southerners did not hate the Negro in the year 1913. People hate their equals, or better still, they hate someone who is mysteriously "superior." The Negro of the South in 1913 was "inferior,"—he was nothing. These Atlantans on the jury, Southerners everywhere, did not hate "nothing."

The Southerner was not to hate the Negro until May 17, 1954, when the U.S. Supreme Court ruled, in effect, that the legal "inferiority" imposed upon the Negro was not only untrue, but unconstitutional.

CHAPTER SIXTEEN

DEFENSE ATTORNEYS Rosser, Arnold, and Haas were ready to put their side of the case to the jury. They felt they enjoyed two advantages over their adversary Dorsey.

Time was a vital factor in Jim Conley's story. Conley swore he first saw the dead Mary Phagan at four minutes to one. The prosecution had contended Frank left the factory at 1:10 P.M. This gave Frank and Conley but fourteen minutes to wrap the body in a cloth and carry it to the front of the factory and down the elevator to the basement. After returning to the second floor, Frank supposedly washed his hands before hiding Conley in a wardrobe at the approach of two factory employees, Corinthia Hall and Emma Clarke Freeman. Then there were notes to write. Conley said he wrote them in a minute and a half or two minutes, but a Pinkerton detective testified that it took Conley six or seven minutes to write one of these notes in jail when it was dictated to him one word at a time. Assuming Conley required only half that time, still he had to write four notes. Nor was the handwriting continuous, since Conley described that Frank interrupted to make erasures. There was also, according to Conley, considerable conversation between the two of them about Frank's wealthy folks in Brooklyn as well as instructions about burning the body. Two hundred dollars was handed back and forth, and each man had smoked a cigarette.

As soon as Conley had finished testifying, Rosser and Arnold introduced Dr. William Owens who had been hired to stage a re-enactment of the crime exactly as Conley had described it on the witness stand. Carrying a sack with a 110-pound weight to simulate the dead girl's body, Owens, in concert with other reputable citizens, found it was impossible to carry out all the actions that Conley swore he and Frank accomplished in fourteen minutes; it took more than thirty-four.

Over Dorsey's strenuous objections, Owen's report was admitted in evidence for the defense.

The second advantage the defense had was their superior witness: Leo Frank. They hoped the jury would find it easier to believe the articulate Cornell graduate than the illiterate roustabout.

At that, Rosser and Arnold almost lost their chance to put Frank on the stand. On the afternoon that the prosecution rested its case, the mob surged around Sheriff Mangum's car taking Frank back to the Tower. Mangum had been a Southern sheriff for too many years not to know a lynch mob. He leaped from the front seat with a drawn gun and cocked it at the menacing men.

"One more move," he warned, "and I fire."

The mob halted momentarily. In that moment, Deputy Sheriff Plennie Miner drove off.

Other than Conley's, the story that had seriously hurt the defense was Monteen Stover's. Rosser and Arnold argued, therefore, that Mary Phagan arrived at the factory *after* Monteen Stover had left. They opened by swearing W. M. Matthews and W. T. Hollis, the motorman and conductor respectively of the English Avenue streetcar that Mary Phagan had boarded on April 26. Both witnesses testified Mary rode downtown alone. Both testified Epps did not get on with her. Both were positive she left the streetcar at twelve-ten; that morning they were running a few minutes late.

The last witness the state had called was C. Brutus Dalton,

who had supposedly participated in the factory seductions. Rosser called Daisy Hopkins, whom Conley swore was one of the girls Frank and Dalton entertained. She swore she knew Frank only by sight and that she had never entered the factory for immoral purposes.

But she made a bad witness. Prosecutor Dorsey made Daisy admit she had been jailed for immoral purposes, though she insisted, "I went to jail because people told tales on me."

Harry Scott, the Pinkerton detective succeeded her. He described the unkempt and ragged appearance of Conley the day he was arrested and how he and the police had constantly pressed the Negro for an elaboration of the crime to make some sense out of his story.

George Epps was next. Arnold began the questioning: "Do you recollect the Sunday the body was found?"

"Yes."

"Do you remember a gentleman, a Mr. Miner, coming to your house and talking to you and your sister?"

"Yes."

"Didn't he ask you the last time either of you had seen Mary?"

"Yes. He asked my sister but he didn't ask me."

"Weren't you there?"

"No, I wasn't there. I was in the house."

"Weren't you standing by your sister and she said the last time Mary Phagan was seen by her was Thursday before the murder and you stood there and said nothing?"

"No, I didn't hear that. I was in the house but I didn't hear all he said to her."

"Come down," said Arnold.

Cross-examining, Dorsey asked, "George, has there been any trouble to get you to come to court?"

"No, sir. I was playing ball when they sent for me yesterday and didn't get the message."

But the defense had caught George in his lie. Arnold questioned John Miner, a reporter for the *Georgian*: "After this girl's body was found, did you go out to this boy Epp's home?"

"I did."

"Did you ask this boy and his sister when they last saw Mary Phagan?"

"Yes."

"Were they together?"

"Yes."

"Is there any doubt they both heard you?"

"No."

"What did they say in reply to your question?"

"The girl said she had seen her Thursday."

"Did the boy say anything?"

"He said he rode to the city with her in the mornings occasionally."

"Did he say anything about riding with her that Saturday?"

"No."

The most effective witness for the defense, besides Frank himself, was his assistant, Herbert Schiff. Younger than his superintendent, Schiff was equally as intelligent and quick.

"Do you remember Thanksgiving Day, 1912?" asked Arnold.

"I do."

"Were you at the factory that day?"

"I was."

"Who else was there?"

"Mr. Frank and myself, an office boy, and Jim Conley. We had asked Jim Conley to come in because some boxes had to be stacked on the fourth floor."

"Do you remember what time Conley left?"

"Yes. About ten o'clock."

"What time did you and Mr. Frank leave?"

"Shortly after twelve o'clock."

"Where did you go?"

"Home. Mr. Frank's Washington streetcar came before my Whitehall and he got on it."

"Do you know of anything he had to do that night?"

"Yes. He was president of B'nai B'rith and it was giving an affair. He had some packages in his hands."

Defense Attorney Arnold introduced into evidence the financial report Frank had prepared on the afternoon of April 26, as well as those he had made out in previous weeks. Arnold's purpose now was to establish that a man who had just committed a murder would not be able to exercise the demanding clarity and precision that compiling such a report required.

Schiff enumerated the various items on the single sheet and testified that their arrangement took great concentration. Frank had to add, divide, and multiply these figures to arrive at the weekly cost of production.

"How many pencils do you produce a week?"

"About three thousand five hundred gross."

"Have you other places?"

"A slat mill in Oakland City and a lead plant on Bell Street."

"Did Frank have to do the bookkeeping for these places?"

"Yes."

Shown the murder notes, Schiff told the jury the paper on which they were written could be found on every floor of the factory. The old order forms were stored in every department because Frank had found it was cheaper than buying new pads.

"Can you sit in Mr. Frank's office and see the clocks?"

"Only half of one of them."

"If that safe door is open, could you see out?"

"No."

"Could Monteen Stover have seen over it if she were looking in from the outer office?"

"It would have been impossible."

Schiff went on to testify that the blood stains found near Barrett's lathe could have been made by any of the employees. The workers suffered frequent cuts from their machines, and the route to the first-aid cabinet took them past Barrett's lathe. Schiff concluded his direct testimony with the statement that the safe of the National Pencil Company could not possibly have contained two hundred dollars that Saturday. The pencil company's available funds had gone into the payroll envelopes. (Frank's own bank book had shown a balance of sixteen dollars.)

Schiff proved formidable on cross-examination, too. Dorsey and Hooper took turns, but Schiff admitted only that Frank confessed his nervousness on Sunday and had called him three times on Monday about hiring the Pinkerton Agency.

Loud laughter interrupted Schiff's testimony during this cross-examination. (Loud laughter inside the courtroom and outside in the adjacent streets interrupted the testimony of all the Jewish witnesses for Frank.) Judge Roan continually rapped for order. Angrily, Arnold charged the bench: "I am going to move that this courtroom be cleared if there is any more of this disturbance. If we have got to take all of this crowd in, we might as well try the case in the open."

The tired Roan said, "Mr. Sheriff, find out who is creating this disturbance and bring them to me. I will see if I can't stop it."

But a mob is more than a brutal bully, a physical being; it is also a pervading spirit. Day by day, Judge Roan and the jury felt it invade their consciousness; day by day Dorsey and his assistants walked more confidently in its approval.

The best Dorsey or Hooper could get from Schiff was the admission that the pencil company foremen thought Conley was worthless, the implication, of course, that Frank kept him on. To the contrary, insisted Schiff. They kept him on because it was hard to replace a Negro roustabout who knew the work.

To substantiate Schiff's testimony about the complicated financial report, the defense later swore in expert accountants, C. E. Pollard and Joel Hunt, who made a detailed study of Frank's completed work sheet. Pollard told the jury that this exacting work must have taken Frank three hours and eleven minutes to execute.

On Monday, August 11, the trial entered its third week. Rosser and Arnold proceeded then to introduce their medical experts * to contend against the testimony of the state's experts. Charles and Louise Samuels explain in *Night Fell on Georgia:*

"Six years before the entire medical profession had lost the respect and trust of a vast number of Americans due to the venal behaviour of the handful of specialists who testified—for fat fees—in the circus-like murder trial in New York of Harry K. Thaw, the millionaire playboy, who had shot Sanford White, the country's most distinguished architect. Again and again these doctors contradicted one another's scientific opinions. The public by and large concluded that the country's most eminent medical men would testify under oath any way they were asked to—if the price was right.

"There was nothing about the medical testimony given for either side in the Frank case to restore America's faith in its doctors. But the great physicians and specialists of Atlanta appear to have been not so much corrupt as ignorant."

The first of these defense experts was Dr. Leroy Childs, a local surgeon. Arnold asked him a theoretical question: Could he determine from a two-inch scalp wound, examined nine days after *rigor mortis* had set in, whether that would have caused unconsciousness.

"It would be a hazardous guess." Under further questioning, Dr. Childs delivered himself of the opinion that the time of Mary Phagan's death could not be set by the state of partially digested cabbage in her stomach because of the consequent hemorrhages and blood congestion she had suffered.

Holding aloft the vial of cabbage, Dorsey asked Dr. Childs about his experience with the digestive tract. Why wasn't he able to set the time of death?

---

* Although the following testimony was not recorded in chronological order, it is presented forthwith for greater clarity.

The doctor replied that the only comparable instance he remembered was forcing emesis (vomiting) on a patient with indigestion caused by cabbage.

"But that stomach was diseased, wasn't it?" asked Dorsey.

"To a certain extent."

That one emesis, Dorsey made the doctor admit, constituted all he knew about cabbage and digestion.

Dr. Thomas Hancock told the jury that he had practiced for twenty-two years and estimated he had performed fourteen thousand surgical operations. "I have examined the private parts of Leo M. Frank," he testified, "and found nothing abnormal. As far as my examination disclosed, he is a normal man sexually."

He, too, doubted the possibility of determining at what time Mary Phagan died from the state of the cabbage she had eaten. He ventured the opinion that the damage done to the walls of Mary Phagan's vagina was caused by the digital examination the county physician and the mortician had necessarily performed. On cross-examination, however, he had to admit he was no expert on sexuality.

Dr. Willis F. Moreland had practiced medicine for twenty-eight years, had taught surgery, and had formerly served as the president of the State Board of Health. He agreed with the two preceding experts: the delayed exhumation of Mary Phagan's body precluded the chances of determining what time she had died. Without knowing how much blood the patient had lost, it was also impossible to tell whether her scalp wound had been inflicted before or after her death.

When Arnold asked, "Do you have any personal feelings against Dr. Harris, the medical expert for the State?" Moreland replied, "No, but I once preferred charges against him for professional dishonesty." Dr. Moreland concluded, "From an examination of the private parts of Leo M. Frank, he appears to be a perfectly normal man."

Professor George Bachman, a native of France, once an instructor in the Jefferson Medical College of Philadelphia, now the head of the Physiological Department of Physicians and Surgeons in the Atlanta Medical College, also had no hesitancy in belittling the testimony of Dr. Harris. Shown the specimen of cabbage, he declared there was no way of telling whether it had been in the stomach six or seven hours. As to Dr. Harris's theory that no digestion had taken place in the small intestine, Dr. Bachman said the formalin in the embalming fluid would have destroyed the ferments of the pancreatic juice.

He was child's play for Dorsey.

"Do you, Dr. Bachman, know the meaning of the word 'amidulin' as used in the description of starch in its various stage of digestion?"

"I never heard of such a word."

"You never did?"

"No, and no one else ever did. It isn't in any dictionary."

"Nor in any medical work?"

"No."

"*Webster's International Dictionary* gives the definition of 'amidulin' as a variety of starch made soluble by heating."

Dr. J. C. Olmstead, a physician for thirty-six years, and Dr. W. S. Kendrick, Dean of the Atlanta Medical College, completed the defense's medical testimony. They too disagreed with Dr. Harris's conclusions regarding the time of Mary Phagan's death. Dr. Kendrick, however, had to tell Dorsey he hadn't read a book on digestion in the past ten years.

Daisy Hopkins, whom the defense had called to rebut the testimony of C. Brutus Dalton, had damaged Frank's case. Consequently, Rosser investigated Dalton. Now at last, the defense had a surprise for Dorsey.

Rosser recalled Dalton and made him admit he had served time on the chain gang in 1894 on three separate counts of stealing. Ashamedly, Dalton also had to confess he had been indicted in 1899 again for stealing and fined $141.46. He was presently under indictment in Warren County for bootlegging.

When Dalton stepped down, trying to avert the glare of Hugh Dorsey, Arnold swore V. S. Cooper, who appeared with his four-year-old son in his lap, J. H. Patrick, W. T. Mitchell, and I. M. Patrick, all life-long neighbors of Dalton. These four swore that Dalton had a reputation for lying and dishonesty and that no one they knew would believe him under oath.

Minola McKnight was the next important witness. She was the cook who had signed an affidavit alleging that Lucile Frank told her Leo had murdered a Gentile factory girl, a statement she had repudiated.

"What time did Mr. Frank come to dinner that Saturday?"

"Mr. Frank came to dinner about twenty minutes after one. That was not the dinner hour, but Mrs. Frank and Mrs. Selig were going off on the two o'clock car. They were already eating when Mr. Frank came in."

"Was your husband Albert McKnight with you in the kitchen at this time?"

"My husband Albert McKnight wasn't in the kitchen that day between one and two at all."

"From the kitchen can you see the mirror in the dining room?"

"Standing in the kitchen door you cannot see the mirror in the dining room. If you move up to the north end of the kitchen, where you can see the mirror, you can't see the dining-room table."

"After Mr. Frank was arrested, what happened to you?"

"After this happened the detectives came out and arrested me and took me to Mr. Dorsey's office where Mr. Dorsey and my husband and another man were."

"What did they ask of you?"

"They tried to get me to say that Mr. Frank would not allow his wife to sleep that night and that he told her to get up and get his gun and let him kill himself and that he made her get out of bed. I told them right there in Mr. Dorsey's office it was a lie."

"Then what did they do?"

"Then they carried me down to the station house in a patrol wagon. They came to me for another statement about half-past eleven or twelve o'clock that night and made me sign something before they turned me loose, but it wasn't true."

"Why did you feel you had to sign it?"

"I signed it to get out of jail because they would not let me out. It was all written out for me before they made me sign it."

She maintained her story through Dorsey's relentless cross-examination. "Yes, I wept and cried. When they first brought me out of jail, they said they did not want anything but the truth. Then they said I had to tell a lot of lies and I told them I would not do it." She pointed at Detective Campbell in the courtroom. "That man sitting right there and a whole lot of men wanted me to tell lies. They wanted me to witness what my husband was saying."

With the next witness Defense Attorneys Rosser and Arnold took their long chance. They called J. Ashley Jones, Frank's insurance agent, who described the report his company received on Frank's character.

Dorsey was on his feet, objecting.

"We mean to introduce the defendant's character as an issue," explained Arnold. Dorsey smiled and smiled, as Arnold's witness, Jones, said, "We would never have insured him unless he was physically fit and morally above reproach."

Putting a defendant's character in evidence is always a risky business. The State must prove acts—not that a man was *capable* of doing something, but that he *did* do it. Moreover the State must argue first, and the defendant gets the last word. Once a defendant argues he is by nature incapable of the act with which the State charges him, the State can challenge that assertion by introducing evidence that the defendant's character is *indeed* capable. Thus the court allows the prosecution to reopen its case in rebuttal, giving the State the last word.

What probably prompted Rosser and Arnold to throw Frank's

character into the balance was the realization that Conley's testimony about sexual perversion had shifted the burden of proof. The defense was in the position of having to "prove" Frank's innocence, instead of Dorsey's having to "prove" Frank's guilt. These brilliant lawyers accepted the challenge. In this way, they reasoned, they might shift the burden back. It was a serious mistake.

When Ashley Jones finished his insurance testimony Dorsey asked, "Didn't your investigators ever report Frank took girls on his lap and caressed them?"

Arnold objected. Roan overruled him.

Dorsey asked eight more questions. "About twelve months ago you never heard of Frank kissing any girls and playing with the nipples on their breasts? Didn't you hear of the time it was said Miss Pearl Darlson about five years ago threw a wrench at Frank when he offered her money? Didn't you hear that Frank played with little girls in his office?"

Jones kept answering an incredulous, "No, sir."

The defendant's mother, Rhea Frank, at this last question leaped from her seat and screamed hysterically at Dorsey, *"No and you haven't either, you gentile dog!"* Much of her following tirade was fortunately lost in the consequent confusion.

"My God, my God," she moaned. Arnold tried to comfort her before Herbert Haas led her from the courtroom.

In the morning, Dorsey addressed the bench before the jury filed in. "Your Honor," he said, "I appreciate the feelings of the wife and mother. I am sorry for them. They suffer a terrible strain. But I must have protection and I think they should be excluded when we are subjected to outbreaks like that yesterday."

"Without criticizing Mrs. Frank," replied Arnold, "I want to state that the solicitor general's examination of this witness was far worse than her emotional outburst. He was undertaking to get in evidence in an illegal way. He was appealing to the crowd and to the feelings of the jury. My friend is zealous—

he is a little overzealous, but that is not a matter for me to criticize. Our jury system is very lame if we admit this sort of evidence."

Roan ruled, "You are entirely right, Mr. Dorsey, in saying you are entitled to protection. Other women were put out because the evidence was of such a nature as to be indecent to be heard by them. It is a matter in the discretion of the court to state whether these ladies should be allowed to remain. I will say that if there are any more such outbreaks as yesterday I shall be forced to exclude them."

One after another the character witnesses took the stand. Alfred A. Lane, a classmate of Frank's at Pratt Institute, testified he had known Frank for fifteen years and that he possessed a good character. Richard A. Wright and Philip Nash, Cornell classmates, told of Frank's reputation for probity and testified that, to their knowledge, there had never been the slightest gossip concerning the defendant. So did a neighbor of the Franks', Harry B. Lewis, then assistant district attorney of the Borough of Brooklyn, later to become a famous jurist. Several of Atlanta's Jews also testified as to his good character. Their appearance required courage. They lived in Atlanta; their livelihoods depended on the good will of the community. The mob hooted at them as each approached and left the witness chair.

Dorsey rarely cross-examined the well-dressed Northerners or the Jewish businessmen from Atlanta. He did press Sig Montag, the president of the National Pencil Company.

"Didn't you notice how nervous Frank was on Saturday?"

"I was nervous, too."

"Didn't you try to rent a horse and buggy from Brown, the West End liveryman, Saturday afternoon, April 26th?"

"I did not."

"You mean you weren't able to rent one?"

"I mean I did not try."

Defense Attorney Rosser next produced a string of alibi witnesses. Lemmie Quinn told his story. Helen Kerns saw Frank on the street at one-ten Saturday. Mrs. M. G. Michael, a neighbor, said hello to Frank before one-thirty. Mrs. Hennie Wolfsheimer saw him walking back to the factory and noticed nothing unusual about him. Cohen Loeb was on the streetcar with Frank when he returned to the factory after lunch and said the defendant had no cuts or scratches.

Fifty of the girls employed at the factory testified about Frank's good character. Mollie Blair, Ethel Stewart, Sarah Barnes, Ina Hays, Eula May Flowers, Elma Hayes, Minnie Foster, Obie Dickerson, Gussie Wallace, and Annie Osman were among them.

Sarah Barnes, in fact, stampeded through Arnold's questioning, determined to speak without interruption. "I know Frank couldn't have committed such a terrible deed," she screamed, waving her little fan. "He never has done any of these things that have been told about him. He has always been a gentleman. I've had to fight for him, almost, a number of times since these awful charges have been made against him. I am willing to fight for him again. I am willing to die in his place."

She made life no easier for Dorsey on cross-examination when she once again repeated her wish to die for Leo Frank.

Rhea Frank, her eyes red, her face lined with anguish, took the stand. Arnold hoped her testimony would convince the jury that the Franks were not "wealthy Jews from Brooklyn" but rather people of moderate means.

Rhea Frank said that she and her husband owned a six thousand dollar home in Brooklyn on which they had assumed a three thousand dollar mortgage. Their only source of income came from the interest on twenty thousand dollars they had saved and invested. She denied they had rich relatives.

Dorsey did not spare her. One of the few moments in the course of the trial when Frank showed what the ordeal cost him occurred during the cross-examination of his mother. Frank kept glaring at Dorsey, hate and annoyance clearly on his face.

Arnold and Rosser might think the interest on twenty thousand dollars was a moderate income, but Atlanta knew better. The mill hands and the tenant farmers and the other factory workers had rarely seen ten dollars at one time, let alone known the chance to assume a mortgage.

"In what business is your husband?"

"He is not in business at present."

"Ah,* he's a capitalist, is he?"

"No, he's not. He's broken in health. That's why he is not here."

"But aren't you all living on capital?"

"I don't know what you mean."

"You know what it means to be a capitalist, don't you?"

"No, I don't," said the confused woman.

When Dorsey finally let her go, the jury and most of Atlanta still thought Leo Frank was a capitalistic Jew from Wall Street. Long before Mary Phagan died, Tom Watson and most of his Populistic followers had convinced themselves and the South that all their problems were created by rich Jews and Northern capitalists in Wall Street. Georgia was finally getting to see one of her tormentors in the person of Leo Frank. Georgia would hear him on Monday: Leo Frank would tell his story to the jury.

---

* Dorsey's "Ah," is in the official transcript.

CHAPTER SEVENTEEN

IN 1913, no defendant charged with a capital crime in Georgia could testify under oath on his own behalf. Neither he nor his wife could be cross-examined. But he could make a statement to the jury.

Frank chose to make that statement, and he prepared it himself. On Monday, August 11th, the beginning of the fourth week of the trial, his attorneys informed Judge Roan of their client's decision. Two long queues formed outside the courtroom early that morning. The lines reminded one reporter of the crowd collecting for a popular, low-priced matinee.

The courtroom was filled. When Frank rose with Arnold and Rosser at 2:00 P.M. to make his request, even the mob outside hushed.

Judge Roan read him the Georgia law. "In criminal procedure the prisoner will have the right to make to the court and jury such statement in the case as he shall deem proper in his defense. It shall not be under oath and shall have such force as the jury shall think right to give it. They may believe it in preference to sworn testimony. The prisoner shall not be compelled to answer any questions on cross-examination. He should feel free to decline to answer them. Now you can make such statements as you see fit."

Frank mounted the witness stand. His statement was a writ-

ten one, but he faced the jury throughout the four hours it took
him to read it.

His statement was as amazing as Conley's testimony. Perhaps
the Leo Frank statement is as amazing as any statement ever
compelled by American criminal jurisprudence.

Frank read it well. For four hours he was the center of attention in a hot, quiet courtroom as Georgia tried to make up its
mind about justice.*

"Gentlemen of the jury: In the year 1884, on the 17th
day of April, I was born in Quero [Cuero], Texas. At the
age of three months, my parents took me to Brooklyn, New
York, and I remained in my home until I came South, to Atlanta, to make my home here. I married in Atlanta, an Atlanta girl, Miss Lucile Selig. The major portion of my married life has been spent at the home of my parents-in-law,
Mr. and Mrs. Selig, at 68 East Georgia Avenue. My married
life has been exceptionally happy—indeed, it has been the
happiest days of my life. My duties as superintendent of
the National Pencil Company were in general as follows:
looking after the operations and seeing that the product
was turned out in quality equal to the standard which is
set by our competitors. I looked after the installation of
new machinery and the purchase of new machinery. In addition to that, I had charge of the office work at the Forsyth Street plant, and general supervision of the lead plant,
which is situated on Bell Street. I looked after the purchase
of the raw materials which are used in the manufacture of
pencils, kept up with the market of those materials, where
the prices fluctuated, so that the purchases could be made
to the best possible advantage.

"On Saturday, April 26th, I arrived at the factory at
about 8:30 A.M. I found Mr. Holloway, the day watchman,

---

* The statement is abridged in the interests of brevity and continuity.

at his usual place and Alonzo Mann, the office boy, in the outer office.

"About 9 o'clock Mr. Darley and Mr. Wade Campbell, the inspector of the factory, came into the outer office, and I stopped what work I was doing that day and went to the outer office and chatted with Mr. Darley and Mr. Campbell for 10 or 15 minutes, and conversed with them, and joked with them, and while I was talking to them, about 9:15, Miss Mattie Smith came in and asked me for her pay envelope, and for that of her sister-in-law, and I went to the safe and unlocked it and got out the package of envelopes that Mr. Schiff had given me the evening before and gave her the required two envelopes, and placed the remaining envelopes that I got out, that were left over from the day previous, in my cash box, where I would have them handy in case others might come in. Mr. Darley left with me for Montags about 9:35 or 9:40, and we passed out of the factory, and stopped at the corner of Hunter and Forsyth Streets, where we each had a drink at Cruickshank's soda water fount, where I bought a package of Favorite cigarettes, and after we had our drink I lighted a cigarette and went on my way to Montag Brothers, where I arrived at 10 o'clock. Returned to the factory alone. On arrival there I went to the second or office floor, and I noticed the clock, it indicated five minutes after eleven. I saw Mr. Holloway there, and I told him he could go as soon as he got ready, and he told me he had some work to do for Harry Denham and Arthur White, who were doing some repair work up on the top floor, and he would do the work first. I then went into the office and found Miss Hattie Hall, who had preceded me over from Montag's and another lady who introduced herself to me as Mrs. Arthur White, and the office boy; Mrs. Arthur White wanted to see her husband. About this time Mrs. Emma Clarke Freeman and Miss Corinthia Hall, two of the girls who worked on the fourth floor, came in, and asked permission to go up-stairs and get Mrs. Freeman's coat, which I readily gave, and I told them at the same time to tell Arthur White that his wife was downstairs. Just before they left the office, Mrs. Emma Freeman and Miss Corinthia Hall came into my office and asked permission to use the telephone. Mrs. Freeman and Miss Hall left the office, as near as may be, at a quarter to twelve, and went out and I started to work reading over the letters and signing the mail and transacting orders.

"There were in the building then Arthur White and Harry Denham and Arthur White's wife on the top floor. From ten to fifteen minutes after Miss Hall left my office, this little girl whom I afterwards found to be Mary Phagan, entered my office and asked for her pay envelope. I asked her for her number and she told me; I went to the cash box and took her envelope out and handed it to her, identifying the envelope by the number. She left my office and apparently had gotten as far as the door from my office leading to the outer office, when she evidently stopped and asked me if the metal had arrived, and I told her no. She continued on her way out, and I heard the sound of her footsteps as she went away. It was a few moments after she asked me this question that I had an impression of a female voice saying something; I don't know which way it came from; just passed away and I had that impression. This little girl had evidently worked in the metal depart-ment by her question and had been laid off owing to the fact that some metal that had been ordered had not arrived at the factory; hence, her question. I only recognized this little girl from having seen her around the plant and did not know her name, simply identifying her envelope from her having called her number to me.

"She had left the plant hardly five minutes when Lem-mie Quinn, the foreman of the plant, came in and told me

that I could not keep him away from the factory, even
though it was a holiday; at this I smiled and kept on working. He asked me if Mr. Schiff had come down and I told
him he had not and he turned around and left. I continued until I finished this work. I looked at my watch and noticed that it was a quarter to one. I called my home up on
the telephone, for I knew that my wife and my mother-in-
law were going to a matinee and I wanted to know when
they would have lunch. Minola [McKnight] answered the
phone that they would have lunch immediately and for me
to come right on home. I gathered my papers together and
went upstairs to see the boys on the top floor. I saw Arthur
White and Harry Denham who had been working up there
and Mr. White's wife. I asked them if they were ready to
go and they said they had enough work to keep them several hours. I noticed that they had laid out some work and
I had to see what work they had done and were going to
do. I asked Mr. White's wife if she was going or would stay
there as I would be obliged to lock up the factory, and
Mrs. White said, no, she would go then. I went down and
gathered up my papers and locked my desk and went
around and washed my hands and put on my hat and coat
and locked the inner door to my office and locked the doors
to the street and started to go home.

"Now, gentlemen, to the best of my recollection from the
time the whistle blew for twelve o'clock until after a quarter to one when I went upstairs and spoke to Arthur White
and Harry Denham, to the best of my recollection, I did
not stir out of the inner office; but it is possible that in order to answer a call of nature or to urinate I may have gone
to the toilet. Those are things that a man does uncon-
sciously and cannot tell how many times nor when he does
it. Now, sitting in my office at my desk, it is impossible
for me to see out into the outer hall when the safe door is
open, as it was that morning, and not only is it impossible

for me to see out, but it is impossible for people to see in and see me there.

"Arrived home about one-twenty. I found that my wife and my mother-in-law were eating their dinner, and my father-in-law had just sat down and started his dinner. After a few minutes my wife and mother-in-law finished their dinner and left and told me good-bye. My father-in-law and myself continued eating our dinner, Minola McKnight serving us. After finishing dinner, I lighted a cigarette and laid down. After a few minutes I got up and walked up Georgia Avenue to get a car. I saw the Washington Street car coming and I ran up and got on the car and talked to Mr. Loeb on the way to town. About the intersection of Washington Street and Hunter Street and the fire engine house there was a couple of cars stalled up ahead of us, the cars were waiting there to see the memorial parade. After it stood there a few minutes, I told Mr. Loeb that I was going to get out and go on as I had work to do. I went on down Hunter Street, when I got down to the corner of Whitehall and Hunter, the parade had started to come around and I had to stay there fifteen or twenty minutes and see the parade. I stood there between half-past two and a few minutes to three o'clock until the parade passed; then I went on down to Jacobs and purchased twenty-five cents worth of cigars; then down Forsyth Street to the factory; unlocked the street door and the inner door and left it open and went on upstairs to tell the boys that I had come back and wanted to know if they were ready to go, and at that time they were preparing to leave. I went immediately down to my office and opened the safe and my desk and hung up my coat and hat and started to work on the financial report.

"I heard the bell ring on the time clock and Arthur White and Harry Denham came into the office and Arthur White borrowed two dollars from me in advance on his wages. I had gotten to work on the financial sheet, figuring it out, when I happened to go out to the lavatory and on returning to the office, I noticed Newt Lee, the watchman, coming from towards the head of the stairs, coming towards me. I looked at the clock and told him to go to the baseball game. Newt Lee greeted me and offered me a banana; I declined the banana and told him that I had no way of letting him know sooner that I was to be there at work and that I changed my mind about going to the ball game. I told him that he could go if he wanted to or he could amuse himself in any way he saw fit for an hour and a half, but to be sure and be back by around six o'clock. He went off down the stair case leading out and I returned to my office. [Here he described at length his work on the financial sheet and orders.]

"I finished this work that I have just outlined at about five minutes to six, and I proceeded to take out the clock strips from the clock which were used that day and replace them. As I was putting these slips into the clock, I saw Newt Lee coming up the stairs, and looking at the clocks, it was as near as may be six o'clock. I finished putting the slip in and as I was washing, heard Newt Lee ring the bell on the clock when he registered his first punch for the night, and he went downstairs to the front door to await my departure. After washing, I went downstairs to the front door. I saw outside on the street Newt Lee in conversation with Mr. J. M. Gantt, a man that I had let go from the office two weeks previous. Newt Lee told me that Mr. Gantt wanted to go back up into the factory, and he had refused him admission, because his instructions were for no one to go back into the factory after he went out, unless he got contrary instructions from Mr. Darley or myself. I asked him what he wanted, he said he had a couple of pairs of shoes, black pair and tan pair, in the shipping room; told Newt Lee it would be all right to pass Gantt in, and Gantt went in, Newt Lee closed the door locking it after him. I then walked up Forsyth Street, posted two letters, got a drink at soda fount, and bought my wife a box of candy. Arrived home about six twenty-five; sat looking at the paper until about six thirty when I called up at the factory to find out if Mr. Gantt had left. Couldn't get Newt Lee then. At seven I again called the factory, got Newt Lee and asked him if Mr. Gantt had gone again, he says, 'Yes.' I asked if everything else was all right at the factory; it was, and then I hung up and had supper. About eight I saw Minola pass out on her way home. That evening, my parents-in-law, Mr. and Mrs. Emil Selig, had company, and among those present were Mr. and Mrs. Morris Goldstein, Mr. and Mrs. M. Marcus, Mrs. A. E. Marcus and Mrs. Ike Strauss. Sat reading in the hall until ten-thirty when I turned out the gas, went into the dining room, bade them all good night, and went upstairs to take my bath, a few minutes later my wife followed me upstairs.

"Sunday, April 27th, I was awakened before seven o'clock by the telephone. The man that spoke was City Detective Starnes; he said, 'Is this Mr. Frank, superintendent of the National Pencil Company?' I says, 'Yes, sir,' he says, 'I want you to come down to the factory right away,' I says, 'What's the trouble, has there been a fire?' He says, 'No, a tragedy, I want you to come down right away'; I says, 'All right,' he says, 'I'll send an automobile for you,' I says, 'All right,' and hung up and went upstairs to dress; was in the midst of dressing when the automobile drove up, the bell rang and my wife went down stairs to answer the door. She had on a night dress with a robe over it. I followed my wife in a minute or two. I asked them what the trouble was, and the man who I afterwards found out was Detective Black, hung his head and didn't say anything. They asked me did I know Mary Phagan, and I told them I didn't, they then said to me, didn't a little girl with long hair hanging down her back come up to your office yesterday some time for her money. I says 'Yes, I do remember such a girl coming up to my office that worked in the tipping room, but I didn't know her name was Mary Phagan.'

" 'Well, we want you to come down right away with us to the factory.'

"I didn't have breakfast, but went right on with them in the automobile. They took me to the undertaker's, as they wanted me to see the body and see if I could identify the little girl. One of the men asked the attendant to show us the way into where the body was, and the attendant went down a long, dark passageway with Mr. Rogers following, then I came, and Black brought up the rear until we got to a place that was apparently the door to a small room— very dark—the attendant went in and suddenly switched on the electric light, and I saw the body of the little girl. Mr. Rogers stood to my right, inside of the room, I stood right in the door, leaning up against the right facing of the door, and Mr. Black was to the left, leaning on the left facing, but a little to my rear, and the attendant, whose name I have since learned was Mr. Gheesling, was on the opposite side of the little cooling table to where I stood. He removed the sheet which was covering the body, and took the head in his hands, turned it over, put his finger exactly where wound in the left side of the head was located. I noticed the hands and arms of the little girl were very dirty—blue and ground with dirt and cinders, the nostrils and mouth just full of sawdust and swollen, and there was a deep scratch over the left eye on the forehead; about the neck there was twine— a piece of cord similar to that which is used at the pencil factory and also a piece of white rag. After looking at the body, I identified that little girl as the one that had been up shortly after noon the day previous and got her money from me. We then left the undertaking establishment, got in the automobile, and rode over to the pencil factory.

"I went to the elevator box—the switch box, so that I could turn on the current, and found it open. I got on the elevator and started to pull the rope to start it going, and it seemed to be caught, and I couldn't move it. However, Mr. Darley was successful in getting it loose, and it started up.

"In the basement, the officers showed us just where the body was found, and in behind the door to the dust bin, they showed us where they found the hat and slipper on the trash pile, and they showed us where the back door, where the door to the rear was opened about 18 inches. We all went back upstairs and Mr. Darley and myself got some cords and some nails and a hammer and went down to the basement again to lock up the back door, so that we could seal the factory from the back and nobody would enter. After returning upstairs, Mr. Darley and myself accompanied Chief Lanford on a tour of inspection through the three upper floors of the factory. We did not notice anything peculiar.

"We removed the clock slip. After putting a new slip in the clock, we all went out of the factory and went downstairs and locked the door and we went to the police headquarters.

"Now, gentlemen, I have heard a great deal, and so have you, in this trial, about how nervous I was that morning. I was nervous, and completely unstrung; imagine, awakened out of my sound sleep, and a run down in the cool of the morning in an automobile driven at top speed, without any food or breakfast, rushing into a dark passageway, coming into a darkened room, and then suddenly an electric light flashed on, and to see the sight that was presented by that poor little child; why, it was a sight that was enough to drive a man to distraction. Of course I was nervous; any man would be nervous if he was a man. We rode to headquarters very quickly and Mr. Darley and I went up to

Chief Lanford's office where I sat and talked and answered every one of their questions freely and frankly, trying to aid and to help them in any way that I could.

"Next morning, arose about seven and washed and shaved and dressed, and while I was dressing the door bell rang, and my wife again answered the door, and there were two detectives down there, one was John Black, and the other, Mr. Haslett, of the city detectives. They told me they wanted me to step down to headquarters with them. On the way down, I asked Detective Haslett what the trouble down at the station house was, and he said: 'Well, Newt Lee has been saying something, and Chief Lanford wanted to ask you a few questions about it'; and I said, 'What did Newt Lee say?' 'Well, Chief Lanford will tell you when you get down there.' When I got down to police headquarters, Chief Lanford hadn't come down yet. I waited around the office possibly an hour, chatting and talking to the officers. Later Chief Lanford came in and says: 'Come here,' and beckoned to me; and I went with him and went into his room, in his office, and while I was in there, to the best of my recollection, anyhow it is my impression now, that this very time slip, on which at that time was written 'taken out at 8:26,' with the two lines under it, had not been erased, was shown to me, and in looking over it and studying it carefully, I found where the interval of an hour had occurred three times during the time that Newt Lee had been punching on that Saturday night, April 26th. When I had first looked at it, I only noticed that every line had a punch on it, but I didn't notice what time the punch marks themselves were on; this time I studied the slip carefully, it was the same slip I had taken out of the clock, Chief Lanford or one of the officers handed it to me at Police Headquarters, which I absolutely identified with the writing which was on it, which you can readily see if you look now, even though it has been erased.

"There seemed to be some altercation about Mr. Rosser coming in that room, and I heard Mr. Rosser say: 'I am going into that room, that man is my client.' That was the first intimation I had that Mr. Rosser was going to look after my interests in this matter. Chief Beavers stated that he wanted me to give him a statement, and he said: 'Mr. Frank, will you give us a statement?' And I said: 'Certainly.'

"After I had given the statement, I overheard Mr. Rosser say: 'Why, it is preposterous, a man who would have done such a deed must be full of scratches and marks and his clothing must be bloody.' I turned and jumped up and showed them my underclothing and my top shirt and my body, I bared it to them all that came within the range of their vision. I had everything open to them, and all they had to do was to look and see it. After that, Mr. Rosser insisted that two of the detectives, Mr. Black and another detective, accompany Mr. Herbert Haas, and myself to my home and look over my soiled clothing for the past week, which I anticipated had not been given to the washwoman.

"They complied with this request. The detectives immediately went upstairs to my room with Mr. Haas and myself, and I took the laundry bag in which my soiled laundry is always kept and emptied it out on the bed, and they examined each and every article of the clothing which I was then wearing, and which was the brown suit I have here, this brown suit is the same suit I wore that Saturday, April 26th, and Monday, April 28th, and I have worn that suit continuously since then until the weather became so hot, and it has neither been pressed nor cleaned since then.

"The detectives were evidently perfectly well satisfied with what they had seen there, and they left without any further remarks with Mr. Haas. After dinner, I telephoned down to the office and to Mr. Schiff, and told him to get Mr. Montag's permission for the Pencil Company to put on

a detective, preferably a Pinkerton detective, to work with
and assist the city detectives in ferreting out the crime.
Then I went down town to the pencil factory. Mr. Quinn
said he would like to take me back to the metal department
on the office floor where the newspapers had said that Mr.
Barrett of the metal department had claimed he had found
blood spots, and where he had found some hair. They then
took me over to the place in front of the dressing room
where it was claimed the blood spots were found. I examined those spots; took a strong electric flash lamp that he
had around there and looked at them and examined them
carefully. With reference to those spots that are claimed to
be blood that Mr. Barrett found, I don't claim they are not
blood, they may have been, they are right close to the ladies' dressing room, and we have had accidents there.
Where people just cut their fingers and they go back to
work, we don't make any record of that, and we have people there cutting their fingers very often, and when they
cut their fingers, their line of travel is right by that place
where Mr. Barrett found those spots, right to the office.

"I returned after making this examination to my office
and gathered up what papers I had to take over to Montag
Brothers, and I took the financial report which I had made
out the Saturday afternoon previous, and I talked it over
with Mr. Sig Montag. I returned from Montag Brothers to
the pencil factory. In a few minutes Mr. Harry Scott of the
Pinkerton Detectives came in and I took him aside into my
office, my private office, and spoke to him in the presence
of Mr. N. V. Darley and Mr. Herbert Schiff. I told him that
I expected that he had seen what had happened at the pencil factory by reading the newspapers and knew all the details. He said he didn't read the newspapers and didn't
know the details, so I sat down and gave him all the details that I could; took him around the building, took him
first back to the metal room and showed him the place

where the hair had been found; showed him the spot in front of the dressing room and took him to the fourth floor; took him down into the basement and made a thorough search, and that included an examination of the elevator well which was at bottom of elevator shaft; then went back and I showed him where the officer said the slipper had been found, the hat had been found and the little girl's body was located. I showed him, in fact, everything that the officers had showed us.

"On Tuesday I arrived at the pencil factory about 8:30; immediately entered upon my routine work sending the various orders to the various places in the factory where they were due to go; a little later detectives Scott and Black came up to the factory and said: 'Mr. Frank, we want you to go down to headquarters with us,' and I went with them. We went down to headquarters and I have been incarcerated ever since.

"Detective Scott and Detective Black showed me a little piece of material of some shirt and asked me if I had a shirt of that material; told them I didn't think I ever had a shirt of that description; they brought in Newt Lee, the nightwatchman from a cell and showed him the cloth, he said he had a shirt like that but didn't remember having worn it for two years. Detectives Scott and Black then opened a package they had and disclosed the full shirt of that material that had all the appearance of being freshly stained with blood, and had a very distinct odor. Newt Lee was taken back to the cell. After a time Chief Lanford came over to me and began an examination of my face and of my head and my hands and my arms. Detective Starnes took me down to the desk sergeant where they searched me and entered my name on the book under a charge of suspicion. Detectives Scott and Black came in at midnight, Tuesday, April 29th, and said: 'Mr. Frank, we would like to talk to you a little bit.' They stressed the possibility of couples having been let into the factory at night by the night watchman, Newt Lee. I told them that I didn't know anything about it, that if I had, I certainly would have put a stop to it long ago. They said: 'Mr. Frank, you have never talked alone with Newt Lee. You are his boss and he respects you. See what you can do with him. We can't get anything more out of him, see if you can.'

"I says: 'All right, I understand what you mean; I will do my best,' because I was only too willing to help. Black says: 'Now put it strong to him, put it strong to him, and tell him to cough up and tell all he knows. Tell him that you are here and that he is here and that he better open up and tell all he knows about happenings at the pencil factory that Saturday night, or you will both go to hell.'

"In a few minutes Detective Starnes brought up Newt Lee from the cell room and handcuffed him to a chair. I spoke to him at some length in there, but I couldn't get anything additional out of him. He said he knew nothing about couples coming in there at night, and remembering the instructions Mr. Black had given me I said: 'Now, Newt, you are here and I am here, and you had better open up and tell all you know, and tell the truth and tell the full truth, because you will get us both into lots of trouble if you don't tell all you know,' and he answered me like an old Negro; 'Before God, Mr. Frank, I am telling you the truth and I have told you all I know.' And the conversation ended right there.

"Within a minute or two afterwards the detectives came back into the room, that is, Detective Scott and Detective Black, and then began questioning Newt Lee, and then it was that I had my first initiation into the third degree of the Atlanta police department. The way that fellow Black cursed at that poor old Negro, Newt Lee, was something awful. He shrieked at him, he hollered at him, he cursed him, and did everything but beat him. Then they took

Newt Lee down to a cell and I went to my cot in the outer room.

"Before closing my statement, I wish to touch upon a couple of insinuations and accusations other than the one on the bill of indictment, that have been leveled against me so far during the trial. The first is this, the fact that I would not talk to the detectives; that I would not see Jim Conley.

"On Sunday morning I went to headquarters twice, willingly, without anybody coming for me; I answered frankly and unreservedly, giving them the benefit of the best of my knowledge. On Monday they came for me; I went down and answered any and all of their questions and gave them a statement which they took down in writing. Tuesday I was at the police station again, and answered every question; talked to anybody who wanted to talk with me about it, and I have even talked with them at midnight when I was just about to go to bed. I spoke to Newt Lee alone, but what was the result? They commenced and they grilled that poor Negro and put words into his mouth that I never said, and twisted not alone the English, but distorted my meaning.

"I decided then and there that if that was the line of conduct they were going to pursue, I would wash my hands of them. On May 1st, was taken to the Fulton County Tower. On May 3rd Detectives Black and Scott came up to my cell; wanted to speak to me alone without any of my friends around. Black said: 'Mr. Frank, we are suspicious of that man Darley. We are watching him; we have been shadowing him. Now open up and tell us what you know about him.' I said: 'Gentlemen, you have come to the wrong man, because Mr. Darley is the soul of honor and as true as steel. He would not do a crime like that, he couldn't do it.' And Black said: 'Come on, Scott, nothing doing,' and off they go.

"That showed me how much reliance could be placed in

either the city detectives or our own Pinkerton detectives, and it was for this reason that I didn't see Conley, sur-rounded with a bevy of city detectives and Mr. Scott, be cause I knew that there would not be an action so trifling, that there was not an action so natural but that they would distort and twist it to be used against me, and that there was not a word that I could utter that they would not de-form and twist and distort to be used against me, but I told them through Mr. Klein that if they got the permis-sion of Mr. Rosser to come, I would speak to them; would speak to Conley and face him or anything they wanted—if they got that permission or brought Mr. Rosser. Now, that is the reason that I have kept my silence, not because I didn't want to speak, but because I didn't want to have things twisted.

"Then that other implication, the one of knowing that Conley could write, and didn't tell the authorities.

"On May 1st I was taken to the Tower. On the same date the negro Conley was arrested. I didn't know anybody had any suspicions about him. His name was not in the papers; I had no inkling that he ever said he couldn't write. I was sitting in that cell in the Fulton County jail, about May 12th or 14th. Mr. Leo Gottheimer, a salesman for the Na-tional Pencil Company, came running over and says, 'Leo, the Pinkerton detectives have suspicions of Conley. He keeps saying he can't write; these fellows over at the fac-tory know well enough that he can write, can't he?' I said: 'Sure he can write.'

" 'We can prove it; the nigger says he can't write and we feel that he can write.'

"I said: 'I know he can write. I have received many notes from him asking me to loan him money. If you will look into a drawer in the safe you will find the card of a jeweler from whom Conley bought a watch on the installment. If you go to that jeweler you may find some sort of a receipt that Conley had to give.'

"Gottheimer took that information to the Pinkertons; they did just as I said; they got the contract with Conley's name on it; Scott then told the Negro to write. The man who found out or paved the way to find out that Jim Conley could write is sitting right here in this chair. That is the truth about it.

"Then that other insinuation, so dastardly that it is beyond the appreciation of a human being, that my wife didn't visit me; the truth is, that on April 29th, when I was taken in custody at headquarters, my wife was there to see me; was downstairs on the first floor; I was up on the top floor. She was there almost in hysterics, having been brought there by her two brothers-in-law, and her father. Rabbi Marx was with me at the time. I consulted with him as to the advisability of allowing my dear wife to come up to the top floor to see me in those surroundings with city detectives, reporters and snapshooters; I thought I would save her that humiliation, because I expected any day to be returned once more to her side at home. Gentlemen, we did all we could do to restrain her in the first days when I was down at the jail from coming on alone down to the jail, but she was perfectly willing to even be locked up with me and share my incarceration.

"Gentlemen, I know nothing whatever of the death of little Mary Phagan. I had no part in causing her death nor do I know how she came to her death after she took her money and left my office. I never even saw Conley in the factory or anywhere else on April 26, 1913.

"The statement of the witness Dalton is utterly false as to coming to my office and being introduced to me by the woman Daisy Hopkins. If Dalton was ever in the factory building with any woman, I didn't know it. I never saw Dalton in my life to know him until this crime.

"The statement of Conley is a tissue of lies from first to last. I know nothing whatever of the cause of the death of Mary Phagan, and Conley's statement as to his coming up and helping me dispose of the body, or that I had anything to do with her or to do with him that day is a monstrous lie.

"The story as to women coming into the factory with me for immoral purposes is a base lie and the few occasions that he claims to have seen me in indecent positions with women is a lie so vile that I have no language with which to fitly denounce it.

"I have no rich relatives in Brooklyn, N.Y. My father is an invalid. My father and mother together are people of very limited means, who have barely enough upon which to live. My father is not able to work. I have no relative who has any means at all, except Mr. M. Frank who lives in Atlanta, Georgia. Nobody has raised a fund to pay the fees of my attorneys. These fees have been paid by the sacrifice in part of the small property which my parents possess.

"Gentlemen, some newspaper men have called me "the Silent Man in the Tower," and I kept my silence and my counsel advisedly, until the proper time and place. The time is now; the place is here; and I have told you the truth, the whole truth."

The statement moved them. There was no sound when Frank finished and walked back to his table to welcome the embraces of his wife, Lucile, who had begun to sob. His mother clutched him, too, and for the second time during the trial, Frank let his emotions take over. He, too, looked as if he would weep. He beckoned to Sheriff Mangum and was passed through the courtroom, shaking hands with his friends and relatives who had come to hear him.

CHAPTER EIGHTEEN

IN THE STATE'S REBUTTAL, Dorsey first of all swore eighteen witnesses who said C. Brutus Dalton was a reformed man with a present reputation for honesty.

That done, he proceeded to swear dozens of the factory girls to impugn the character of Leo Frank.

Irene Jackson, an 18-year-old ex-employee, testified, "Emily Mayfield and I were in the ladies dressing room of the factory one morning when the door opened suddenly and Frank came in. I was fully dressed but Emily stood in her underskirt. Frank said nothing and walked out. Another time I was in the dressing room with my sister who was lying down. Frank came in but walked out again, saying nothing. The third time I was in the dressing room with Mamie Kitchens when Frank came in. I was not dressed. He pushed open the door without knocking, looked at us and left."

Mamie Kitchens corroborated this story. She said Frank stood there, staring at her, and laughed.

Dorsey even imported Dewey Hewell, a 16-year-old girl who was serving a sentence in the Home of the Good Shepherd in Cincinnati. She came to Atlanta, heralded by headlines, and appeared in court accompanied by a police matron. She had worked in the pencil factory four months, she told the jury, during which time she saw Frank talk to Mary Phagan two or three times. "He called her Mary. He would stand pretty close to her and lean over in her face."

Equally as damaging was the testimony of a farmer, Will Turner, who had worked briefly for the National Pencil Company. Turner swore he saw Leo Frank talking to Mary Phagan on the second floor about the middle of March. There was nobody else in the metal room when he saw Frank stop the girl. She told him she had to go back to work, but he said he was the superintendent of the pencil factory and that he wanted to talk to her.

"What did Mary Phagan look like?" asked Rosser on cross-examination.

All Turner could remember was that she had light hair. He could not remember the names of any other girls in the factory, nor could he say who told him Mary Phagan's name.

Dorsey tried discrediting the testimony of Rachel Carson, a forewoman on the second floor, who had been one of the defense's staunchest character witnesses. "I propose to show," announced the solicitor general, "that this woman brought here to swear to Frank's good character had been seen entering a dressing room with him when no one else was in there and that she and Frank remained in there by themselves for fifteen to twenty minutes at a time."

Miss Carson denied this but was contradicted by two other girls, Maggie Griffin and Myrtis Cato.

Not one of these girls who told the jury Frank was lascivious was cross-examined. Defense Attorneys Rosser, Arnold, and Haas waited through their testimony. Certainly it was damaging. Certainly it endangered Frank's fate.

"The puzzling failure of the defense attorneys," write the Samuelses, "to cross-examine these witnesses is one of the main reasons given by some students of the case for the jury's verdict."

But it is not a puzzling failure. The jury itself had become part of the mob that ringed the courthouse, the mob that loved little Mary Phagan, the factory girl. All these witnesses, still in their teens, were stand-ins for the ravished Mary. Bullying them would have prejudiced Frank's case even more.

Atlanta thought it was cruel enough that Frank hired these young Southern girls, thought it was criminal that he could have sexually exploited them. It is doubtful any cross-examination would have made the jury disbelieve them.

What Rosser and Arnold and Haas counted on was that the defense had made a good case for Frank's innocence, and they were banking on Judge Roan to buttress that case with his charge. Of course, the jury would believe these girls testifying for the prosecution. The defense was hoping the jury could not bring itself to believe the word of the Negro.

CHAPTER NINETEEN

IN SUMMATION, the prosecution had the better of it. F. A. Hooper argued first for the State, followed by Arnold and Rosser for the defense, and Dorsey's summation closed the trial.

Hooper's argument was brief. In essence, he said Leo Frank had tried to sacrifice two Negroes, Newt Lee and Jim Conley, as well as one white man, John Gantt, to save his own life.

"As a citizen of Atlanta, I am not proud of conditions that existed in that factory! What was its moral atmosphere? The character of it appeals wonderfully to us as we seek the truth.

"The defense has produced numbers of girl workers who told us of Frank's character. They say it is good. That is only negative because he has never harmed them. They do not know him. But, while we are considering their stories, there are the stories of others—girls who left his factory because of his character and his conduct toward them. They say his character is bad. You have from the two your choice of either. Those who still are there—those who have never been harmed—and those who have left because of him and his character.

"That pencil factory was a great place for a man without a conscience. It was a great place for Frank, his handsome assistant, Mr. Darley, and the able Mr. Schiff. We find that Frank had coupled himself up for nightly meetings with Dalton, who now has, it seems, turned respectable. My friends, no doubt, will argue that it was strange a man of such business and social posi-

Leo Frank at his installation as president of the Atlanta B'nai B'rith, 1912.

Leo Frank on trial for the murder of Mary Phagan. Behind him, his wife Lucile.

Lucile Selig Frank, wife of the defendant. She was faithful to her husband and to Atlanta until her death in 1957.

Mrs. Rudolph (Rhea)
Frank in Atlanta dur-
ing her son's trial.

Governor John M. Slaton on his inauguration day, June, 1913.

Tom Watson, the Populist leader, on the porch of his mansion, Hickory
Hill, Thomson, Georgia, in 1914.

Part of the affidavit of the prosecution's chief witness, James Conley. For the first time in the South, a Negro's affidavit brought a white man to trial on a capital charge.

The reason I have not told this before is I thought Mr. Frank would get out and help me out, but it seems that he is not going to get out and I have decided to tell the whole truth about this matter.

While I was looking at the money in my hand Mr. Frank said let me have that and I will make it all right with you monday live and nothing happens" & he took the money back & I asked him if that was the way he done and he said he would give it back Monday

Sworn to and subscribed before me this 29 day of May, 1913.

James Conley

G C Febuary

Notary Public, Fulton County, Georgia.

The lynching. Compare the expression of the photographer with that of the fellow in overalls and the shirt-sleeved boy next to him. Copies of this photo, taken by a member of the lynch mob, were sold throughout the South for the next ten years.

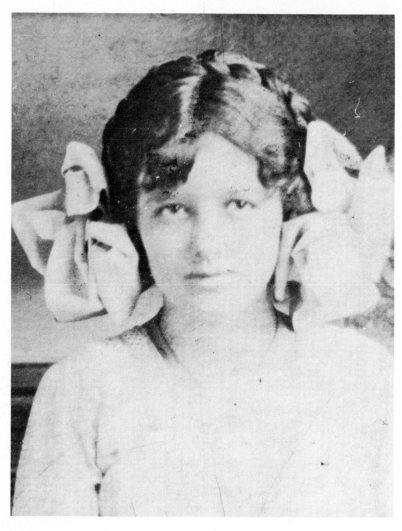

Little Mary Phagan, fourteen-year-old factory employee, a few months before her death. Her hair was a dark reddish-blond.

tion should consort with such a character. It will be a good argument, likely, but probe a little deeper and see if Dalton was not the kind of man required by a dual personality such as possessed by Frank?

"This factory was under the control of this man Frank. It is a house of bad reputation. You find other acts of this sort committed therein. It is unsavory. Frank is its head. He contends he did not know Mary Phagan. Why, every day as he walked through the floor on which his office was situated, he passed by her at her machine. You find, gentlemen, that he often stopped at her place of duty to show her this or to show her that, to help her in her work. Not only that, but he followed her out of her beaten path—following like some wild animal, telling her of his superiority, coaxing, persuading, all the while she strove to return to her work at her machine. You will notice on this diagram that every time he crossed the floor he passed this beautiful girl, looking upon her with the eye of lust.

"I will be fair with Frank. When he followed the child back into the metal room, he didn't know that it would necessitate force to accomplish his purpose. I don't believe he originally had murder in his heart.

"There was a scream. Jim Conley heard it. Just for the sake of knowing how harrowing it was, I wish you jurymen could hear a similar scream.

"Frank said Newt Lee's time slip was correctly punched, that it was all right, and others agreed to it. He said, 'That clears you, Newt.'

"What next occurred to him? He saw he was getting into a fix, and he had better take a shot at Newt. What happens? Another slip turns up. He says he was mistaken at first. There were lapses in the punches on the slip, showing time enough unaccounted for to allow Newt to go home.

"Policeman Black had suspicions. He goes to Newt Lee's home. He unlocks the door with his keys, and looks in the house and on the trash pile, and in the bottom of the barrel, with a lot of things piled on top of it, he found a bloody shirt! How did it get there? Newt Lee accounts for his time Sunday. No suspicion attaches to Newt Lee. He is a free man. How did that bloody shirt get there? It had to be planted. Gentlemen, it was planted! Here are the two propositions, gentlemen. If Newt Lee was to be made the goat, suspicion had to be directed to him. Somebody had to plant that suspicion.

"He would sacrifice Newt Lee that he might live!

"The Bible says, 'What will not a man give for his life?' He was willing to give the life of Newt Lee that his own life might be spared. He was willing to give the life of Gantt that he might live. Was not Gantt arrested a few days after?

"But not once at that time did he think of giving the life of Jim Conley. But somebody found Jim Conley washing a shirt to go to the trial, and that was where Jim got into trouble. He is the man about whom it appeared that the whole fight would center. If he could convince you that Jim confessed the murder to him, that would let Frank out! Yet where is Mincey? * Gentlemen, this has been a long testimony which you have had to sit through, and I do not wish to take up any more of your time than necessary.

"Gentlemen, the only belief required of you is the same sort of belief that you would have upon the street, at your places of business, or in your homes, and on this belief you are to act. Simply use your common sense in the jury box. I thank you."

Many students of the Frank case have argued that Reuben Arnold made a serious mistake in his summation by introducing the Jewish issue. Arnold argued Frank was hounded and prosecuted because he was a Jew.

This argument was not a mistake. That Frank was a Jew was the paramount interest about him from the moment the papers told Atlanta he was questioned by police. Arnold made the ob-

* Mincey it will be remembered was supposed to be the Defense's star witness, the man who heard Conley confess on Saturday afternoon, April 26. Never sworn, Mincey, an obvious fraud and publicity seeker, dealt the defense a staggering blow.

vious, the necessary, argument: the truth was that if Frank had not been Jewish he would never have been tried.

As far as trial testimony goes, it was Dorsey who introduced Frank's Jewishness. He questioned Mrs. Frank about the supposedly rich relatives in Brooklyn. The jury knew what the prosecutor was talking about. And in his rebuttal, Dorsey swore one James Kendley, a streetcar conductor, to contradict the testimony of conductor and motorman Hollis and Matthews, who had testified that Mary Phagan alighted from their streetcar at twelve-ten. Kendley proved a psychotic anti-Semite.

What the big, blond Arnold didn't realize until too late was that Dorsey was also an anti-Semite.

Arnold began:

"I'll tell you right now, if Frank hadn't been a Jew there would never have been any prosecution against him. I'm asking my own people to turn him loose, asking them to do justice to a Jew, and I'm not a Jew, but I would rather die before doing injustice to a Jew.

"Oh, well, the whole case is a mystery, a deep mystery, but there is one thing pretty plain, and that is that whoever wrote those notes committed the crime. Those notes certainly had some connection with the murder, and whoever wrote those notes committed the crime."

Here he undertook a detailed elaboration of how the police had worked over the story that Jim Conley had told on the stand. Conley's ability to recall detail, Arnold argued, was all the work of the police. In each of his three affidavits Conley recalled concrete details, all of which were later admitted lies.

"I want to ask this much: Could Frank have remained at the head of his concern if he had been as loose morally as the state has striven to show? If he had carried on with the girls of the place as my friend alleged, wouldn't the entire working force have been demoralized, ruined? He may have looked into this dressing room, as the little Jackson girl says, but, if he did, it was done to see that the girls weren't loitering. There were no lavatories, no toilets, no baths in these dressing rooms. The girls only changed their top garments. He wouldn't have seen much if he had peered into the place. You can go to Piedmont Park any day and see girls and women with a whole lot less on their persons. And at the shows any night you can see the actresses with almost nothing on. Everything brought against Frank was some act he did openly and in broad daylight, and an act against which no kick was made.

"I tell you that they have mistreated this poor Mrs. Leo Frank terribly. They have insinuated that she would not come to the Tower to see Frank—had deserted him. When we know that she stayed away from the jail at Frank's own request because he did not want to submit her to the humiliation of seeing him locked up and to the vulgar gaze of the morbid and to the cameras of the newspapermen. The most awful thing in the whole case is the way this family has been mistreated! The way they invaded Frank's home and manipulated his servants. I deny that the people who did this are representative of the 175,000 people of Fulton County! We are a fair people, and we are a chivalrous people. Such acts as these are not in our natures.

"The man that wrote those murder notes is the man who killed that girl. Prove that man was there and that he wrote the notes and you know who killed the girl. Well, Conley acknowledges he wrote the notes and witnesses have proved he was there and he admits that, too. That negro was in the building near the elevator shaft; it took but two steps for him to grab that little girl's mesh bag. She probably held on to it and struggled with him. A moment later he had struck her in the eye and she had fallen. It is the work of a moment for Conley to throw her down the elevator shaft.

"Away with your filth and your dirty, shameful evidence of perversion; your low street gossip, and come back to the time— the time-element in the case.

"Now, I don't believe the little Stover girl ever went into the inner office. She was a sweet, innocent, timid little girl, and she just peeped into the office from the outer one, and if Frank was in there, the safe door hid him from her view, or if he was not there, he might have stepped out for just a moment.

"Now, gentlemen, I've about finished this chapter, and I know it's been long and hard on you and I know it's been hard on me, too; I'm almost broken down, but it means a lot to that man over there. It means a lot to him, and don't forget that. This case has been made up of just two things—prejudice and perjury. I've never seen such malice, such personal hatred in all my life, and I don't think anyone ever has. The crime itself is dreadful, too horrible to talk about, and God grant that the murderer may be found out, and I think he has. I think we can point to Jim Conley and say there is the man.

"But, above all, gentlemen, let's follow the law in this matter. In circumstantial cases you can't convict a man as long as there's any other possible theory for the crime of which he is accused, and you can't find Frank guilty if there's a chance that Conley is the murderer. The State has nothing on which to base their case but Conley, and we've shown Conley a liar. Write your verdict of not guilty and your consciences will give your approval."

For three and a half hours on Friday, August 22, the huge Luther Rosser pleaded for Frank's life. His voice was husky, but he spoke incisively. He grew bitter in his attack on Dorsey's methods, and heaped scorn and sarcasm on Jim Conley, declaring it was a shame to the city and state that the word of a "filthy, criminal, lying Negro" should be taken in an effort to hang a man and that the state would regret it for many a day.

"Well, gentlemen, the older I get the gentler I get and I wouldn't think or say anything wrong about those misleading little girls who swore Frank was a bad man. I guess they thought they were telling the truth. Well, did Miss Maggie Griffin really think Frank was a vicious man and yet work there three years with him? Don't you think she heard things against him after the crime was committed and that when she got up here and

looked through the heated atmosphere of this trial, she did not
see the real truth? And Miss Myrtis Cato, she was there two
months. I wonder what she could know about Frank in that
time. There was Mrs. Donegan and Miss Johnson and another
girl there about two months, and Nellie Pettis, who never
worked there at all, and Mary Wallace, there three days, and
Estelle Wallace, there a week and Carrie Smith, who like Miss
Cato, worked there three years. These are the only ones in
the hundreds who have worked there since 1908 who will say
that Frank has a bad character. Why, you could find more people to say that the Bishop of Atlanta, I believe, had a bad character, than have been brought against Frank.

"You noticed they were not able to get any men to come from
the factory and swear against Frank. Men are harder to whee-
dle than are little girls. Does anybody doubt that if that factory had been the bed of vice that they call it, that the long-
legged Gantt would have known of it? They had Gantt on the
stand twice, and, well, you know Gantt was discharged from the
factory, of course you weren't told why in plain words, but you
all know why. Well, Frank is not liked by Gantt and Gantt
would have loved to tell something against his former employer,
but he couldn't.

"Gentlemen, take a look at this spectacle, if you can. Here is
a Jewish boy from the North. He is unacquainted with the
South. He came here alone and without friends and he stood
alone. This murder happened in his place of business. He told
the Pinkertons to find the man, trusting to them entirely, no
matter where or what they found might strike. He is defenseless
and helpless. He knows his innocence and is willing to find the
murderer. They try to place the murder on him. God, all merci-
ful and all powerful, look upon a scene like this!

"The thing that arises in this case to fatigue my indignation
is that men born of such parents should believe the statement
of Conley against the statement of Frank. Who is Conley? Who
was Conley as he used to be and as you have seen him? He was

a dirty, filthy, black, drunken, lying nigger. Black knows that. Starnes knows that. Chief Beavers knows it. Who was it that made this dirty nigger come up here looking so slick? Why didn't they let you see him as he was? They shaved him, washed him and dressed him up. Gentlemen of the jury, the charge of moral perversion against a man is a terrible thing for him, but it is even more so when that man has a wife and mother to be affected by it. Dalton, even Dalton did not say this against Frank. It was just Conley.

"Gentlemen, I want only the straight truth here, and I have yet to believe that the truth has to be watched and cultivated by these detectives and by seven visits of the solicitor general. I don't believe any man, no matter what his race, ought to be tried under such testimony. If I was raising sheep and feared for my lambs, I might hang a yellow dog on it. I might do it in the daytime, but when things got quiet at night and I got to thinking, I'd be ashamed of myself. You have been overly kind to me, gentlemen. True, you have been up against a situation like that old Sol Russell used to describe when he would say, 'Well, I've lectured off and on for forty years, and the benches always stuck it out, but they was screwed to the floor.' You gentlemen have been practically in that fix, but I feel, nevertheless, that you have been peculiarly kind, and I thank you."

On Friday afternoon, August 22, Hugh Dorsey began his summation. He spoke until court adjourned at 5:30 P.M., for six hours on Saturday, and for another three on Monday morning.

It was a white-hot Philippic, not incisive or analytic, but exhausting and emotional rhetoric, pure and simple. And as such it was brilliant. William Faulkner called the South a myth and James McBride Dabbs calls it a poem. The South is also its own rhetorical invention. Dorsey's was precisely the speech that would spur a juror to vote guilty.

Arnold and Rosser had to interrupt Dorsey's summation constantly. They charged he had commented on subjects other than

were introduced into evidence. Garrulously, Dorsey would wave
them aside.

Dorsey began by denying any anti-Semitic prejudice and then
promptly launched into a resume of the careers of Jewish
criminals.

"We would not have dared to come into this presence and
ask the conviction of a man because he was a Gentile, a Jew or a
Negro. Oh, no two men ever had any greater pleasure shown on
their faces than did Mr. Arnold and Mr. Rosser when they
started to question Kendley and began to get before the Court
something about prejudice against the Jews. They seized with
avidity the suggestion that Frank was a Jew.

"Remember, they put it before this Court, and we did not;
the word Jew never escaped our lips. I say that the race this
man comes from is as good as ours; his forefathers were civilized
and living in cities and following laws when ours were roaming
at large in the forest and eating human flesh. I say his race is
just as good as ours, but no better. I honor the race that produced Disraeli, the greatest of British statesmen; that produced
Judah P. Benjamin, as great a lawyer as England or America
ever saw; I honor the Straus brothers; I roomed with one of
his race at college; one of my partners is of his race. I served on
the board of trustees of Grady hospital with Mr. Hirsch, and I
know others, too many to count, but when Lieutenant Becker
wished to make away with his enemies, he sought men of this
man's race.

"Then, you will recall Abe Hummel, the rascally lawyer, and
Reuff, another scoundrel, and Schwartz, who killed a little girl
in New York, and scores of others, and you will find that this
great race is as amenable to the same laws as any others of the
white race or as the black race is.

"They rise to heights sublime, but they also sink to the lowest
depths of degradation!"

He proceeded then to give the jury a detailed interpretation of the meaning of the Georgia criminal law. He discussed the issue of a man's good character.

"Now, gentlemen, put yourself in this man's place. If you are a man of good character, and twenty people come in here and state that you are of bad character, your counsel have got the right to ask them who they ever heard talking about you and what they ever heard said and what they ever saw. Is it possible, I'll ask you in the name of common sense, that you would permit your counsel to sit mute? You wouldn't do it, would you? If a man says that I am a person of bad character, I want to know, curiosity makes me want to know, and if it's proclaimed, published to the world and it's a lie, I want to nail the lie—to show that he never saw it, and never heard it and knows nothing about it. And yet, three able counsel and an innocent man, and twenty or more girls all of whom had worked in the factory but none of whom work there at this time, except one on the fourth floor, tell you that that man had a bad character, and had a bad character for lasciviousness—the uncontrolled and uncontrollable passion that led him on to kill poor Mary Phagan."

When Judge Roan interrupted to ask if he was nearly through, Dorsey, in genuine surprise, informed the Court he had not yet begun to touch on the State's case. Roan ordered an adjournment until Saturday.

Saturday morning Dorsey cited case histories where a man of reputed character *lost* reputation when he placed that character before a jury. Brilliantly, he chose Oscar Wilde as an example: "Oscar Wilde, an Irish knight, a literary man, brilliant, the author of works that will go down the ages—*Lady Windemere's Fan, De Profundis*—which later he wrote while confined in jail. He was a man who had the effrontery and the boldness—when the Marquis of Queensbury saw that there was something wrong between this intellectual giant and his son and sought to break up their companionship—Wilde sued the Marquis for damages, which brought retaliation on the part of the Marquis for criminal practices on the part of Wilde, this intellectual giant. Wherever the English language is read, the effrontery, the boldness, the coolness of this man, Oscar Wilde, as he stood the cross-examination of the ablest lawyers of England—an effrontery that is characteristic of the man of his type—that examination will remain the subject matter of study for lawyers and for people who are interested in that type of pervert. Not even Oscar Wilde's wife—for he was married and had two children— suspected that he was guilty of such immoral practices, and, as I say, it never would have been brought to light probably, because committed in secret."

Solicitor General Dorsey finally started to explain the State's evidence, distorting it as he went along, challenged constantly by Arnold or Rosser.

Said Dorsey: "You have Lemmie Quinn arriving, not on the minute, but, to serve your purposes, from 12:20 to 12:22; but that, gentlemen, conflicts with the evidence of Mrs. Freeman and the other young lady, who placed Quinn by their evidence, in the factory before that time."

Mr. Arnold: "There isn't a word of evidence to that effect; those ladies were there at 11:35 and left at 11:45, Corinthia Hall and Mrs. Freeman, they left there at 11:45, and it was after they had eaten lunch and were about to pay their fare that they ever saw Quinn, at the little cafe, the Busy Bee. Dorsey says that they saw Quinn over at the factory before 12, as I understand it."

Mr. Dorsey: "Yes sir, by his evidence."

Mr. Arnold: "That's absolutely incorrect, they never saw Quinn there and never swore they did."

Mr. Dorsey: "No, they didn't see him there, I doubt if anybody else saw him there either."

Mr. Arnold: "If a crowd of people here laugh every time we say anything, how are we to hear the Court? He has made a whole lot of little mis-statements, but I let those pass, but I'm going to interrupt him on every substantial one he makes."

Diabolically, Dorsey read aloud the letter Frank had written to his uncle, Moses Frank:

"ATLANTA, GA., APRIL 26, 1913.

DEAR UNCLE:

I trust that this finds you and dear Tante well after arriving safely in New York. I hope that you found all the dear ones well in Brooklyn and I await a letter from you telling me how you find things there. Lucile and I are well.

It is too short a time since you left for anything startling to have developed down here. The opera has Atlanta in its grip, but that ends today. I've heard a rumor that opera will not be given again in a hurry here.

Today was "Yontiff" [holiday] here, and the thin gray line of veterans, smaller each year, braved the rather chilly weather to do honor to their fallen comrades.

Enclosed you will find last week's report. The shipments still keep up well, tho' the result is not what one would wish. There is nothing new in the factory, etc., to report. Enclosed please find the price list you desired.

The next letter from me, you should get on board ship. After that I will write to the address you gave me in Frankfurt.

With much love to you both, in which Lucile joins me, I am

Your affectionate nephew,

LEO M. FRANK"

Dorsey continued: "But whether or not he made out that financial sheet, I'll tell you something that he did do Saturday afternoon, when he was waiting up there for old Jim to come back to burn that body, I'll tell you something that he did do—and don't forget the envelope and don't forget the way that the paper was folded, either, don't forget it.

"Listen to this: 'I trust this finds you and dear Tante (that's

the German for aunt) well after arriving safe in New York. I
hope you found all the dear ones well in Brooklyn.'

"Didn't have any wealthy people in Brooklyn, eh? This uncle
of his was mighty near Brooklyn, the very time old Jim says he
looked up and said, 'I have wealthy people in Brooklyn.'

" 'It is too short a time,' he says, 'since you left for anything
startling to have developed down here.' Too short! Too short!
Startling! But 'Too short a time,' and that itself shows that the
dastardly deed was done in an incredibly short time. And do
you tell me, honest men, fair men, courageous men, true Georgians, seeking to do your duty, that that phrase, penned by that
man to his uncle on Saturday afternoon, didn't come from a conscience that was its own accuser?

" 'It is too short a time since you left for anything startling to
have developed down here.' What do you think of that? And
then listen to this—as if that old gentleman, his uncle, cared
anything for this proposition, this old millionaire traveling
abroad to Germany for his health, this man from Brooklyn; and
do you tell me that this old gentleman, expecting to sail for Europe, the man who wanted the price list and financial sheet,
cared anything for those old heroes in gray? And isn't this sentence itself significant: 'Today was Yontiff [holiday] here, and
the thin gray line of veterans here braved the rather chilly
weather to do honor to their fallen comrades'; and this from
Leo M. Frank, the statistician, to the old man, the millionaire,
or nearly so, who cared so little about the thin gray line of veterans, but who cared all for how much money had been gotten in
by the pencil factory."

Dorsey neglected to tell the jury that Moses Frank was a
Confederate veteran. He also neglected to tell the jury that
Moses Frank, a Confederate veteran, had insisted on investing
his money in Atlanta. In a letter to Sig Montag old Mr. Frank
had written; "The South and Atlanta must have capital investment."

Over and over again that Saturday, Dorsey defended the work

of the police in the case, citing their impartiality. Like a pendulum, he would swing then to Leo Frank's "degeneracy."

"When Frank wanted to get him to go down into the dark cellar and burn that body by himself, and old Jim says, 'I'll go if you go, but if I go down there and burn that body, somebody might come along and catch me and then what kind of a fix will I be in?' And I'll tell you right now, if Jim Conley had gone down in that cellar and had undertaken to have burned that body, as sure as the smoke would have curled upward out of that funnel toward heaven, just so certain would Leo M. Frank have been down there with these same detectives, and Jim Conley would have been without a shadow of defense."

The last two hours of Saturday Dorsey spent in rehashing Albert McKnight's testimony and on insisting that Minola's repudiation clearly indicated that the Seligs had bribed her.

Continuing his summation on Monday, he attacked Frank's innocence through Lucile Frank.

"This defendant stated to you, after His Honor had excluded our evidence and properly, I think, that his wife visited him at the police station. He says that she was there almost in hysterics, having been brought there by her father and two brothers-in-law and Rabbi Marx—no, 'Rabbi Marx was with me, I consulted with him as to the advisability of allowing my dear wife to come up to the top floor to see those surroundings, city detectives, reporters and snapshooters.' He doesn't prove that by a living soul and relies merely upon his own statement. If they could have proven it by Rabbi Marx, who was there and advised him, why didn't they do it? Do you tell me that there lives a true wife, conscious of her husband's innocence, that wouldn't have gone through snapshooters, reporters and everything else, to have seen him—"

MR. ARNOLD. "I must object to as unfair and outrageous an argument as that, that his wife didn't go there through any consciousness of guilt on his part. I have sat here and heard the unfairest argument I have ever heard, and I can't object to it, but I do object to his making any allusion to the failure of the wife to go and see him; it's unfair, it isn't the way to treat a man on trial for his life."

THE COURT. "Is there any evidence to that effect?"

MR. DORSEY. "Here is the statement I have read."

MR. ARNOLD. "I object to his drawing any conclusions from his wife going or not going, one way or the other, it's an outrage upon law and decency and fairness."

THE COURT. "Whatever was in the evidence or the statement I must allow it."

MR. DORSEY. " 'Let the galled jade wince.'——"

MR. ARNOLD. "I object to that, I'm not a 'galled jade,' and I've got a right to object. I'm not galled at all, and that statement is entirely uncalled for."

MR. DORSEY. "Frank said that his wife never went back there because she was afraid that the snapshooters would get her picture—because she didn't want to go through the line of snapshooters. I tell you, gentlemen of the jury, that there never lived a woman, conscious of the rectitude and innocence of her husband, who wouldn't have gone to him through snapshooters, reporters and over the advice of any rabbi under the sun."

He finished up with Jim Conley.

"The existence of the notes alone sustains Jim Conley, because no Negro ever in the history of the race, after having perpetrated rape or robbery, ever wrote a note to cover up the crime. The note paper on which it is written, paper found in abundance on the office floor and near the office of this man Frank, sustains Jim Conley. The diction of the notes, 'this Negro did this,' and old Jim throughout his statement says 'I done,' sustains Jim Conley."

MR. ROSSER. "I have looked the record up, and Jim Conley says 'I did it,' time and time again. He said 'I disremember whether I did or didn't,' he says 'I did it'——"

MR. DORSEY. "They would have to prove that record before I would believe it."

MR. ROSSER. "He says time and time again, 'I disremember whether I did or not'; he says 'I did it,' page after page, sometimes three times on a page. I've got the record, too. Of course, if the Almighty God was to say it you would deny it."

MR. DORSEY. "Who reported it?"

MR. ROSSER. "Pages 496——" [Mr. Rosser here read a list of page numbers containing the statement referred to.]

MR. DORSEY. "Who reported it, that's what I want to know."

MR. ARNOLD. "This is the official report and it's the correct report, taken down by the official stenographer, and he said, 'Now when the lady comes I'll stamp like I did before,' 'I says all right, I'll do just as you say and I did.' "

MR. DORSEY. "He's quoting Frank here, 'and he says now when the lady comes I'll stamp like I did.' "

MR. ARNOLD. " 'I says all right, I'll do just as you say and I did as he said.' He has got it both ways, 'I did it,' and 'I done it,' you can find it both ways."

MR. DORSEY. "The jury heard that examination and the cross-examination of Jim Conley, and every time it was put to him he says 'I done it.' "

MR. ROSSER. "And I assert that's not true, the stenographer took it down and he took it down correctly."

MR. DORSEY. "I'm not bound by this stenographer."

MR. ROSSER. "I know, you are not bound by any rule of right in the universe."

THE COURT. "If there's any dispute about the correctness of this report, I will have the stenographer come here." Roan then called the stenographer, Parry.

MR. PARRY. "I reported 1 to 31 myself, and I think I can make a statement that will satisfy Mr. Dorsey: The shorthand character for 'did' is very different from 'done,' there's no reason for a reporter confusing those two. Now, at the bottom of this page—I see I reported it myself, and that was what he said, quoting, 'All right, I'll do just as you say and I did as he said.' Now, as I say, my characters for 'did' and 'done' are very different and shouldn't be confused—no reason for their being confused."

THE COURT. "Well, is that reported or not correctly?"

MR. PARRY. "That was taken as he said it and written out as he said it."

MR. DORSEY. "Let it go, then, I'll trust the jury on it.

"Your Honor, I have done my duty. I have no apology to make. Your Honor, so far as the State is concerned, may now charge this jury—this jury who have sworn that they were impartial and unbiased, this jury who, in this presence, have taken the oath that they would well and truly try the issue formed on this bill of indictment between the State of Georgia and Leo M. Frank, charged with the murder of Mary Phagan; and I predict, may it please Your Honor, that under the law that you give in charge and under the honest opinion of the jury of the evidence produced, there can be but one verdict, and that is: We the jury find the defendant, Leo M. Frank, guilty! guilty! guilty!"

Dorsey had timed his speech perfectly. The church bells all over Atlanta promptly clanged at noon. As he pronounced his "guilty! guilty! guilty!" his peroration was punctuated by the clamor of pealing bells.

"The superstitious—and there were many of them present—" write the Samuelses, "recalled that it was precisely at that moment, twelve noon, that Mary Phagan had walked into the factory to her death; to them it was a sign God wished the child avenged."

With that pronouncement of "guilty! guilty! guilty!" there were only two men in either the courtroom or among the clamoring crowd in the streets who did not know what verdict that jury would bring in: those men were Judge Leonard S. Roan and the defendant, Leo M. Frank.

CHAPTER TWENTY

DORSEY FINISHED and retired to his table, rubbing his face in a handkerchief, Hooper and Stephens congratulating him.

Defense Attorney Arnold asked Judge Roan to excuse the jury. "I make a motion for a mistrial," the defense lawyer said. He said the defense had asked at the beginning of the trial that the courtroom be cleared. He reminded Roan that when Conley's testimony was ruled entirely admissible, the audience had cheered, and the jury only twenty feet away, in another room not sealed, had to have understood the significance of those cheers.

Arnold went on to charge that on August 22, when the jury was only two hundred feet north of the courthouse on South Pryor Street, a large crowd had congregated in front and begun chanting "Hooray for Dorsey!" On August 23, when the jury was eating its lunch at the German Cafe which was but one hundred feet from the courthouse, another crowd had set up a loud cheer for Dorsey.

Such demonstrations, Arnold argued, tended to coerce and intimidate the jury. "The behavior of the spectators throughout this trial has been disgraceful," he concluded. "This man has had anything in the world but a fair trial. I am not afraid of the crowd and I hope no one else is, but their demonstrations *do* intimidate the jury."

Solicitor General Dorsey was on his feet immediately. There

were shouts, to be sure, he told the judge, but he had never heard any for himself. The judge had it within his power to charge the jury to pay no attention to any demonstration, just as he had charged them to pay no attention to the newspaper headline they inadvertently saw.

Judge Roan let Arnold swear in R. V. Davers, one of the deputies in charge of the jury on the preceding Friday. The jury might have heard the cheers, said Davers, he himself did, but he did not hear shouts of "Hooray for Dorsey."

Another of the deputies, Charles F. Huber, testified he did not know until Saturday of the cheers on Friday; his statement was greeted with loud laughter.

"Why, your Honor," shouted Arnold, "you can't even keep them quiet now, here in the courtroom. I wish to state in the record, Mr. Stenographer, that while a witness was being examined in support of a motion, quite a demonstration took place unfavorable to the defendant. We want an opportunity to complete our showing of this motion. Some of the other deputies are not here."

"I will overrule this motion," said Judge Roan. "I will charge the jury. Before I do, I want to see all counsel in my chambers."

Attorneys Rosser, Arnold, and Haas, along with the prosecuting staff of Dorsey, Stephens, and Hooper followed the judge into an anteroom. Roan showed them three letters; each was signed by one of the editors of Atlanta's three papers, each speculated on what would happen if the jury found Frank not guilty. "Gentlemen," said Roan, "I think we know. The defendant would be lynched."

Not even Dorsey pretended otherwise.

"What solution can you suggest?" Arnold asked.

"I have two," Roan said. "I shall alert the commander of the National Guard unit. And I shall ask that neither Frank nor you, Mr. Rosser, nor you, Mr. Haas, nor you, Mr. Arnold, be present in the court when the jury returns its verdict. I fear for all your lives."

"I don't think Frank will waive that right," said Rosser.

"Don't advise him he is waiving it," snapped the old man.

"He wants vindication."

"And I want to preserve law and order."

The defense attorneys finally agreed. When Frank left after Roan's charge, he did not know he would not face his jury.

Back in the courtroom, Roan summoned the jury. Waiting to hear the charge, however, the jury saw Roan consult with Adj. Gen. J. Van Holt Nash, commanding officer of the Fifth National Guard, who was in uniform and with Police Chief Beavers. Later, in their appeals, Frank's lawyers charged that this scene was bound to have frightened the jury members.

In his charge to the jury, Judge Roan said that they would have to consider Frank's character as they would consider any other substantial fact. If they returned a verdict of guilty and said nothing more, the Court would have to sentence the defendant to the extreme penalty.

The jury retired. Before beginning their deliberations, they walked to the German Cafe for lunch again. They were back in the jury room by one thirty-five. An hour later they sent for documents. A little after three they cast their first ballot: eleven for conviction, one in doubt. At three-thirty, they balloted again: twelve for conviction, no recommendation for mercy.

At four fifty-six, the foreman, F. E. Winburn, rose and in answer to Roan's question, replied, "We the jury find the defendant guilty of the murder of Mary Phagan."

From the Court windows, a reporter leaped to shout to his colleagues collected in an office across the street, "Guilty!"

A roar rose from the two thousand people surrounding the Court. The cheers were deafening. Roan remarked that never in his experience had he witnessed such a demonstration. He instructed one of the deputies to close the windows so the Court could hear as the prosecutor polled the jury.

As Dorsey polled, he began to weep. He asked each member of the jury, "Is this your verdict?" One by one they answered, "It

is." As he asked the sixth juror, tears rolled down the solicitor
general's cheeks, and his chin quivered. He told friends he was
thinking of the condemned man's wife and mother.

Each of the jurors congratulated Dorsey when he finished.
"Mr. Sheriff," said Judge Roan, "I will pass sentence tomorrow. I'll let you know in time to have the defendant here."
He turned to the jury. "It was the longest trial I ever participated in and I dare say you ever have or ever will. The State
will now furnish the scrip. Let's see, how many days?"

"Twenty-nine," answered two members of the jury.

"Mr. Sheriff," said the judge, "make out the scrip. Two dollars a day for twenty-nine days."

While the jury posed for photographers, J. W. Coleman,
stepfather of the murdered girl, walked over to them and shook
each and every hand as he had at the conclusion of the coroner's
inquest. None of the reporters, however, could make out what
he was saying.

C. P. Connolly described Atlanta that afternoon in *The
Truth About the Frank Case:*

"When the verdict was rendered, street-car employees
quit their street cars to join the crowds that cheered;
women in fashionable groups in Atlanta's stores and at
semisocial functions clapped their hands. It was a Roman
holiday in Atlanta. The news of the verdict was chalked
up on the score board at the baseball game, and a wild
demonstration of approval ensued in the grandstand and
in the bleachers. Hundreds cake-walked for an hour in
front of the factory of which Frank had been superintendent and where the girl had been murdered. Telephone bells
rang incessantly. 'It looked as if every man, woman, and
child in Atlanta wanted to use the telephone as soon as
the verdict was rendered,' said an official of the Southern
Bell Telephone Company. More than three times the number of telephone connections were called for on that Mon-

day afternoon than on any previous day in the history of the company in Atlanta."

Dorsey left the courtroom. On the steps, he was met by an enthusiastic crowd which the police could not yet disperse. The crowd surged around him, and he was hoisted aloft and carried across the street to his office in the Kiser Building.

An hour later, when Dorsey left, the crowd was still there. Dorsey tipped his hat to them and crossed the street, amidst tumultuous cheering, to A. E. Stephens, who was waiting in an auto. The crowd broke through the cordon of police, all of them trying to shake Dorsey's hand. Dorsey waved to the crowd, shook hands with Detectives Starnes and Campbell, and the car rolled away.

In his cell in the Tower, Leo Frank waited, confidently expecting acquittal. His wife, his mother, and Rabbi David Marx were with him. He did not know he was not to return to the courtroom until Dr. Joseph Rosenberg, his family physician, who had run through the streets of Atlanta, appeared. "Leo," the doctor said breathlessly, "the jury has found you guilty."

"My God," said Frank, "even the jury was influenced by that mob."

Lucile Frank fainted. When Leo and the doctor revived her, she was shaken by hysterics. Calmed, she left with her father and went to the home of her brother-in-law, Charles Ursenbach. The shades at the Selig home on 68 East Georgia Street, were drawn and remained drawn for the next few months.

All Frank would say to the reporters was, "I am as innocent of this crime as I was a year ago."

At ten-thirty the next morning, Sheriff Mangum and Deputy Sheriff Plennie Miner took Frank to court to have Judge Roan pronounce sentence. His wife and mother followed in another car. Entering the courtroom, Frank asked Defense Attorney Rosser, "What shall I say?"

"That your case is in the hands of your counsel," replied Rosser.

There were not more than thirty people in the room when Roan mounted the bench.

Frank faced him.

"Your counsel inform me," said Roan, "that they will move for a new trial. In the meantime, it is my sworn duty to pass sentence on you. I have tried to give you a fair trial. I may have erred but I have done my duty as my conscience dictated. Have you anything to say?"

"I am innocent. Further than that, I will state that my case is in the hands of my counsel."

Roan read the sentence from a sheet of white paper: ". . . that on the tenth day of October, the defendant Leo Frank be executed by the Sheriff of Fulton County between the hours of ten o'clock and two P.M. That he be hanged by the neck until he is dead and may God have mercy on your soul."

Frank sank back in a chair. Two of his friends, Julian Boehm and Leo Strauss, comforted him.

When Defense Attorney Arnold told Roan he wanted to make a motion for a new trial, the Judge said he would hear arguments on October 4.

"That at least will extend the time of execution," breathed Rosser to Frank.

After sentencing Frank, Roan signed an order for Newt Lee's release. Lee had been in jail since April 27. "All I know is I'm going to look for work," said Lee to the reporters when he picked up his possessions from the police desk. "I sure got to work to live. I feel weak, just in my body, boss. I feel all right in my head because I never did have nothing to do with the murder."

On August 26, Rosser and Arnold published a protest in the three Atlanta newspapers:

"We deem it not amiss to make a short statement, as the attorneys of Leo M. Frank, to the public. The trial which has just occurred and which has resulted in Mr. Frank's

conviction, was a farce and not in any way a trial. In saying this, we do not make the least criticism of Judge Roan,
who presided. Judge Roan is one of the best men in
Georgia and is an able and conscientious judge. The
temper of the public mind was such that it invaded the
court room and invaded the streets and made itself manifest
at every turn the jury made; and it was just as impossible
for this jury to escape the effects of this public feeling as if
they had been turned loose and had been permitted to
mingle with the people. In doing this we are making no
criticism of the jury. They were only men and uncon-
sciously this prejudice rendered any other verdict impossible. It would have required a jury of Stoics, a jury of
Spartans to have withstood this situation. The time ought
to come when this man will get a fair trial, and we profoundly believe that it will. The final judgment of the
American people is a fair one. It is sometimes delayed in
coming, but it comes. We entered into this case with the
profound conviction of Mr. Frank's innocence. The result
has not changed our opinion. Every step of the trial has
intensified and fortified our profound conviction of his innocence."

That Saturday, still-celebrating Atlantans gave a public bar-
becue in honor of Hugh Dorsey and the twelve jurors who
found Frank guilty. Police Chief Beavers was there. So was
Chief of Detectives Newport Lanford.

A few months later, Judge Roan sentenced Jim Conley to
one year on the chain gang as an accessory after the fact in the
murder of Mary Phagan.

CHAPTER TWENTY-ONE

THE ORDEAL was to last two more years. At one point, absolutely exasperated, Leo Frank asked reporters rhetorically, "If they had found Conley's gun beside her body, would they have convicted me? If they had found a shred of Jim Conley's shirt in her clenched hands, would they have convicted me? But they found his handwriting beside her and for this they have convicted me."

His essential rigidity stood him in good stead. He was rarely bitter and always self-contained. While he had always been perfunctorily Jewish, now he became deeply religious. He found great comfort in his faith. His patience seemed endless, and his ability to receive bad news equally won him admiration.

That is not to say he had no right to bitterness. Certainly he had been denied a fair trial. He had been denied his right to a reasonable doubt. And more. He knew he had been victimized by policemen who, the night they picked up the murder notes beside the body of Mary Phagan, held in their hands the identity of the killer.

Leo Frank knew he faced the hangman and the noose because initially the police misread those notes. As new evidence was later to prove, they never *looked* at those murder notes. One does not need to be a Freudian psychoanalyst to realize those two notes were the murderer's attempt to divert suspicion from himself and were, at one and the same time, his own confession.

Some years later Henry A. Alexander, an Atlanta lawyer who helped prepare Frank's appeals to the higher courts, published an eight-page pamphlet in which he reprinted the notes, and in his commentary offered the opinion that it is hard to believe they were ever dictated by a white man.

"Mam," read the first note, written on a sheet from a lined order pad, "that negro hire doun here did this i went to make water and he push me doun that hole a long tall negro black that hoo it was long sleam tall negro i wright while play with me."

With errors corrected, Alexander made this of the note: "Mama, that Negro hired down here did this. I went to make water and he pushed me down that hole, a long tall Negro, black, that who it was, long slim tall Negro. I write while play with me."

Alexander speculated that the murderer dimly realized how a girl mortally injured or dead could have done any writing or how he, the murderer—standing over her and watching every movement—came to permit her to write notes which would incriminate him. The reader of the notes was expected to believe that Mary Phagan wrote them without the murderer seeing her do it because he was "playing" with her.

The second note, written on a lined white sheet, read: "he said he wood love me and land down play like night witch did it but that long tall black negro did buy his slef."

Again correcting the errors and supplying two words, Alexander read: "He said he would love me laying down [and would] play like night witch did it but that long tall black Negro did it by himself."

The fundamental mistake the police made in reading these notes came when Newt Lee gasped that the murderer was trying to put the blame on him, the night watchman.

"While the writer of these notes made repeated errors in his spelling, he made none in correctly reproducing the sound of words and it is extremely unlikely he meant 'night watchman' when he wrote 'night witch,' and that if he had intended to write 'night watchman' he would have spelled it as it sounds. If the word 'night watchman' was intended, how account for the entire absence of any letters corresponding to the syllable 'man'? It seems to the writer of this article that in this expression there is disclosed a piece of superstition characteristic of the Negro of the plantation and totally foreign to the white man. The idea the girl was killed by a night witch, or, as the note expresses it, that the 'long tall black negro' would play 'like the night witch did it' is inconceivable as the thought of the white man." [1]

Admittedly, this analysis is not without pro-Frank pleading, but it is not on that account without merit.

The Reverend Luther Otterbein Bricker, the pastor of Mary Phagan's church in Bellwood, whose reminiscences of the Frank trial were quoted earlier in Chapter Six, lends corroboration to Mr. Alexander. In the same article which defended Frank's innocence, Bricker wrote:

> "The general public took it for granted that the words 'night witch' were Negro for 'night watchman.' We had an old Negro woman working for us as cook and I asked her one day, 'Rebecca, what do colored people mean by night witch?' She replied, 'When children cry out in their sleep at night, it means the night witches are riding them, and if you don't go and wake them up, they will be found dead the next morning with a cord around their necks.' Now I, a Southerner, born and bred and raised among Negroes, had never heard such a thing as that." [2]

Frank's defense was on the right track when they tried to secure the services of Albert L. Osborne, already famous as an

[1] Henry A. Alexander, *Some Facts About the Murder Notes in the Phagan Case* (privately printed, Atlanta, Ga., no date).
[2] Bricker, *op. cit.*

examiner of handwriting documents. This same Osborne, some twenty years later, was to prove the worth of his reputation when he described to the police almost exactly the kind of man who wrote the Lindbergh ransom note.

Osborne, a man of integrity, said it would be improper for him to appear in Frank's defense because the prosecution had sought him first and paid him a fee and expenses. But significantly, Dorsey, who used everything against Frank, did not call Osborne. Osborne had reported to the solicitor general that he was sure the notes were not only written by, but originated in, the mind of a semiliterate.

Considering how accurate Osborne proved himself, not only in the Lindbergh kidnapping but in the famous Duveen art dealer case, he was probably right. For it is inconceivable that a college graduate would not have transferred a single intimation of his intelligence, background, diction, or education in a lightning-fast dictation of 128 words in the two and a half minutes that the prosecution contended it took.

On May 18, 1915, when the Supreme Court of the United States turned down Frank's last appeal, Osborne wrote Governor John M. Slaton a letter on Frank's behalf in which he said the writing in the notes "in arrangement, margin, spacing, composition and general character is characteristically illiterate. If it is characteristically illiterate, it is the natural result of the operation of an untrained hand and an ignorant brain. If one takes a few pages of these two documents and looks at them as a whole, considers their character in every particular, and then attempts to picture the conditions under which they were written and the purpose for which they were written, one considers the two stories that Conley told, first that he could not write and then that he wrote one of the notes, and then finally consider the fact that the notes failed to accomplish their purpose in throwing off suspicion, then it seems to me clear that they were the work of an unassisted ignorant mind thinking in an unskilled, clumsy way to remove suspicion from himself.

"This question of determining identity from ideas and language is a comparatively new subject. It is not treated in any of the technical books as far as I know. It seems to me a proper subject for investigation, and I have endeavored to consider it in as careful and scientific a manner as I am capable of employing, and I have applied it to the same principles which apply in investigations of other questions of similar character." *

The defense attorneys exercised a crucial indifference to these notes. When they studied them for Frank's appeals they would find under the microscope the new evidence which they should have produced at Frank's trial to provide the one reasonable doubt that could have won Frank an acquittal.

A reasonable doubt is a doubt for which there is a reason. The reasonable doubt in Frank's case was that the murder took place on the second floor. The defense first tried to prove that it was inconceivable that Frank and Conley in less than twenty minutes could have: accomplished the desperate and worrisome task of wrapping a corpse in a crocus-sack, carrying it through a factory, and taking it down to the basement by elevator, dragging it back 136 feet to a coal heap, then returning to the second floor; composed four murder notes; and then held a substantial discussion about money. Nor did the defense concentrate on proving explicitly, instead of by half-hearted indirection, that the elevator was not used that Saturday. Conley confessed evacuating his bowels in the elevator shaft that morning, and this excrement was in its natural state when the detectives discovered the body on Sunday. When the detectives took Frank to the basement later Sunday morning, the elevator mashed this dung, and the basement was pervaded with its smell, conclusive proof this was the first time the elevator had been used since Friday.

To the higher courts, the defense attorneys offered new evidence that the order pad on which the first murder note was written was never on the second floor. But the courts sacrificed

---

* Among the John M. Slaton papers, courtesy of the Georgia Department of Archives and History, Atlanta.

Frank because this evidence had never been offered to his trial jury.

The defense did not realize that the Leo Frank case literally hypnotized Hugh Dorsey. Luther Z. Rosser was the best all-around lawyer in Atlanta. He was also Hugh Dorsey's brother-in-law, and when Frank retained Rosser to represent his interests Dorsey felt the challenge. Dorsey had recently lost important cases for the State and he wanted to redeem himself by besting Rosser. From the time Rosser entered the police station, Dorsey ceased to have a judicious cell in his brain.

Unaware lawyers, however, were not at the core of Leo Frank's bad luck.

PART 2

CHAPTER TWENTY—TWO

ON THE DAY Leo Frank was arrested, a rumor gained circulation and continued to circulate for the next two years, never missing a beat. Every farmer, blacksmith, mill hand, motorman, and mechanic sooner or later said, "Frank will never hang. He is rich, and Mary Phagan has no friends." Though prominent clergymen were to beg for a fair trial for Frank, though the rest of the United States asked Georgia to reconsider, the hatred this rumor generated was too much to overcome.

Leo M. Frank was the son of a well-to-do family in New York, the nephew of a millionaire, or as Solicitor General Dorsey said, "a near millionaire." When the unsubstantiated charges of sexual perversion fixed suspicion on the factory superintendent, those most inflamed were the working men and farmers who immediately saw a symbol of all their troubles—the Northern capitalist who was not only keeping the Southerner in poverty, but who was also exploiting Southern womanhood.

Georgia was poor. The mill hands in the cities and the one-gallus farmers in the rural areas lived in virtual peonage. They believed rich men in the North kept them poor. Frank was one of those men, and the resentment against him had mixed economic and sexual overtones.

The farmer was in the grip of the crop lien system, mortgaging his harvest to the merchant who supplied clothes, food, and seed. This farmer paid the prices the merchant demanded, and he sold his harvest only through the merchant, who alone determined the time and method of disposal.

And now, in 1913, even the banks and the merchants could not finance the cotton crop. Only two years before the murder of Mary Phagan, Joseph Brown, running against Hoke Smith, won the gubernatorial race with the slogan, "Hoke for hunger; Brown for bread," and "bread" was not used metaphorically.

There was little to hope for on the farms, and when the farmers moved to the city to work in the factories there was little more there. And now the Georgians suspected that the rich could despoil their daughters with impunity.

Already there was considerable agitation about Southern women in industry. "Our women are being introduced to the evils of factory life," came from the pulpit. From the charitable and fraternal organizations came the abortive efforts to shorten the woman's working day, to pay a better wage, to abolish child labor. But it must be remembered the one-gallus farmer and the mill hand were as effectively segregated from the mainstream of society as the Negro. The mill villages had separate schools and separate churches; rural Georgia had almost no schools, and farmers had to pay their ministers in kind.

Thirty years before, these marginal tenant farmers started a revolution against such inequities. The revolution went by the name of Populism. The leader of this revolution was Tom Watson, who founded the People's Party in Georgia.

Born in 1856, Watson saw scalawags and carpetbaggers take over his father's plantation during the Reconstruction. He saw his brother in the fields lashed by an overseer. Self-educated, he became a lawyer, a noted backwoods criminal lawyer at that, and began to speak out. He spoke the language of the mill people and the farmers, but it would be a mistake to think of Tom Watson as a hillbilly or redneck.

"He saw the mill town shacks," wrote Ralph McGill in *Tom Watson: The People's Man,* "and the miserable people in them while others wrote of the poetry of the new industrial smoke in the soft Southern sky. He cried out that the 'New South' was forging the machinery of exploitation but the newspapers never published his speeches in any detail and distorted what little they did print." [1]

Yet in 1890, Tom Watson served in the 52nd Congress. He had amazingly put together a coalition of poor white and Negro tenant farmers, a coalition which was to form the nucleus of the Populist Party.

Tom Watson reached these people. He told them: "Now the People's Party says to these two men, 'You are kept apart that you may be separately fleeced of your earnings. You are made to hate each other because upon that hatred is rested the keystone of the arch of financial despotism which enslaves you both. You are deceived and blinded that you may not see how this race antagonism perpetuates a monetary system which beggars both.' " [2]

Watson nominated Negroes for seats on the State Executive Committee of the Populist Party arguing—and winning—"Tell me the use of educating these people as citizens if they are never to exercise the rights of citizens." [3] He was the only Southerner of his time, and since, to hear the cheers of naturalized citizens strung along the Lower East Side of New York. In 1904, the Populist Party nominated him for President and he gave his acceptance speech at Cooper Union in New York City where Judge Samuel Seabury introduced him. At the end of this mass meeting, the officials of the Hebrew Trades Unions went out of their way to shake his hand. In Chicago, Clarence Darrow told an audience Watson was a "beacon of light to those in doubt."

In Georgia, Watson led an agrarian revolution that frightened the Democratic politicians in the city whose support came

---

[1] "American Movers and Shakers No. 6," *The New Republic* (August 23, 1948).
[2] Quoted in Woodward, *op. cit.*, p. 220.
[3] *Ibid.*, p. 221.

from the railroads, the financiers, the banks, and the mill and
factory owners. Twice, in 1892 and 1894, these politicians literally stole from Watson his election to Congress. They gerryman-
dered his district, and they voted wagonload after wagonload of
city Negroes to gain the plurality for their candidate.

In 1896, William Jennings Bryan, the surprise presidential
nominee of the Democratic Party, proved a powerful attraction
to western Populists, particularly when he promised the vice-
presidential nomination to Watson in return for Populist support. Watson always distrusted the Great Commoner, but he
accepted. The Democrats, once adopting the Populist platform,
proceeded to give the vice-presidential nomination to the con-
servative Arthur Sewall. The Populists at their convention, left
with little choice, endorsed Bryan and nominated Watson as
his running mate on a separate ticket.

Nationally, Watson won a little over 200,000 votes in 1896;
in 1904 as the presidential candidate only 117,000. Populism was
dying. This demise and Bryan's betrayal broke Watson. For in
truth, there would have been no William Jennings Bryan if
Tom Watson had come from Ohio or Illinois. Bryan wanted to
save the country with the panacea of free silver; Watson with
conservation programs, farm subsidies, an eight-hour day, and
free public schools.

"Late in his career," writes Hodding Carter in *The Angry
Scar*, "Tom Watson wrote what should be the epitaph of any
Southern liberal who might dare to preach and practice civil
equality and be rendered politically impotent thereby: 'Consider the advantages of the position Bryan had over me. His
field of work was the plastic, restlessly growing West; mine was
the hide-bound, rock-ribbed Bourbon South. Besides, Bryan had
no everlasting and overshadowing Negro question to hamper
and handicap his problems. I had.' " [4]

Already the bitterness was there. The Negro denied Watson

---

[4] Hodding Carter, *The Angry Scar* (Doubleday, 1959), p. 146.

not only the triumph of his Populist Party but his own personal quest for power.

The tragedy that engulfed Mary Phagan, and later Leo Frank, his family, the Jews of Atlanta, and Governor John M. Slaton, engulfed Tom Watson as well. Watson, too, is one of the tragic figures of the Frank case because he is the South's own tragedy.

Watson had a great and invigorating talent. He had vision far beyond that possessed by the hack politicians of his time, yet, like so many others of the South who could have been equally as great, he was self-ruined, self-betrayed, and self-corrupted by the spectre of race. The political disappointments between 1896 and 1904 finally deranged him. "After the victory of the Republicans," continues Ralph McGill, "Watson retired to Hickory Hill. He was in debt. He felt his mind was going. He was defeated and, for the first time in his life, he accepted defeat, and crept brooding into his tent. He began to write, in brilliant erratic style, books that sold well." [5]

He wrote a *History of France,* a biography of Napoleon and one of Thomas Jefferson which he dedicated, with deep affection, to William Randolph Hearst. (Eleven years later, when Hearst's *Georgian* joined the *Atlanta Journal* in demanding a new trial for Leo Frank, Watson wrote: "William Randolph Hearst is a half-Jew under orders from Nathan Straus.")

Tom Watson returned to Hickory Hill a liberal in 1904 and in 1906 he came out the forerunner of the new Klan. And not only did he come out a Klansman, but a Klansman who was a political boss with immense power.

Watson had led a surge and though it had slackened, Populism had not completely died. The city politicians knew they could not fix black districts forever. They began in the 1890s to urge disfranchisement of the Negro as a remedy for Populism. Politicians, editors, and mill owners suddenly discovered the races had a "natural" antipathy. City councils began introduc-

---

[5] McGill, *op. cit.*

ing segregation ordinances, and legislatures, poll taxes. Editorials proclaimed the Negro a beast and a brute.

Cynically, the embittered Watson promised not to oppose these disfranchisement laws if the gubernatorial candidates would urge Populist reforms. Watson even apologized for his defection, writing, "White men had to unite before they could divide."

Within a decade, the city politicians had succeeded; the Negro was completely disfranchised. But the city politicians had outwitted themselves. As C. Vann Woodward wrote, "With the Negro vote eliminated, Watson and the Populists stood much in the same relation toward the two factions of the Democratic Party as the Negro had held toward the Populists and the Democrats: the Populists held the balance of power." [6]

It was Tom Watson who controlled the "Old Pops" of rural Georgia, controlled them because he could speak in words that the poor of the South could understand. They could understand Watson hammering away at "Wall Street," "Railroads," and "Big Money."

In his *Jeffersonian Magazine* and in his *Jeffersonian Weekly*, Watson began to beat down the Negro. He identified the Negro with all the vices, demanding a repressive policy for his now politically impotent and friendless one-time ally. He argued for a repression so complete that "the great masses of the Negroes would gradually reconcile themselves to the condition of a recognized peasantry—a laboring class." The superiority of the Aryan, he wrote, was menaced by the "hideous, ominous, national menace of Negro domination."

Booker T. Washington was written off as imitative as an ape; bestial as a gorilla. Lynch law was a good sin, it showed that a sense of justice yet lived among the people. Thus the editorials in the *Jeffersonian*.

Most of the whites in Georgia who had repudiated Tom Wat-

---

[6] Woodward, *op. cit.*, p. 372.

son when he walked with the Negro loved every word. And the Negroes who once crowded around the stump to touch Tom Watson's sleeve lived in fear of angry men stalking the countryside with a noose.

And what happened to agrarian reform? Did the new Watson ease the burden of the cotton farmer, mill hand, and average poverty-stricken redneck? Once the disfranchisement of the Negro was complete, Populism was replaced by something much better—white supremacy. To the ordinary white man it became more valuable than minimum wage, or a moratorium on a farm mortgage; indeed, more valuable than money. A man can lose money; he can not lose white supremacy. It was an entailed estate handed down from father to son.

Nor was white supremacy Tom Watson's only gift to the mill hands and tenant farmers. From 1907 on, Tom Watson became as closely identified in the public mind with the anti-Catholic crusade as he had once been with the Populist movement.

"Same Old Story," wrote Watson in his *Jeffersonian* for April 14, 1914. "Skeleton in Basement of Catholic Home." It did not matter to Watson that the news item in the Savannah paper which inspired the story concerned the *building* of a Catholic convent on grounds that had once been a cemetery.

The Pope was always "Jimmy Cheezy" in the *Jeffersonian*, the nuns were always ravished by black priests. In 1910, Watson started a series which was to run twenty-seven months, "The Roman Catholic Hierarchy—The Deadliest Menace to Our Liberties and Our Civilization." One example of 1912:

"Through his questions, the priest learns which of his fair penitents are tempted to indulge in sexual inclinations. Remember that the priest is often a powerfully sexed man, who lives on rich food, drinks red wine, and does no manual labor. He is alone with a beautiful, well-shaped young woman who tells him that she is tormented by carnal desire. Her low voice is in his ear; the rustle of her skirts and the scent of her hair kindle flames. She will never tell what he says or does. She believes that he cannot sin. She believes that *he* can forgive her sin. She has been taught that in obeying him, she is serving God." [7]

This campaign, which continued unabated, was so influential not only in Georgia, but throughout the old Confederate states, that anti-Catholicism was to dominate the thinking of the Southern white Protestant for the next two generations. Over and over, the political platforms of Watson's candidates promised there would be no Catholics on the ticket, that no Catholics would receive patronage. Watson's attacks on the Catholic Church were so obscene and inflammatory that the United States Postmaster General twice during World War I ordered inquiries and suspended the *Jeffersonian* from the mails (Watson won his case on the constitutional grounds of freedom of the press).

But Watson had done his work well. His anti-Catholic crusade was now so effective that the Georgia state legislature passed the bill he had demanded conferring the authority on grand juries to investigate Catholic convents. The few legislators who rebelled at this tyranny were later defeated at the polls.

And, of course, there were the Jews. When Tom Watson came upon Leo Frank he was directly responsible for fomenting the only European-type pogrom against a Jewish community in the history of the United States.

[7] Quoted in Woodward, *op. cit.*, p. 421.

CHAPTER TWENTY-THREE

TOM WATSON made no editorial comment about either Leo Frank's arrest or trial. All anyone heard him say about Frank during the early stages of the case was that he was surprised the defense had not sought a change of venue, since in Atlanta Frank had about "as much chance for his life as a snowball in Hell. It would be like trying a rat before an old cat and a litter of her kittens." [1]

In fact, one of Watson's flacks, William W. Brewton, in an adulatory biography, says Watson was once approached to take the case. Probably. Every prominent lawyer in Georgia was approached. Since Rosser was undeniably the best criminal lawyer in the state, he was the obvious man. Brewton says Watson could have won Frank's acquittal. This is doubtful. If Luther Rosser couldn't, it is hard to see how Tom Watson, who had not practiced law in twenty years, could.

With the verdict of guilty, the Frank case took on a new coloration. Throughout the country many began to consider the evidence impartially.

There were Georgians, too, who realized that anti-Semitic bigotry had figured importantly if not decisively in Frank's trial. The Jewish community, both in Atlanta and in the United

---

[1] William W. Brewton (Vail-Ballou), *The Life of Thomas Watson* (published by the author, Atlanta, 1926), p. 174.

States at large, realized one of its members had been the victim of prejudice.

The decent people of Georgia hoped Frank would find redress in the higher courts. The mob had dispersed. The fever was gone. Or so the "good people" thought.

Even the press had sobered. With the exception of Herbert Asbury, a reporter for the *Georgian* and Britt Craig of the *Constitution*, who was making a career of having discovered Mary Phagan's corpse, the working reporters closest to the case thought Frank innocent. One of these reporters was Harold Ross, who later founded *The New Yorker*. Ross had moved from Atlanta to the San Francisco *Chronicle* in 1914, where he wrote an impassioned article asserting Frank's innocence.*

The power structure of the city, when it thought about Leo Frank, thought he would be saved by the judicial process. But Judge Roan turned down the defense's plea for a new trial. The Georgia Supreme Court proved no more amenable. The situation was serious. Georgia's reputation as well as Leo Frank's life were at stake.

On March 14, 1914, the *Atlanta Journal* came to Frank's defense, stating in a lead editorial written by the *Journal's* editor that Frank deserved a new trial; without it, his execution would amount to judicial murder.

The *Journal* and its editors were political foes of Tom Watson, who read the editorial and misinterpreted its purpose. The *Journal's* editorial defending Frank appeared at that moment when Watson was trying to decide whether to back Hugh Dorsey or Nat Harris against the candidate the city politicians and the *Journal* would back for the governorship in 1915. Watson saw the editorial as a challenge.

"If Atlanta politicians and editors are crazy enough to make war on Dorsey because he did his duty in the Frank case, LET WAR BEGIN." [2]

---

* Appendix C.
[2] *Jeffersonian*, March 14, 1914.

Watson berated the *Journal*. And the *Journal*, soon losing circulation, desisted in its efforts to secure a new trial for Leo Frank. But Watson had just begun. Like Foster Coates, the editor of Hearst's *Georgian*, who saw that little Mary Phagan would sell newspapers, Tom Watson saw that Leo Frank would sell them just as well. More than that, Watson realized the fate of Leo Frank could make or unmake politicians. This old Populist, wracked by his failure, a chronic drunk now, found in anti-Semitism the tidal wave he needed to ride back to personal power. He was soon to prove himself the most talented hate-monger the American South has ever had the misfortune to produce.*

---

* Anti-Semitic demagogues in the United States have invariably conducted their crusades through weekly or monthly publications. Beginning May, 1920, Henry Ford's weekly, the *Dearborn Independent*, published a series of anti-Semitic fabrications under the general title, "The International Jew." Recanting several years later, Henry Ford delivered to Louis Marshall an apology to the Jews and retracted these calumnies. Despite Ford's protest, however, he could not stop the newly-organized Nazi Party in Germany from republishing these articles in the German, Polish, and Hungarian languages.

Another serious attempt to make political capital out of anti-Semitism came in 1936 when the Roman Catholic priest, Charles E. Coughlin of Royal Oak, Michigan, began publishing *Social Justice. Social Justice* reprinted a series of articles which had originally appeared in the *Voelkischer Beobachter*. The *Voelkischer Beobachter*, whose editorial policy was dictated by Nazi Propaganda Minister Joseph Goebbels, had lifted these articles from the *Dearborn Independent*. George Cardinal Mundelein of Chicago, the Catholic scholar, Msgr. John A. Ryan, the Committee of Catholic Laymen to Fight Anti-Semitism, and finally the Vatican itself effectively repudiated Father Coughlin. (The American Jewish Committee reports that in 1965 the *Dearborn Independent*'s anti-Semitic articles are being widely distributed in Spanish, in Argentina, and other Latin-American countries.)

There have been other anti-Semitic weekly and monthly publications, though of lesser importance. These included Gerald L. K. Smith's *Cross and Flag*, William Dudley Pelley's *Liberation*, and Conde McGinley's *Common Sense*.

Tom Watson, Henry Ford, and Father Coughlin charged that Jews were capitalists and bankers. Smith, Pelley, and McGinley charged Jews were subverting the capitalistic system.

None of these hate mongers had the advantage Watson enjoyed. Watson had an actual Jew, a living symbol, who was awaiting execution for allegedly having murdered a fourteen-year-old Southern virgin.

Since the Supreme Court decision of May 17, 1954, which ruled against public school segregation, a dozen anti-Semitic publications in the South

"Frank belongs to the Jewish aristocracy," wrote Watson, "and it was determined by rich Jews that no aristocrat of their race should die for the death of a working girl! Yes, Mary Phagan was only a factory girl: there was no glamor of wealth or fashion about her. She had no millionaire uncle: she had no Athens [Georgia] kinsmen to raise fifty thousand dollars for her: no mighty connections. While the Sodomite who took her sweet life basks in the warmth of Today, the poor child's dainty flesh has fed the worms." [3]

"Over and over," writes C. Vann Woodward, "Watson reviewed the evidence in the case: the torn garment, 'spotted with virginal blood,' the tuft of hair, the crumpled white form. Rumors, half-truths, special pleading, merciless slander, every device known to the skilled criminal lawyer—he employed." [4]

Watson warred not only to keep his rednecks in tumult but to silence the decent people of Georgia. Watson won. When the rest of the country asked Georgia to reconsider justice in the Frank Case, the endemic xenophobia of the redneck came to the fore. Interference, they cried. Tom Watson championed this complaint.

Beginning with his weekly *Jeffersonian* in March of 1914 until Frank was lynched in August of 1915, and for five years after that until he was elected to the United States Senate, Tom Watson kept one theme alive: "Our Little Girl—ours by the Eternal God—has been pursued to a hideous death and bloody grave by this filthy perverted Jew of New York."

Not only did Watson revive his political fortunes with antiSemitism, but he made money at it. *"The Jeffersonian,"* says

have tried, unsuccessfully, to revive the hatred Watson originally incited in the Frank case. The National States Rights Party of Birmingham, Alabama, devoted the entire February, 1961, issue of its publication, *The Thunderbolt: The White Man's Viewpoint*, to the Leo Frank case. The story, with photographs of all the principals involved, insisted that Leo Frank was part of the conspiracy to "mongrelize" Southern white womanhood and that the decision of the "Warren Court" in outlawing segregation was to avenge his lynching.

[3] *Jeffersonian*, October 15 and December 3, 1914.
[4] Woodward, *op. cit.*, p. 439.

C. Vann Woodward, "melted like snowflakes. Eager crowds in small towns met the incoming trains to buy their 'Jeffs' as soon as they arrived. The circulation of Watson's weekly leaped from around 25,000 at the beginning of the Frank crusade to 87,000 for the week ending September 4, 1915. The price per copy to dealers increased from one to one-and-a-half and then to two cents. At this rate a convincing itemized estimate shows that at its maximum circulation the paper made a profit of $1,123.75 per week." [5]

In the May 14, 1914, issue, Watson used a photo of Frank that had obviously been retouched: no eyeglasses, eyes popping, thickened lips, disheveled hair. Below this began the editorial: 'You could tell that Frank is a lascivious pervert, guilty of the crime that caused the Almighty to blast the Cities of the Plain, by a study of the accompanying picture; look at those bulging, satyr eyes, the protruding sensual lips; and also the animal jaw."

Though Watson was devoting most of his space to Leo Frank, he did not forget his parallel campaigns against Negroes and Catholics. When C. P. Connolly wrote in *Collier's* that his investigation had convinced him of Frank's innocence, Watson replied: "Of course Connolly is a Catholic, a Fourth Degree Knight of Columbus. Connolly and Straus, Catholic and Jew, kiss the Pope's toe. We Georgians save our kisses for our wives and children. We will make certain that no other Georgia girl, budding into womanhood, will die a horrible death defending her virtue against a rich depraved Sodomite Jew." In the same issue he published a lengthy article, "Jesus Was No Jew." [6]

While modern anti-Semitism is in one part a reaction against Christianity, it is in another part an attack on liberal democracy. Often anti-Semitism is a chosen weapon in a political-economic conflict.

In Czarist Russia, the grinding poverty and the humiliating defeat by the Japanese in 1905 impelled the Czar's minister to

---

5 Woodward, *op. cit.*, p. 442.
6 *Jeffersonian*, December 4, 1914.

upgrade political anti-Semitism to the already high level of the endemic religious anti-Semitism. In France, the anti-Semitic hysteria over the Dreyfus case was whipped up in a country harrowed by fear of a new invasion and defeat by Germany. The Dreyfus case exploded upon the public after the failure of a series of rightist plots engineered by the Army. In Germany, the anti-Semitism of the Nazis who massacred six million Jews was seized upon to "explain" the devastating defeat of the German war machine in 1918 and the consequent inflation and paralyzing economic depression that followed. And in the United States, in the Georgia of 1913, the terrible poverty of the tenant farmer and mill hand made it possible for a demagogue to arouse an entire community against a defendant in a capital case on the grounds that he was a *wealthy* Jew, that his parents owned stocks and bonds, and that his uncle was a millionaire.

Whether from the far right or far left, the anti-Semitic campaign has always involved a talented writer. In Russia, it was Sergei Nilus, with the forged *Protocols of Zion;* in France, Edouard Drumont in *La Libre Parole;* in Germany, Joseph Goebbels in the *Voelkischer Beobachter;* and in Georgia, Tom Watson in the *Jeffersonian.*

So intense were Tom Watson's anti-Semitic tirades that he was eventually to attack the very institution he set out to defend: Southern womanhood. He was within the year to slander and vilify Mrs. John M. Slaton, and to slander and vilify her in a way no other Southerner would have dared to slander or vilify a white woman.

CHAPTER TWENTY-FOUR

TRUE, no Jews were assaulted on the streets of Atlanta, although physical violence was averted on one occasion only through careful planning by the Jewish community. What hurt the Jews of Georgia was a boycott, inspired by Watson's editorials and effectively planned by an organization calling itself the Knights of Mary Phagan.

Throughout Georgia, the Knights distributed circulars reading: "Buy your clothing from Americans. Don't give your money to save a Jew Sodomite."

The boycott took its inspiration from Tom Watson's symbol of Nathan Straus as the typical Jewish capitalist and exploiter. Straus had joined with Samuel Untermeyer, Rabbi Stephen S. Wise, and many others, including Senators William Borah and Philander Knox, in demanding a new trial for Leo Frank. But Straus was certainly not as deeply committed to the case as two other nationally prominent Jews—A. D. Lasker and Louis Marshall. Watson, however, knew that the names Lasker and Marshall had little meaning for Georgians. In fact he would have had to explain that "Lasker" and "Marshall" were "Jewish" names.

Nathan Straus, on the other hand, was well known in Georgia. He and his brothers, Isidor and Oscar, were raised in Talbotton, Georgia, where their father had settled as a merchant in 1850. After the Civil War, the Straus family moved to New York, where their crockery store which they started in 1866 was

to grow eventually into the vast R. H. Macy enterprise. The
Strauses often visited Georgia. When Mr. and Mrs. Isidor Straus
went down on the *Titanic,* every Georgia paper expressed its
condolences editorially. Two years earlier Nathan Straus had fi-
nanced a study of the facilities in Georgia for the pasteurization
of milk. In interviews and feature stories, the press often called
Straus "the famous Jewish philanthropist."

Over the next five years Watson bitterly attacked Nathan
Straus in almost every issue of his two *Jeffersonian* journals. His
readers knew what old Tom was talking about—Jews.

Watson dismissed Nathan Straus's statement given to the press
in the heat of the Frank agitation in which the philanthropist
said he was still proud to be a Georgian, that he still had confidence in the decent people of the state. Watson replied in the
Jeffersonian of July 15, 1914: "Nathan Straus is a traitor to
Georgia." Watson adduced the proof of treason: "I was greatly
surprised on entering the restaurant of R. H. Macy which is
owned by Nathan Straus, to find Negroes were being served at
regular tables, and that white girls were compelled to wait on
them. . . . This condition does not exist in any first-class hotel
in the city of New York—*except in the Nathan Straus store who
makes white women servants of Negro men.*"

As Watson stepped up his anti-Semitic campaign, some Jewish families found it necessary to leave Georgia. David Hoffman,
a business executive in Norwalk, Connecticut, recalls in a personal letter to this author the decision of his father to leave
Americus, Georgia, in 1917. The elder Hoffman owned a store.
The boycott had cut into his livelihood. Hoffman saw no future
for himself in Georgia and left. There were many others.

If the anti-Semitic campaign hurt the Jews it hurt Georgia
even more. The pain suffered by a few families moving away
is minimal compared to the deprivation the state suffered.

One large Jewish-owned firm, the Empire Plow Company,
which manufactured wheelbarrows and other farm and construction equipment, had some time before purchased a tract of land

for a new plant near Atlanta when Tom Watson initiated his crusade. This company abandoned its plans for building in the South because of the attendant anti-Semitism that made even hiring an architect difficult. The Empire Plow Company went instead to Cleveland, Ohio, where it still operates.

There were other instances of firms, not Jewish-owned, that decided the *milieu* of Georgia was too hostile and inflammatory for risking a capital investment.

But far more serious than any of these economic factors was the indisputable fact that Tom Watson made an entire Jewish community feel insecure for the first time in America. The Jews of Atlanta lived with this insecurity and fear for an entire generation.

Morris Abram, once a leading lawyer of Atlanta, now president of the American Jewish Committee, recalled for the New York *Post* his boyhood in Georgia. "I grew up in the shadow of the Leo Frank lynching. He was innocent but was convicted in no small measure because he was a Jew." [1]

There were Jews in Atlanta before there was an Atlanta. Jacob Haas came to America from Germany in 1803, settled in Georgia in a town called Marthasville, later renamed Atlanta. A daughter, Carolina, born to the Haas family, was the first white girl born in the newly named city. For some years Mr. Haas and his partner, Henry Levi, operated a store in Decatur, Georgia.

There were Jews in Georgia a hundred years earlier. On July 10, 1733, a vessel containing a handful of Jewish immigrants from England berthed in Savannah. After considerable opposition from the directors of the company holding the Royal Charter, these Spanish and Portuguese Jews fleeing the Inquisition, finally settled in the coastal town. They had come at their own expense at the same time another group of immigrants left England as charity wards of James Oglethorpe, who was trying to relieve the congestion of the London prisons.

With independence, nowhere in America were Jews made

1 New York *Post*, June 30, 1963.

more welcome than in Georgia. Indeed, the entire South had always been philo-Semitic.

In the North, the Jewish immigrant had to wait until his children became Americanized before the family entered the open society. But the Protestant fundamentalism of the South greeted the Jew with unusual generosity. As the Jew went about his business, peddling from home to home, or selling merchandise, his Gentile neighbors saw in him a living witness of all the Biblical truths about Moses, Isaiah, Jeremiah, and the Second Coming of Jesus.

The Jew in the South was nearly always self-employed. Far into the late 1940s, Southern Jews, in the main, represented a single proprietary class, which lent them immediate identity with the Gentile managers and owners, the power structure, of the community.

Social segregation between Jew and Gentile remained rigid, of course, but the Jew's economic status suggested a quasi-equality with the banker, the lawyer, and the president of the chamber of commerce.

It was precisely this identity that militated against the Jew whenever demagogic orators held forth against "Wall Street" or "international bankers."

"Our Negro brethren, too, are being held in bondage by Rothschild," said North Carolina's Elias Carr in almost every speech. Carr became governor of North Carolina (1893–97) as a Democrat who promised to silence the Populists by employing, at least, their rhetorical anti-Semitism.

Unlike the economic structure in metropolitan centers of the North, the Southerner saw no Jewish garment workers, garbage collectors, street cleaners, policemen, janitors, clerks, or truck drivers; furthermore, in the absence of the Jewish slum or ghetto of a Northern city, a demagogue such as Watson easily made the poor of the South believe, "The Jews have all the money."

In 1913, there were approximately 3500 Jews in Atlanta,

about 900 families, representing the largest Jewish population of any city in the South. The arrest of Leo Frank on the charge of the murder of a little factory girl brought deep concern to the Jewish community; it aroused the fear that has been part of Jewish life through history—the fear that the delinquency of one will endanger the security of all.

The fear was heightened when Frank's guilt was assumed from the beginning, based on the exaggerated stories in the newspapers. Five prominent members of the Jewish community were on the grand jury which indicted him. DeWitt Roberts, in his fine essay on the Frank case, for the Anti-Defamation League, writes: "Apparently, except for close personal associates, his family and in-laws, Herbert and Leonard Haas, some of the members of the *Journal* staff, and Rabbi Marx, no one believed Frank innocent until after his conviction." [2]

Even after the crowds shouted, "Hang the Jew," and a tent evangelist thundered at the open window to the spectators in the courtroom, "The Jew is the synagogue of Satan," many Jews of Atlanta still wrote letters to the American Jewish Committee, and to Abe Cahan of the *Jewish Daily Forward,* urging them to use their influence with the Jews of the North to stay out of it, protesting, ". . . it will hurt us if you interfere."

Initially, the Jews of Atlanta felt no sympathy for Leo Frank. Jews usually shun a co-religionist involved in a criminal case as one who has brought shame and possible disaster on the congregation. The French Jews broke their silence in the Dreyfus case only after Clemenceau and Zola became champions of the accused captain. In Atlanta, Tom Watson had already involved them all with his anti-Semitic campaign, but they began actively to support Frank's fight for freedom only after thousands of the leading lawyers of America, including a surprisingly large number of Southerners outside of Atlanta, publicly demanded a new trial.

At the trial itself, Frank's Jewishness first emerged as a cause

2 DeWitt Roberts, *The Story of Mass Hysteria* (Atlanta, Ga., 1948).

for his conviction during Dorsey's cross-examination of his mother, Mrs. Rudolph Frank. The solicitor general always claimed it was the defense that initially called attention to Frank's Jewishness. Dorsey was simply evasive. One cannot dismiss the fact that every prosecution witness described Frank as "rubbing his hands."

Jim Conley said three times that Frank was "rubbing his hands."

Detectives Starnes, Black, and Rogers each testified that when they first met Frank ". . . he was rubbing his hands." Yet during thirty days of courtroom tension Leo Frank did not rub his hands once, even before he had heard the first of the eleven references to this mannerism.

In 1913 vaudeville was in its heyday. The stage was filled with the stage Irishman—red nose, floppy pants, carrying a can of beer; and the stage Jew—black caftan, oversized derby, rubbing his hands over money. The repetition by witnesses, every one of whom said he specifically remembered Frank "rubbing his hands," strains belief. It makes one speculate whether the witnesses had been reminded by some vaudeville buff—perhaps Dorsey or Stephens: "Remember one thing, Jews are always rubbing their hands."

One witness testified that she had seen Frank on the street with Jim Conley.

"How did you know it was Frank?" asked Dorsey.

"Because as they walked along he had his face very close to the Negro, and that's how I knew he was a Jew."

Under the most favorable courtroom conditions, no Southern jury would have understood what Defense Attorney Reuben Arnold meant when he said the prosecution was asking the jury to believe the word of a Negro against a "white man." The jury would have been similarly confused if Arnold had argued thus on behalf of an Italian, Greek, Arab, or Syrian. By definition, a white man in the South is a white Anglo-Saxon Protestant and only a white Anglo-Saxon Protestant.

The tradition of Jewish self-help, hitherto reported in the Georgia press with respect and admiration, now helped strengthen Georgia's determination to hang Leo Frank. With cotton selling at five cents a pound, with thousands of Georgians actually worrying about their daily bread, the *Georgian* all too nonchalantly described a huge fund-raising campaign among the Jews of America to send Passover food to Palestine.

It would have been difficult to convince the poverty-stricken Georgians in 1913 that on the Lower East Side of New York where the majority of the Jewish immigrants lived that most of the Jewish school children were having their noonday meal at one of the free milk stations established by the Straus family.

It would have been equally difficult to convince them that Jews do not band together to save a Jewish criminal. Solicitor General Dorsey, referred to the Becker-Rosenthal case in New York as an example of Jewish gangsterism, but was careful not to mention the fact that the gunmen would never even have been arrested if it hadn't been for the lone efforts of the editor of the New York *World*, Herbert Bayard Swope, who was himself Jewish.

When Jews outside Georgia became involved in the Frank case, it was not on the question of Frank's innocence or guilt. They became involved because anti-Semitism was being disseminated by a talented publicist. This outbreak threatened not only the nine hundred Jewish families in the city of Atlanta but the entire Jewish community in America.

Extracts from the minutes of the executive committee of the American Jewish Committee reveal that the Leo Frank case first came before it in June of 1913, when Dr. Lee K. Frankel described the situation in Atlanta. After discussion, it was resolved that the committee take no action. It was none of their business. Leo Frank was the business of Georgia. But a month later, the obvious anti-Semitism that accompanied the trial, reported upon by competent newspapermen, alerted Jews everywhere to the inherent danger. Even then, however, the American Jewish

Committee formally decided in executive session that whatever aid they extended Frank should be extended as individuals, not as an organization. All over America this was the decision of the Jewish fraternal orders.

The Jew who eventually assumed the vast expense of Frank's appeals was Albert D. Lasker, the president of the famous Lord and Thomas advertising agency in Chicago. Albert Lasker spent two years worrying about Leo Frank to the exclusion of his other civic and philanthropic activities, even to the exclusion of his own business. He established committees that worked out ways and means to influence public opinion. Lasker induced Jane Addams, Thomas A. Edison, Arthur Brisbane, and others to participate in a campaign to aid Frank and carried on a limitless correspondence with Mark Sullivan, Adolph Ochs, Louis Wiley, Jacob Schiff, and Julius Rosenwald about the case.

Originally, Lasker promised Leonard Haas that the defense could count on him for $25,000. Others were not so generous. John Gunther in his biography of Lasker, *Taken at the Flood*, estimates the case cost Lasker $100,000.[3] In examining some additional data, particularly the correspondence between Lasker and Herbert Haas,[4] I estimate that Lasker's total outlay was closer to $160,000. Leo Frank's uncle, Moses Frank, was the second largest contributor with $50,000.

Lasker personally rehired William J. Burns for the defense. It was a reasonable decision since it was impossible to get cooperation from private detective agencies in Atlanta. As an outside investigator of great fame, Burns might find witnesses, perhaps even find the guilty man. Still it worked to Frank's disadvantage. Atlantans charged the Jews with trying to "bribe" Frank out of jail, asking who but rich Jews could afford William J. Burns, the head of the Justice Department's Bureau of Investigation (not yet designated the FBI).

---

[3] John Gunther, *Taken at the Flood* (Harper and Brothers, 1960).
[4] Lasker-Haas Correspondence, American Jewish Archives, Cincinnati Campus, Hebrew-Union College—Jewish Institute of Religion.

CHAPTER TWENTY-FOUR

231

Burns himself never grasped the true situation. He was totally ignorant of the South, its people, and its mores. When he arrived in Atlanta, a city already incensed over outside interference, he calmly announced this was a simple case and he would have no trouble solving it. This offhand manner of treating the murder of a little girl, already a Southern legend, turned the hostility of the Georgians into hatred, a hatred so violent that Burns himself came within an ace of being lynched.

Burns visited Marietta, where Mary Phagan had lived, and some town people recognized him. They reviled him as a Jew lover, and one Bob Howell, later to set upon the corpse of Leo Frank, attacked the detective, punched him and chased him to the courthouse, with a rapidly growing mob swelling behind him. Howell shouted: "Lynch him." Within minutes, hundreds of people were shrieking for Burns's blood.

Fortunately, someone telephoned for Judge Newton Morris, Marietta's leading citizen. Judge Morris came on the run, and for at least the tenth time in his career, delivered an anti-mob speech. This remarkable man was almost always successful in such situations because he spoke their language. "Boys, this man Burns didn't kill Mary Phagan. Frank did. Are you going to hang Burns and leave Frank in jail? Besides, Burns is a federal man and if you kill him the government will send marshals down here. They'll arrest you and put you in federal prisons where you will never see your wives and children again and you'll go through all of this just for hanging a man who didn't kill Mary Phagan."

In a few minutes, Judge Morris had the mob under control. He and a deputy sheriff spirited William J. Burns away.

Burns cost the defense $25,000. But Burns had accomplished some solid work. The Samuelses write that Burns posted a $5,000 reward to anyone who could prove Frank's perversion:

"The $5,000 reward—which no one ever attempted to collect—convinced thousands of people that the immorality charges against Frank had been dreamed up by the police. But Burns did more: he produced evidence that convinced additional thousands that Jim Conley, not Frank, was the pervert in the case and the murderer of Mary Phagan. The evidence came from a Negro woman, Annie Maude Carter, who had met the sweeper while they were both in jail. Miss Carter had been sent to jail for highway robbery the previous October and often talked through the bars to Conley, whose cell she passed daily. That spring of 1914 she was out on bail, pending an appeal.

"She asserted that Conley had confessed the crime to her after he had asked her to marry him. On getting out of jail, Miss Carter said that she had tried to tell her story at police headquarters and that Lanford and two of his men had taken an affidavit from her.

"Even more valuable from a legal point of view were one hundred obscene letters suggesting acts of perversion which Annie Maude Carter turned over to the Burns detectives, saying that Conley had passed them to her while they were both in jail. Burns showed them to the reporters, pointing out the similarity in the handwriting to the notes found near the body." [5]

Conley wrote these letters in February of 1914, a day after he had met Annie Maude Carter in court. Initially, she rebuffed him but then answered his correspondence in the mistaken hope that Conley would furnish her with money for an appeal. On his part, Conley was in love and in each letter asked Annie Maude Carter to marry him, sometimes addressing her as "Mrs. Conley." He turned away her pleas for money and insisted on professing his love and his sexual prowess. While repetitive, no one can help missing the truth; these are complex letters from a depraved yet articulate man.

"I still love you," Conley wrote in the first of these after An-

[5] Samuels, *op. cit.*, p. 186.

nie Maude Carter had rebuffed him, "and will always love you but I must not have a wife that will tell people to kiss her ass."

When she grew desperate for money, Conley promised it to her, swearing he would get it from "white friends" and from the State. "Give your heart to God," he concluded, "and your ass to me."

Sexual perversion occurs over and over again: "Now baby if you don't get out on no bond or if you do get out on bond you have that right hip for me cause if you hold your fat ass on the bottom and make papa go like a kitty cat then you have won a good man, that's me. I will try to give you this world, but if you let papa put his long ugly dick up your fat ass and play on your right and left hip, just like a monkey playing on a trapeze, then Honey Papa will be done played hell with you."

Conley always called her a "little girl," though she was probably more than his contemporary: "All I want is a woman that can work her ass and I believe you can. So don't worry about that other—No woman—and I don't want her I want you, that is if you will be a good litle girl." *

Despite this clear similarity to the murder notes, no state official or court moved to give Frank a new trial.

The near-lynching, coupled with his own pomposity prohibited any further investigation Burns might have proposed. He withdrew from the case. In fact, Judge Ben H. Hill of the Fulton Superior Court indicted Burns's Atlanta director, Daniel Lehon, for contempt, charging that by transporting Annie Maude Carter out of the State, he had taken her out of the court's jurisdiction.

Burns's blunders did not distress Lasker. The great contribution Lasker and the Haas brothers made to Leo Frank's defense was to persuade Louis Marshall, the leading constitutional au-

---

* I am indebted to the Georgia State Board of Pardons and to the committee members of this Board, Rebecca L. Garrett, Chairman, Walter O. Brooks, and J. W. Claxton who declassified Jim Conley's letters written to Miss Carter. This is the first time in fifty years any reporter or writer has had access to this important evidence.

thority in the country, to argue Frank's appeal before the United
States Supreme Court.

How important this argument was eventually to prove to the
American concept of *due process* became evident eight years
after the lynching of Leo Frank.

CHAPTER TWENTY-FIVE

SOMETIME BEFORE the Frank case went to the jury, Judge Leonard Roan had a momentary premonition that something more powerful than law had invaded his courtroom. He remarked to one of the defense counselors, "Why, if Christ and all his angels came to show this man innocent, they would still vote him guilty."

The conviction troubled Roan. Just before he heard arguments on the motion for a new trial, he confided in his friend, Judge Fred C. Foster, that the Frank case had materially affected his health. Roan insisted to Foster, as he indeed insisted to another friend, Judge Arthur G. Powell, that Frank was probably innocent. He wanted to grant the motion for a new trial.

Foster reminded Roan that Frank had no grounds for a new trial, that justice for Frank lay in the equity of criminal law and the only equity was the pardoning power of the governor.

"If you grant this motion," Foster said, "you may save Frank's life, but the chances are you would not. You would preserve the integrity of the courts, but at an awful cost, not that any price is too high. Exactly what happened at the pencil factory that day is known only to Conley. A new trial would serve only to postpone the danger and augment it." [1]

---

[1] A memorandum filed by Allen Lumpkin Henson with the Anti-Defamation League in New York City. Henson also repeated this story in his biography, *Confessions of a Criminal Lawyer* (Vantage Press, 1959), pp. 59–77.

Roan was still undecided when Arnold and Rosser presented their arguments in late October. The defense urged a new trial on the grounds that a mob spirit had pervaded the first one and that two jurors, A. H. Henslee and M. Johenning, voted the defendant guilty out of anti-Semitic prejudice. Arnold and Rosser produced depositions from Atlanta Gentiles who swore they had heard these jurors make prejudicial remarks about "the Jews" both before and after voting for conviction.

On October 31, 1913, Judge Roan denied the motion. Still, he had his doubts which he expressed in a bill of exceptions: "I have given this case long consideration. It has given me more concern than any other case I was ever in and I want to say here, that although I heard the evidence and the arguments during these thirty days, I do not know whether Leo Frank is innocent or guilty. But I was not the one to be convinced. The jury was convinced and I must approve the verdict and overrule the motion."

Roan was too literal. Chief Justice Thomas J. Simmons of Georgia had some years before set aside an outrageous verdict with the remark that *it took thirteen men to deprive any man of his life or property in Georgia.*

Had Roan, however, as the trial judge, included these doubts in the order that overruled the new trial, one of the higher courts in Georgia would perforce have had to grant Frank relief and give him another chance before a jury. But every higher court would rule that a bill of exceptions was not the proper way for a trial judge to communicate his doubts about a defendant's guilt.

Leo Frank, the innocent man convicted of murder, would eventually have to resign himself to the hangman's noose. But his case, as a problematic one for American jurisprudence, would live on to plague and bother the courts.

Discussing the implications of the Frank case in *American State Trials,* John D. Lawson described the jury system as the

best solution for determining guilt or innocence civilization has
yet devised:

"But the agitation in the Frank case was a protest against
this historical and well-ordered method. It was a clamor
that questions of guilt or innocence should be decided not
by established tribunals but by popular vote. It was a demand that those tribunals should solve the problem, not
according to the opinions of its judges, founded upon the
evidence, but upon the views of the multitude, founded
upon sentiment and rhetoric. . . .

"When the condemned man appealed to higher courts, he
contended he was innocent and asked that those who sat in
the high tribunals—because they were presumed to have all
those qualifications which the twelve jurors lacked—should
examine the evidence and pass upon the question of his
guilt or innocence of the crime with which he was
charged. . . .

"But to this appeal, judge after judge turned a deaf
ear. . . . A man's life or liberty, the question of his guilt or
innocence, depend not upon the evidence or upon the idea
of justice, but upon whether or not somebody has put the
necessary thing in the right document or the wrong one.
The people of Georgia, in establishing their Supreme Court,
must have believed they were creating a higher tribunal,
where beyond the prejudice of particular localities a convicted man would have justice administered in its highest
form. . . . When will our appellate judges recognize that
their duty is to do justice, not simply see that the judicial
machine is run according to rule? Not so long as in American courts, Procedure is King; for while the claims of this
tyrant are respected, it matters not what may become of justice." [2]

---

[2] John D. Lawson, *American State Trials* (Thomas Law Book Company,
St. Louis, 1918), Vol. X, Introduction, pp. VI–XI.

In all, Frank would petition the higher courts of Georgia and the United States thirteen times and never find redress.* After Roan refused Frank a new trial, his lawyers took the case to the Supreme Court of Georgia. The defense alleged 103 errors which the court grouped into seventeen categories and, on February 17, 1914, decided none was sufficiently good cause for another trial.

In its ruling, the Georgia Supreme Court commented first on Judge Roan's doubt: "The jury found the accused guilty. The court was called upon to determine whether, under the record, the defendant should be granted a new trial. He refused it, and the rule in such cases is that, even if the court should consider a case weak, yet if he overrules the motion for a new trial, his legal judgment will control."

Next, the justices of the Georgia higher court turned their attention to the main arguments of the defense: that Conley's testimony about Frank's alleged sexual perversion was inadmissible.

"According to the witness," went the majority opinion read by Justice Atkinson, "here was a statement by the accused in connection with homicide and its cause, arising from its lecherous desires and the effort to accomplish them. However black it may

---

* On October 31, 1913, Roan denied the motion for a new trial; February 17, 1914, the Supreme Court of Georgia affirmed the verdict of the lower court and on February 25 unanimously overruled a motion for rehearing. On March 7 Frank was sentenced for a second time. An extraordinary motion for a new trial was filed on April 16. Judge Ben H. Hill denied this motion on April 22. Frank's sanity was examined on April 25; he was declared sane. On November 14, the Georgia Supreme Court again denied a new trial and on November 18, refused to review the case on a writ of error. Mr. Justice Lamar of the United States Supreme Court on November 25 refused to accept the application for argument on a writ of error. Mr. Justice Holmes on November 25 also refused to accept the application. On December 7, the full bench of the United States Supreme Court turned down this appeal for review. Frank was resentenced on December 9. On December 21, United States District Judge W. T. Newman refused a petition for a writ of *habeas corpus*. Mr. Justice Lamar, on December 28 accepted on behalf of the Court the petition for *habeas corpus* proceedings. On April 19, 1915, the United States Supreme Court affirmed the decision of the District Court against Leo Frank. The vote was seven to two.

indicate the conduct of the accused to have been, there was no reason why the jury should have been left in the dark in regard to it."

The court had split, however; Justices Atkinson, Evans, Lumpkin, and Hill voting to uphold the conviction; Chief Justice Fish and Justice Beck dissenting.

In their dissent, Justices Fish and Beck asked: "Was it competent for Conley to testify directly in connection with the homicide that the defendant said, 'Of course you know I ain't built like other men?' We think not. If the guilty cannot be convicted without breaking down the barriers which the law has erected for the protection of every person accused of crime, it is better they should escape rather than that the life or liberty of an innocent person be imperiled."

The majority were ruling admissible a statement Frank obviously never made. It is nonsense to believe that Leo Frank, a Cornell graduate would confide he wasn't "built like other men" to a Negro janitor, an irresponsible semiliterate who had been fined six times during the past twelve months for drunk and disorderly conduct. In addition, Frank *was* built like other men according to reputable physicians who testified in his behalf at the trial. Conley may have been aware of the legends concerning circumcision. Even to this day, the myth persists among some rural and mountain folk, white and black, that circumcision somehow alters a man's sex. True, judges can know nothing about what a particular man may or may not do sexually. Men often boast of sexual conquest, but only under the most thorough scientific inquiry, which guarantees anonymity, do they ever admit the details. Furthermore that Frank would display perversion to his janitor and then confess it to him, hardly fits with what everyone did know about Leo Frank, that he was a particularly proud and humorless man, an extremely careful man, who made certain that every piece of paper in home and factory was in its proper place. Yet when Frank asked the higher courts to assess the evidence qualitatively, the courts refused and and only assessed it quantitatively.

Nor did the Georgia Supreme Court believe the roaring bullying mob had any intimidating effect upon the jury.[3]

Rabbi Marx, Lucile Frank, Emil Selig (Lucile's father) , and
J. M. Goldstein, an Atlanta lawyer who helped prepare the
appeal, went to the Tower to tell Frank. "Frank received the
news," remarked Goldstein, "as calmly as if it were an everyday
event. He was perfectly composed and confident that he would
ultimately be cleared of all suspicion of guilt."

Tom Watson hailed the decision. He castigated Judge Roan's
publicly declared doubt: "Judge Roan is out of his mind. He
cannot think for himself." [4] Judge Roan, of course, was not "out
of his mind," but indeed his health had broken, and he died a
year later.

The denial of a new trial frightened respectable Georgians.
The three papers came to Frank's aid, each of them, the *Journal,*
the *Georgian,* and the *Constitution* editorializing that Frank deserved another hearing.

E. H. Michael, speaker pro-tem of the Georgia House of Representatives, charged: "There was a thirst for the blood of Mary
Phagan's murderer. So intense was this feeling that the very
atmosphere in and about the court house was charged with the
sulphurous fumes of anger. I was in the court house several
times during the trial, and the spirit, the feeling, the thought
of the crowd affected me. Without reason I found myself prejudiced against Frank. Prejudiced, not from facts and testimony,
but by popular belief and hostile feeling manifested by the
crowd. Frank may be guilty, he may be innocent. Certainly he
has not had a fair trial. Let's give him one."

But Representative Michael was more the exception than the
rule. The *Daily Telegraph* of Macon, Georgia, temporized: "If
a mistake is made involving a single human life, it would be

---

[3] Frank v. State (Feb. 17, 1914) , 141 Ga. 243.
[4] *Jeffersonian,* March 30, 1914.

deplorable; but it is better such a mistake should be made than that our legal system should be brought into disrepute."

Again Frank came to court, this time to hear Judge Ben Hill pronounce sentence. On March 7, 1914, Judge Hill set the date for Frank's hanging for April 17. Besides the officials of the court, only Dorsey and his staff and defense counsels Rosser, both Haases, and Reuben Arnold were present. There had been no public announcement of the resentencing.

Frank made a statement: "I trust your Honor will understand that I speak impersonally, addressing my words more to the bench as representing the majesty of the law of Georgia than to the gentleman now on the bench. I well know your Honor has naught to do with the various vicissitudes of my case.

"In your Honor's presence, representing human law, and in the presence of the Supreme Judge who at this very moment is casting the light of His omnipotent and omnipresent eye upon me from His throne on high, I assert I am innocent of little Mary Phagan's death and have no knowledge of how it occurred.

"Your Honor, an astounding and outrageous state of affairs obtained previous to and during my trial. On the streets rumor and gossip carried vile, vicious and damning stories concerning me and my life. These stories were absolutely false, and they did me great harm, as they beclouded and obsessed the public mind and outraged it against me. From a public in this state of mind the jury that tried me was chosen. Not alone were these stories circulated on the street, but to the shame of our community be it said these vile insinuations crept into my very trial in the courtroom, creeping in insidiously, like a thief in the night. The virus of these damning insinuations entered the minds of the twelve men and stole away their judicial frame of mind and their moral courage. The issues at bar were lost. The poison of unspeakable things took their place.

"Your Honor, in this presence and before God, I earnestly ask that God in His mercy may deal lightly with those who

242   A LITTLE GIRL IS DEAD

unwittingly, I trust, have erred against me, and will deal with
them according to His divine judgment. If the State and the law
wills that my life be taken as a blood-atonement for the poor
little child who was killed by another, then it remains for me
only to die with whatever fortitude my manhood will allow.
But I am innocent of this crime, and the future will prove it.
I am now ready for your Honor's sentence." [5]

Frank's defense attorneys were far from having exhausted
their resources. They put another motion before Judge Hill for
a new trial, basing this appeal on the discovery of new evidence.
The evidence was considerable. It consisted of affidavits signed
by several prosecution witnesses repudiating their trial testimony. Since perjury in a murder trial was itself a capital offense
in Georgia in 1913, this was concrete evidence. And the defense
also introduced several affidavits from employees of the National
Pencil Company who swore the police tried to suborn their
testimony. Edith Carter deposed that one month before the
trial, Hugh Dorsey and Detectives Starnes and Campbell called
upon her at home and tried in every way to get her to state that
she had quit the factory because of some act of Mr. Frank. She
insisted she left the factory of her own accord and not because
of any act or word that Mr. Frank had said or done. Mrs. Mattie
Miller swore that A. S. Colyar of the solicitor general's staff,
had offered her $1,000 "to make a statement to the effect that
Mr. Frank had intercourse with me at various times in his
office."

Among the prosecution witnesses who retracted testimony
was Mamie Kitchens, Dewey Hewell, Ruth Robinson, Marie
Karst, C. Brutus Dalton, and George Epps (who soon recanted
his retraction).

One must remember, as the Samuelses remember in *Night
Fell on Georgia,* that, "If Dorsey and his police suborned perjury
from state witnesses as charged—and there seems little doubt

[5] State of Georgia v. Leo M. Frank, 141 Ga. 243, March 7, 1914.

that this was done in instance after instance—they could hardly have prosecuted the 'turncoats' without risking exposure of the role they themselves played." [6]

Nor was this all the new evidence. Frank's lawyers quoted Dr. Harris's opinion that the hairs found on the lathe were not those of Mary Phagan. Harris had testified for the State, but no lawyer during the trial had put the question directly to him whether the strands were those of the murdered girl.

The defense also produced for Judge Hill's inspection the notes Conley had written in jail to Annie Maude Carter which closely resembled in diction, handwriting, and content the murder notes found beside Mary Phagan's body.

Most important of all, the new evidence the defense had gathered was the final proof that the murder notes could not have been written on the second floor as Conley alleged.

A microscopic analysis of the first murder note, written on a brownish-yellow order pad, the dateline of which read "Atlanta, Ga. 190—" revealed the faint impression of a signature. The signature was that of H. F. Becker, a master machinist for the National Pencil Company, between the years 1908 and 1912. Becker's duties included buying machine parts and material for the factory. A canvass of all the firms to which requisitions had been sent by Becker revealed the original order, of which the murder note was a carbon, was signed by Becker on September 16, 1909. The serial number of Becker's order was 1018 and had been sent to the Cotton States Belting and Supply Company. Becker deposed, moreover, that he had packed up and bundled all his carbons bearing the date 190— and bundled them to the basement for burning when the decade changed.

All to no avail. By a constitutional amendment adopted in 1906, no higher court in Georgia could reverse a verdict on other than errors of law. Hill ruled that the new evidence was no indication of procedural errors; the Supreme Court of Georgia upheld him, and Mr. Justice Lamar of the United

_____
[6] Samuels, *op. cit.*, p. 184.

States Supreme Court refused the petition granting a review.[7]

On December 9, 1914, for the third time, Leo Frank heard a judge sentence him to hang. In a published statement, Frank said: "Can it be that the law, and our system of its administration is so inexorable that truth and innocence may never be heard after once the die is cast? Is the technical finesse of the law to forever preclude a hearing of the facts, and human right to be trampled beneath the judicial feet? If this is so, and I cannot believe it, then our twentieth century civilization is but a myth, and the divine spark in each human breast a fairy tale. Then in truth we hark back hundreds of years in human progress to when the arena and 'thumbs down' was the last word of law. It just cannot be that way! The revolving years of twenty-odd centuries must have brought a juster heritage than a condition barbaric in its essential details." [8]

Frank was indulging no rhetorical flair. Every time his lawyers moved into the courts for a review, Georgians mounted fresh attacks upon him. Georgia was readying for the spring elections and former Governor Joseph Brown, trying to re-establish his political fortunes, published a demand that the State stop its delay and execute Frank forthwith.

Frank replied in an open letter: "I have read your remarkable attack upon me. I use the word 'remarkable' advisedly, for no ex-Governor of Georgia ever before used his influence in an effort to destroy the life of one of his fellow citizens. When I read that tirade—unfair, cruel, and untruthful—I remembered that, when Prometheus was bound to the rock, it was the vulture and not the eagle, that stuck its beak into his vitals. I have suffered much; some good men have condemned me, but they have done so in sorrow. It has been reserved to you voluntarily, ignorantly, in passion and prejudice to kick me on toward the

---

[7] Frank v. State, 83 S. E. Rep. 645.
[8] C. P. Connolly, op. cit., pp. 13–14.

gallows that you may lessen your political debts and regain, if possible, some of the political ground you have lost." [9]

Tom Watson had transformed Leo Frank into a burning political issue. Even Sheriff Wheeler Mangum, always sympathetic to Frank and no doubt believing in his innocence, was constrained upon the occasion of his re-election as Sheriff of Fulton County, to take a three-quarter page advertisement in the Atlanta papers to assure the citizenry he had dispensed no special favors. Mangum assured the populace that if Frank was not handcuffed it was because the sheriff's office never handcuffed any defendants, save the desperate; if he and Deputy Miner drove Frank to and from the courthouse, it was to prevent a lynching at the hands of the mob on Pryor Street; if Frank had visitors in the Tower, so did all the prisoners on trial.

At this point, in denying Frank's appeal, the Georgia Supreme Court ruled on the question of Frank's absence from the courtroom when his verdict was returned. No Georgia tribunal had considered as yet this question of law. The State Supreme Court held that the defendant's absence ought to have been raised during the trial; not raised then, it could not be raised at all.

But the defense contended Frank had a right to face the jury of his peers, a right he had neither waived nor authorized anyone to waive for him. Again the attorneys handling Frank's appeal went through the Georgia courts, each of which turned them down. These lawyers petitioned the United States District Court for the northern district of Georgia, arguing Leo Frank was held in custody in violation of the Constitution of the United States, especially that clause which declares no state shall deprive a person of life, liberty, or property without due process of law.

The district court decided that upon "the defendant's own

---

[9] Leo M. Frank letter to Joseph Brown, through courtesy of Georgia Department of Archives and History, Atlanta.

showing"—that he had not objected at the proper time—he was not entitled to relief.

The remedies had been exhausted, save for the Supreme Court of the United States. Leonard Haas, after consulting with A. D. Lasker, went to see Louis Marshall who agreed, without fee, to handle Frank's petition to the United States Supreme Court on appeal from the U. S. District Court's decision.

No one in American Jewish life occupied the position Louis Marshall did from 1905 to 1930. No Jew, in fact, has ever achieved his prominence as a constitutional lawyer with a world-wide reputation, nor has anyone since achieved Marshall's personal influence in the American Jewish community. He was president of the American Jewish Committee at the same time that his briefs were read as models in every American law school.

Marshall was immediately sympathetic when he heard of Leo Frank's conviction. Even before Frank stood trial, Marshall wrote Justice Irving Lehman on July 8, 1913: [10]

"My attention has been called to the Frank case as President of the American Jewish Committee. Obviously it would be most unfortunate if anything were done in this case from the standpoint of the Jews. Whatever is done must be done as a matter of justice, and any action that is taken should emanate from Jewish and non-Jewish sources as individuals."

To Albert Lasker, Marshall wrote, "Frank had been tried in proper form but he had not had a fair trial and therefore, due process should mean not merely a right to be heard before a court, but it must be before a court that is not paralyzed by mob domination."

Marshall was also aware that not only the higher courts in Georgia, but the moral climate as well, imperiled Leo Frank's chances. To his friend Simon Wolf, he wrote, "This matter

---

[10] All the Marshall letters quoted come from the Marshall Correspondence, courtesy of the American Jewish Archives, Cincinnati campus, Hebrew Union College—Jewish Institute of Religion.

involves the good name of Georgia. It is equally important that other prejudices should not be enlisted. Nobody knows better than you how sensitive the South is to criticism from other portions of the country, especially in the North. If, therefore, through indiscretions, there should be published throughout the North articles which criticize the courts of Georgia, it would inevitably injure the cause of Frank." *

   The Frank case was as difficult as any Marshall ever encountered. He wrote to Adolph Krauss: "There is a strange fatality which surrounds the Frank case so that everything goes by contraries." Again to Justice Irving Lehman, he confided: "What really convicted Frank was the suggestion that he was a Jewish capitalist engaged in abnormal sexual practices."

   Marshall was sure the issue Frank had raised about his absence from the courtroom at the time the verdict was rendered was more than a technical and procedural plea. On the contrary, Marshall would argue this issue centered on the foundations of American justice. Frank had been deprived of a constitutional right; he had not received due process. The defense had so far only questioned the State process by which Frank was excluded from the courtroom, and the Supreme Court had decided the equity or inequity of a state process was for state courts to decide. Now Marshall petitioned the U. S. Supreme Court for a writ of *habeas corpus*, arguing that Frank was detained illegally since he had been deprived of rights guaranteed him by the Federal Constitution.

   Marshall based this plea on the Federal Act of 1867 which gave Federal Courts *habeas corpus* jurisdiction over state prison-

---

* Marshall knew whereof he spoke. The South has always been sensitive of criticism from *without*, mainly because so few *within* dared speak. Thousands of Georgians believed Leo Frank did not have a fair trial; just as thousands more believed that the Supreme Court decision outlawing racial segregation in the public schools was not only just but necessary. But few of these are ever able to express their convictions unless they are willing to surrender career, home, and future.

ers when state courts failed to grant relief. If the Supreme Court would entertain this argument, then Marshall was sure he would open up for investigation *all* of Frank's rights, including the fact that the verdict was contrary to the evidence and that the defendant did not have a fair trial.

And indeed, Marshall did succeed in having the Supreme Court hear arguments for Leo Frank. Mr. Justice Lamar finally reasoned: "The Supreme Court of the United States has never determined whether on a charge of murder in a state court the due process clause of the Federal Constitution guarantees the defendant the right to be present when the verdict is rendered."

In May of 1914, Marshall outlined his strategy to his Atlanta colleague, Henry A. Alexander: "I am strongly of the opinion that the record which is to be carried to the Supreme Court of the United States should be something more than the presentation of a bare question of law. However meritorious the constitutional question on which we are relying may be, I feel that it should be accompanied into the court at Washington with something more than the mere dry bones of a legal abstraction. It should be surrounded by an atmosphere which would bestow upon the case a human interest, which would enable the Judges to feel that, if they should decide the legal question in our favor, they would at the same time do justice concretely as well as theoretically. Judges, even of our highest courts, are human and at the present day especially, seek to avoid the criticism that in their judgments they do not sufficiently regard the right and wrong of a case, but are prone to follow ancient precedents not consonant with modern requirements.

"Our chance of success would, in my judgment, be infinitely strengthened if we can present a correct photograph, or rather a kinetoscope, of the entire trial to indicate that the gross violation of the defendant's legal and constitutional rights followed logically from conditions for which he was not responsible, and from an effort to destroy him by evidence which, on its very face, bears the earmarks of suspicion, and which was calculated to create prejudice and public clamor to such a degree as to frighten even the court and the counsel engaged in the trial. *If a court is satisfied that a prisoner has not had a fair trial, it will be apt to seize on a legal proposition which it might otherwise be disposed to overlook in order that the interests of justice might not suffer.*" (Author's italics.)

On February 25, 1915, Marshall argued Frank's case. On April 19, 1915, the majority of the Court ruled against Frank's petition[11]

Mr. Justice Pitney spoke for the majority. He held that the state of Georgia had a corrective process by which it had considered Frank's constitutional rights. State process had determined Leo Frank had a fair trial. If the courts of Georgia certified Frank's equity, the Supreme Court required nothing more.

There were two dissenting Justices—Oliver Wendell Holmes and Charles Evans Hughes. Holmes's dissenting opinion focused directly on the issue Louis Marshall had raised.

"Mob law," said Holmes, "does not become due process of law by securing the assent of a terrorized jury. We are not speaking of mere disorder or mere irregularities in procedure, but of a case where the processes of justice are actually subverted. . . .

"Supposing the alleged facts to be true, we are of the opinion, if they were before the Georgia Supreme Court, it sanctioned a situation upon which the courts of the United States should act, and if for any reason they were not before the Supreme Court [i. e.—a point of procedure kept the Georgia court from considering them], it is our duty to act upon them now, and to declare lynch law as little valid when practiced by a regularly drawn jury as when administered by one elected by a mob intent on death." *

---

[11] Leo M. Frank v. C. Wheeler Mangum, 237 U.S. 309–35.
* Appendix A.

Marshall had failed to save Leo Frank the man, but Leo Frank, the legal problem, persevered. The Supreme Court had recourse to *Frank v. Mangum* less than ten years later in the case of *Moore v. Dempsey.*

A group of Negro sharecroppers met in a church in Phillips County, Arkansas, deciding to hire a lawyer to protect their rights against white landlords. A mob descended upon the church and lynched several of these Negroes. Five Negroes were spared when a white committee promised the mob to hang them after a trial. To carry out this promise, the committee called Negro witnesses and beat and tortured them until the victims promised to testify as the committee wanted. The courtroom was filled with angry white citizens. Outside hundreds milled about, shouting threats to anyone who interfered with the desired result. The trial of these five Negroes before an all-white jury took forty-five minutes. After five minutes, the jury brought back the verdict of guilty of murder in the first degree against all defendants.[12]

The United States Supreme Court reversed the verdict in 1923. Mr. Justice Holmes now spoke for the majority and, citing his dissent in the Frank case, ruled that the Negroes had been deprived of life and liberty without due process of law. A mob-dominated trial is no trial at all; the Fourteenth Amendment to the Constitution guarantees everyone a fair trial.

Walter White, the then executive director of the National Association for the Advancement of Colored People, wrote Louis Marshall in 1923 to thank him for the *Frank v. Mangum* *habeas corpus* proceedings which now saved the lives of five Negroes.

Marshall replied: "Yes, *Moore v. Dempsey* is exceedingly gratifying to me in view of the fact that it has given the Supreme Court an opportunity to adopt the principle for which I con-

---

[12] Leo Pfeffer, *This Honorable Court* (Beacon Press, Boston, 1965), pp. 252–253.

tended in *Frank v. Mangum* and which was advocated in the dissenting opinion rendered in that case by Justices Holmes and Hughes. The stone that the builders rejected has now become the chief of the corner. Due process of law means, not merely a right to be heard before a court, but that it must be before a court that is not paralyzed by mob domination."

So recently as March 18, 1963, the United States Supreme Court again relied on the Holmes dissent in the Frank case. In this instance, the Supreme Court affirmed a Circuit Court decision on appeal by the United States Attorney, granting a writ of *habeas corpus* in the case of *Fay v. Charles Noia*.[13]

The Supreme Court held that due process is not necessarily accomplished by going through a form (i.e. the state processes of granting the opportunity of relief), that, in fact, *habeas corpus* isolates the constitutional question without reference to other questions. Mr. Justice Brennan, for the majority, cited the Holmes dissent in the Frank case. Thus, this dissent filed by Justices Holmes and Hughes on Louis Marshall's brief on behalf of Leo M. Frank is now the law of the land.

But in 1915 Louis Marshall had failed. Marshall optimistically wrote Leo Frank: "It is inconceivable that, with two judges of the Supreme Court of Georgia dissenting on the main appeal, and two justices of the United States Supreme Court dissenting on the Constitutional questions, executive clemency will be denied. The uniform practice of all governors has been, to grant commutation wherever there has been a dissent in a Court of Appeals from the judgment affirming a conviction."

The fate of Leo Frank was now in the hands of the Georgia State Board of Pardons and Governor John M. Slaton.

---

[13] Fay v. Noia (March, 1963), 423 U. S. 107.

CHAPTER TWENTY–SIX

JUDGE HILL set June 22, 1915, as the date for Frank's execution. The defense lawyers petitioned the Georgia State Prison Commissioners to commute Frank's sentence to life imprisonment.

The hearing was held in Atlanta. Commissioners Davison, Rainey, and Patterson convened the hearing at 9:00 A.M. on May 31. Of these three men, only Patterson was a lawyer, a judge of the Fulton County Superior Court.

The room was not large enough to accommodate all the delegations come to seek mercy for Leo Frank. There were petitioners from Massachusetts and New York and several more from Georgia. While the commission itself had no authority to commute Frank's sentence, its recommendations usually guided the Governor.

The defense lawyers recounted the arguments they had offered the Georgia Supreme Court and the Supreme Court of the United States. Frank's adherents addressed the commissioners, too. One of these was Coroner Paul Donehoo, who said he had never believed Frank the murderer of Mary Phagan. Another was Hooper Alexander, the United States District Attorney for Georgia.

Though the trenches had scarred the face of Europe, Leo Frank's fate took World War I off the American front page. The growing agitation throughout the rest of the country for justice for Leo Frank now reached a climax. Every Northern paper asked how Georgia would administer justice. Time was running out both for Leo Frank and the State.

No doubt the notoriety of the case hurt Frank, since it hardened Georgia's conscience, made many determined to punish the Jewish capitalist. But if Leo Frank did not have his day in court, at least he was exerting a ponderable weight on the public conscience.

There were grave doubts about his guilt. Everyone now knew that the trial judge had doubted, but Judge Roan died on March 23. Those who sought justice for Frank counted this a misfortune. Roan, whose health and conscience had broken over the case, had written to Frank's lawyers.

J. H. Howard, a former Congressman, asked the commissioners' permission to read Roan's letter. Granted. "It is possible," the judge had written Rosser, "that I showed undue deference to the opinion of the jury in the case when I allowed their verdict to stand. I was still in a state of uncertainty and so expressed myself. My search for the truth, though diligent and earnest, has not been successful. The execution of any person whose guilt has not been satisfactorily proved is too terrible to contemplate. I do not believe that a person should meet the extreme penalty of the law until the court, the jury, the governor shall all have been satisfied of that person's guilt. Hence, at the proper time I shall express and enlarge upon these views directly to the Governor and the Prison Commission. However, if for any reason I am prevented from doing this, you are at liberty to use this letter at the hearing."

Obviously the old judge knew something. He did not enlarge upon what he knew because his knowledge probably came from someone who had received it as privileged information. He was trying to communicate that something now. His friends eulogized Roan as a man unafraid of the mob. Roan may well have been unafraid of mobs, but the mob still affected him and his judgment. The truth about men who defy mobs is that they in-

variably are the men with the most to lose. Roan was not one
of these. He was, at Frank's trial, an old man, sick and weary,
virtually powerless.

No one opposed commutation.

But the next morning, former Governor Joseph Brown and
Herbert Clay, Solicitor General of the Blue Ridge Circuit,
headed a delegation of fifty men from Cobb County and demanded the commission reopen the hearing. They argued that
Georgia's courts would forever be dishonored if Frank's punishment was less than hanging.

On June 10, 1915, the commission, by a vote of two to one,
decided against clemency. That left Leo Frank twelve days to
live, and the one man who could spare his life, Governor John
M. Slaton, had twenty days left of his term. Slaton was to be
succeeded by Nat Harris. There was no question of what Harris
would do if Slaton postponed the execution. Harris promised
his constituents, as he had promised Tom Watson, that the
Frank case was a Georgia matter and he would consider it on
a Georgia basis.

Exactly what it was that Judge Roan was trying to tell the
prison commission and John Slaton was not clear until three
decades later, in 1943, long after Roan had died and Frank had
been lynched, when Arthur G. Powell caused a mild sensation
by bringing up the Frank case in his book, *I Can Go Home
Again*.[1]

Powell had served several terms as a judge on the Georgia
Court of Appeals; he was a noted Southern lawyer who had
contributed several important textbooks and he had been a
good friend of Judge Roan.

Powell in his autobiography recalled the irritable mob around
the courthouse, howling for Frank's life, and how this debasing
spectacle affected Roan's health. During the trial, Roan had
several times asked Powell's help on points of law. When Roan
was preparing his charge to the jury, Powell was with him on

---

[1] (University of North Carolina Press, Chapel Hill, 1943), p. 291.

the bench. Roan turned to him and said, "This man's innocence is proved to a mathematical certainty."

"I am one of the few people who know that Leo Frank is innocent of the crime for which he was convicted and lynched [Powell wrote]. Subsequent to the trial, and after his conviction had been affirmed by the Supreme Court, I learned who killed Mary Phagan, but the information came to me in such a way that, though I wish I could do so, I can never reveal it as long as certain persons are alive. We lawyers when we are admitted to the bar, take an oath never to reveal the communications made to us by our clients: and this includes facts revealed in the attempt to employ the lawyer though he refuses employment. If the lawyer were to be so forgetful as to attempt to tell it in court, the judge would be compelled under the law not to receive the evidence. The law on this subject may or may not be wise—there are some who think it is not—but naturally, since it is the law, we lawyers and the judges cannot honorably disobey it. Without ever having discussed with Governor Slaton the facts which were revealed to me, I have reason to believe from a thing contained in the statement he made with [Frank's] commutation, that, in some way, these facts came to him and influenced his action. I expect to write out what I know and seal it up for the day may yet come, after certain deaths occur, when more can be told than I can tell you now."

Editors everywhere demanded Judge Powell make his facts public, but the seventy-year-old jurist refused. To several of his associates, however, he hinted he would probably send the information to his Georgia-born friend, Professor Howard W. Odum, Dean of the Sociology Department at the University of North Carolina. Odum died in 1956, and except for a few friendly letters from Powell, who died in 1951, no such memorandum was in his otherwise voluminous papers.

What happened?

The "disappearance" of this memorandum aroused the conscience of Irving M. Engel, well-known New York lawyer and Jewish leader, a president of the American Jewish Committee in the 1950s. Engel wrote a personal letter to a friend in Atlanta, M. F. Goldstein, the senior member of Powell's law firm: Did Goldstein have any knowledge of Powell's memorandum about the Leo Frank case? [2]

Indeed, replied Mr. Goldstein, he knew all about the Powell memorandum: "I accept full responsibility for advising Judge Powell to destroy the memorandum because with the state of public feeling, no one would have believed the truth of it and it would merely have resulted in renewing the agitation which, by that time, had died down."

Goldstein went on to add that the evidence was second and third hand, and no one who had any prejudice about the case would have believed it, and no one who was convinced of Frank's innocence would have been helped.

To which Engel replied: "It seems to me that the fact that the state of Georgia first convicted and then lynched an innocent man should have been given the widest possible publicity. The memorandum to which you refer would not have been released in any event until after Judge Powell's death. By that time, the excited state of public feeling, to which you refer, had died down and I do not see that any harm could have been done releasing the memorandum. On the contrary, it would have impinged on the conscience of many Georgians."

Pierre van Paassen encountered similar inhibitions when he studied the Frank case in 1922. In *To Number Our Days* he says that when he found *his* evidence of Frank's innocence, he offered to write a series of articles for the Atlanta *Constitution* and that Clark Howell, the editor, agreed to publish them. "The entire Jewish community," writes van Paassen, "still felt nervous about the case. Several Jewish lawyers in Atlanta told

---

[2] Irving M. Engel, correspondence on Frank case, 1958–1963.

me if I wrote the articles the old resentments might be stirred up and, who knows, some of the unknown lynchers might recognize themselves as participants in my description of the lynching. It was better, said the Jewish leaders, to leave sleeping lions alone; they actually pleaded with Clark Howell to stop me from reviving interest in the Frank case. They claimed this was bound to have evil repercussions on the Jewish community." [3] *

Mr. Goldstein and the Jewish leaders might have saved themselves the trouble. Allen Lumpkin Henson, in his autobiography *Confessions of a Criminal Lawyer*, revealed exactly what the information was that Judge Roan had about Frank that Powell secreted in a memorandum and then destroyed, that Slaton eventually came to possess.

William Smith, Conley's court-appointed lawyer, came to Roan and told the judge that Conley had confessed the murder to him the first time they talked. Conley said he had been drinking heavily, and he had approached a little girl who fought him. "He stated he didn't know how long the struggle lasted, but that he remembered fighting back. Then, he said, his mind went blank, and he didn't remember anything until he came to himself down in the basement. He looked around and there was the girl, lying still, with a cord around her neck. He looked at her for a long time, and decided she was dead. He was scared. He didn't wait for Newt Lee, but hid the body the best he could and left by the alley entrance." [4]

If William Smith had told this to Judge Roan after Frank's conviction, certainly Roan somehow communicated it to Governor Slaton before Frank's scheduled execution. No court in America could admit this testimony in evidence. No court did

---

[3] Van Paassen, *op. cit.*, pp. 237–238.
* In fact, when I discussed the Frank case with Leo Gottheimer, who daily saw Frank in his cell in the Tower on behalf of the pencil company and the Montags, he said to me wistfully, "Harry, I wish you wouldn't write that book. It will only stir things up again." Gottheimer lives in Charlotte, and he is an eminent and successful citizen. His children are all happily married. *But nothing it seems is as habit-forming as fear.*
[4] Henson, *op. cit.*, pp. 64–65.

listen, only the Governor of the State of Georgia. And, in fact, Slaton did not need this information.

Next to the dissent of Justice Oliver Wendell Holmes, Governor Slaton's order of Frank's commutation is the most remarkable legal document to come out of the Leo Frank case.

CHAPTER TWENTY–SEVEN

JOHN MARSHALL SLATON was born on Christmas Day in 1876 on a plantation in Meriwether County, Georgia. He was the son of Major William Slaton, a Confederate war hero and for many years the superintendent of schools in Atlanta.

Young Slaton worked for three years in the railroad office of R. C. Robson to accumulate enough money to pay his tuition through the University of Georgia Law School. In 1898 he married Mrs. Sarah Grant Jackson, a widow, whose father had amassed a more than modest fortune as one of the first brokers of Georgia's convict lease system whereby prisoners were let as laborers to manufacturers and plantation owners. Slaton himself, as a corporate law expert, became a rich man in his own right, and entered politics. He served first in the Georgia House and then in the Senate.

In 1911, when Hoke Smith went from the governorship to the United States Senate, Slaton, as president of the Georgia Senate, became acting governor. During this short term, he handled all of the state's revenues, and for the first time since the Civil War, the Georgia treasury showed a surplus of $400,000. More importantly, as Slaton liked to boast, all the teachers had been paid.

Slaton described himself as a good, strong Grover Cleveland Democrat and declared, "I am in favor of preserving the fundamentals of states' rights though I firmly believe our only hope in this or any era is maintenance of the power of the Supreme Court."

He had never lost an election. Georgia admired him. Against his own individual and family interests, he left the chair when he was president of the Senate to cast the deciding vote by which Georgia ratified the Federal Income Tax Amendment.

Slaton was governor in his own right from June 28, 1913, when, with Tom Watson's support, he won overwhelmingly, until June 26, 1915. He could not succeed himself (although during Nat Harris's term of office Georgia amended its constitution so that Hugh Dorsey would eventually win two terms). There was every reason for Slaton to expect he would succeed either to a federal judgeship or to the United States Senate—until the night of June 10, 1915, when the prison board sent him its denial of clemency for Leo Frank. With this denial came a letter from Judge Patterson, one of the commissioners, who flatly asserted Frank was innocent.

On the next day, the 11th, Slaton announced he would hold hearings beginning June 12 to consider commutation.

At this point, Tom Watson sent emissaries to Slaton with a promise to put him in the United States Senate if he would let Frank hang.*

Watson's motive was twofold: he was making money on the case through his *Jeffersonian*, and his candidate, Nat Harris, who had won the gubernatorial election, had campaigned strongly on the promise to punish "Jew perverts, capitalists, and Northerners."

But Watson never came near comprehending the conscience of John M. Slaton. During his administration, Slaton had let some men hang and had saved others. Slaton always applied himself to a close study of trial and appeal records in capital cases. In the grisly tragedy that befell Leo Frank and Georgia, Slaton was the only man who tried objectively to determine

---

* According to Slaton's close friends, Judge Arthur G. Powell and Allen Lumpkin Henson.

Frank's guilt or innocence. Even had Slaton wanted to accede to Watson's request, letting Frank hang would not have been simple. The entire nation was waiting. Leo Frank was America's Dreyfus Case. Daily, thousands of letters poured into the governor's office. A politically astute man would certainly have to make some defense, if nothing more, about so fateful a decision.

Frank's defenders and his adversaries both resorted to chain letters to influence the Governor. One of the chain letters that demanded Frank's hanging originated in Blakeley, Georgia. It was sent to thousands of people throughout the state with the instructions to rewrite the message "in your own hand." It read, in part, "Is this tidal wave to release Leo Frank the result of the well-managed and manipulated press bureau preying on the people, coupled with the strength of Frank's eight attorneys who are parading as Georgia's greatest citizens or not? Let Georgia law be enforced by Georgia people." [1]

A majority of Georgians, influenced by Tom Watson, firmly believed that an organization existed among the Jews, "reaching from ocean to ocean," as they put it, dedicated not only to rescuing Leo Frank from the law but also to carving out of Georgia an autonomous Jewish state. These people readily copied out form letters.

A Mr. Edward Clarkson of Atlanta, the resident manager of the Standard Accident Insurance Company of Detroit, also constructed a form letter which he circulated among his agents, urging all of them to sign it. This letter read: "I have followed this case with more or less care and it is my opinion, unbiased by any personal interest therein, that Leo M. Frank is innocent of the crime of which he has been convicted. I therefore urge that in the exercise of your prerogative you use that blessed quality of mercy."

Some of the anti-Frank letters urged the Governor not to in-

---

[1] The letters sent to Governor Slaton and quoted herein were made available to the author by the Georgia Department of Archives and History at Atlanta.

terfere because the commutation would result in lynching. A letter from A. L. Johnson is typical: "There's a dangerous feeling all through the state concerning Leo Frank. If you do not let the law take its course there will be mob violence."

Thousands of interested Georgians inundated the Governor's office with personal communications. Joe Dobbins, of Chamblee, reminded Slaton, "You told me if you could ever do me a favor of any kind, you would gladly do so. I beg you to save the life of Leo Frank because of the mob spirit which was so prevalent around the courthouse during his case."

By far the most influential letter the Governor received came from the now-deceased Judge Roan. The letter sent from the Brookshire Hill Sanitarium, North Adams, Massachusetts, was sent to Luther Rosser, but addressed to the State Prison Board. One paragraph was obviously written for the benefit of Governor Slaton; "I recommend executive clemency in the case of Leo M. Frank. I wish today to recommend to you and the Governor to commute Frank's sentence to life imprisonment."

R. L. Camp, of Dublin, Georgia, wrote, "It is a good thing little folks are not elevated to the Gubernatorial chair in Georgia for if I were Governor I would pardon Leo Frank under my personal conviction he is innocent. We know, as lawyers, that this entire fight in the higher courts relates back to the mere affirmation of the technical regularity of his trial in the court below, which in substantial truth was nothing but a complete farce."

There were poignant letters from Frank's family: from Rhea Frank, "With a mother's tortured heart, I come before you to plead for my son, Leo. I know he is innocent of this terrible charge. I implore you to let him live so that he may prove his innocence to the entire world"; and from Frank's wife, "I married my husband because I loved him and honored him. During the years of our married life we have felt and suffered much. I have never had cause to other than love and honor him. Today convicted of a crime which I who know him best know he could not have committed, I love him, if possible, more than ever before."

All in all, however, the letters demanding the Governor not interfere with the judgments of the court outnumbered those which asked clemency.

When Dorsey and Stephens appeared in his office, arguing that the verdict should stand, Slaton made them accompany him to the National Pencil Company where, holding the testimony in his hand, step by step the Governor re-enacted the State's allegations. Finished, Slaton mutely shook his head at Dorsey, and Dorsey shrugged and offered no argument.

As the week wore on and Slaton still reserved his decision, he began to receive letters threatening him and his wife and promising his home would be destroyed if he did not let Frank hang. The Governor was coming to realize that commuting Frank's sentence was more than political hazard, it was political suicide. But he reached his decision that Saturday, June 19. He worked in his study until two o'clock Sunday morning, exhausting two secretaries, drawing his order of commutation and preparing a statement. Judge Roan's letter, the re-enactment, the new evidence, and the information gleaned one way or another from William Smith, decided him.

When he finished he went upstairs to his bedroom where his wife, whom he called Sally, was still awake.

"Have you reached a decision?" she asked.

"Yes," he said, "it may mean death or worse but I have ordered the sentence commuted."

She kissed him and said, "I would rather be the widow of a brave and honorable man than the wife of a coward." [2]

Slaton had chosen the hardest of the three courses open to him. He could simply have postponed Frank's execution and let his successor, Nat Harris, deal with it. An easier course by

---

[2] Quoted from Arthur G. Powell's book, *op. cit.*, to which Slaton attested accuracy.

far was to have commuted the sentence with a simple paragraph citing that where there is a dissent on an appeal in a capital case, it is customary for the governor to commute. But Slaton chose to submit a lengthy review going over in detail all of the evidence and the testimony. That review insisted on the reasonable doubt if not on Frank's innocence. Slaton dated the order of commutation June 21, the following Monday.*

Slaton wrote:

"Many newspapers and multitudes of people have attacked the State of Georgia, because of the conviction of Leo M. Frank and have declared the conviction to have been through the domination of a mob and with no evidence to support the verdict. This opinion has been formed to a great extent by those who have not read the evidence and who are unacquainted with the judicial procedure in our State.

"The murder committed was a most heinous one. A young girl was strangled to death by a cord tied around her throat and the offender deserves the punishment of death. The only question is as to the identity of the criminal.

"The responsibility is upon the people of Georgia to protect the lives of her citizens and to maintain the dignity of her laws, and if the choice must be made between the approbation of citizens of other States and the enforcement of our laws against offenders whether powerful or weak, we must choose the latter alternative.

"When Frank was indicted and the air was filled with rumors as to the murder and mutilation of the dead girl, there was intense feeling and to such extent that my predecessor, Governor Brown, stated in argument before me that he had the Military ready to protect the defendant.

"The most startling and spectacular evidence in the case was that given by a Negro, Jim Conley, a man 27 years of

---

* Appendix B. The text above is an abbreviated version.

age, and one who frequently had been in the chain gang. Conley had worked at the Factory for about two years and was thoroughly acquainted with it. He had worked in the basement about two months and had run the elevator about a year and a half.

"Conley mentioned several people, including male and female employees, who went up the steps to the second floor where Frank's office was located. He said that Mary Phagan went up the stairs and he heard in a few minutes foot steps going back to the Metal Room, which is from 150 to 200 feet from the office. He heard a scream and then he dozed off. In a few minutes Frank stamped and then Conley locked the door and then Frank whistled, at which time Conley unlocked the door and went up the steps. Frank was shivering and trembling and told Conley, 'I wanted to be with her and I guess I struck her too hard and she fell and hit her head against something, and I do not know how bad she got hurt. Of course, you know I ain't built like other men.'

"Conley described Frank as having been in position which Conley thought indicated perversion, but the facts set out by Conley do not demand such conclusion.

"Frank put his character in issue and the State introduced ten witnesses attacking Frank's character, some of whom were Factory employees, who testified that Frank's reputation for lasciviousness was bad and some told that he had been seen making advances to Mary Phagan, whom Frank had professed to the Detectives, either not to have known, or to have been slightly acquainted with. Other witnesses testified that Frank had improperly gone into the dressing room of the girls. Some witnesses who answered on direct examination that Frank's reputation for lasciviousness was bad, were not cross examined as to details, and this was made the subject of comment before the jury.

"One fact in the case, and that of most important force

in arriving at the truth, contradicts Conley's testimony. It is disagreeable to refer to it, but delicacy must yield to necessity when human life is at stake.

"The mystery in the case is the question as to how Mary Phagan's body got into the basement. It was found 136 feet away from the elevator and the face gave evidence of being dragged through dirt and cinders. She had dirt in her eyes and mouth. Conley testified that he and Frank took the body down to the basement in the elevator on the afternoon of April 26th, 1913, and leaves for inference that Frank removed the body 136 feet toward the end of the building, where the body was found at a spot near the back door which led out towards the street in the rear. Conley swears he did not return to the basement, but went back up in the elevator, while Frank went back on the ladder, constituting the only two methods of ingress and egress to the basement, excepting through the back door. This was between one and two o'clock on the afternoon of April 26th.

"Conley testified that on the *morning* of April 26th he went down into the basement to relieve his bowels and utilized the elevator shaft for the purpose.

"On the morning of April 27th at 3 o'clock, when the Detectives came down into the basement *by way of the ladder,* they inspected the premises, including the shaft, and they found there human excrement in natural condition.

"Subsequently, when they used the elevator, which everybody, including Conley, who had run the elevator for 1½ years, admits, only stops by hitting the ground in the basement, the elevator struck the excrement and mashed it, thus demonstrating that *the elevator had not been used since Conley had been there.* Solicitor General Dorsey, Mr. Howard and myself visited the Pencil Factory and went down this elevator and we found it hit the bottom. I went again with my Secretary with the same result.

"In addition, there was found in the elevator shaft at 3 o'clock Sunday morning, the parasol, which was unhurt, and a ball of cord which had not been mashed.

"Conley in his affidavits before the Detectives testified he wrapped up the body in a crocus sack at the suggestion of Frank, but on the trial, he testified he wrapped up the body in a piece of bed-tick "like the shirt of the Solicitor General." The only reason for such change of testimony, unless it be the truth, was that a crocus sack unless split open would be too small for the purpose. If he split open the crocus sack with a knife, this would suggest the use of a knife in cutting the drawers of the girl.

"So the question arises, whether there was any bed-tick in the Pencil Factory? and no reason can be offered why bed-tick should be in a Pencil Factory. It has no function there. Had such unusual cloth been in the Factory, it certainly must have been known, but nobody has ever found it.

"At the time of the trial, it was not observed that the death note written on brown paper was an order blank, with the date line, 'Atlanta, Ga.——, 190——.'

"Subsequently the paper was put under a magnifying glass and in blue pencil, it was found that one Becker's name was written there. He had been employed at the Factory on the fourth floor. Investigation was made and Becker testified that he worked for the Pencil Factory from 1908 until 1912, and the order blank was #1018. During that entire time, he signed orders for goods and supplies. The brown paper on which the Death Note was written bears his signature, and at the time he left Atlanta in 1912, the entire supply of blanks containing the figures "190—," had already been put in use. Becker makes affidavit that before leaving Atlanta, he personally packed up all of the duplicate orders which had been filled and performed their functions, and sent them down to the basement to be burned. Whether the order was carried out, he did not know.

"This evidence was never passed upon by the jury and developed since the trial. It was strongly corroborative of the theory of the defense that the death notes were written, not in Frank's office, but in the basement.

"Monteen Stover swears that she came into Frank's office at 12:05 and remained until 12:10, and did not see Frank or anybody. She is unimpeached, and the only way to reconcile her evidence would be that she entered Frank's office, as she states for the first time in her life, and did not go into the inner room, where Frank claimed to have been at work. If Frank were at work at his desk, he could not be seen from the outer room. Monteen Stover said she wore tennis shoes and her steps may not have attracted him.

"However, the pertinency of Monteen Stover's testimony is that Mary Phagan had come to get her pay and Frank had gone with her back to the Metal Room and was in process of killing her while Monteen Stover was in his office, and this was at a time when he had declared he was in his office.

"The evidence loses its pertinency, if Mary Phagan had not arrived at the time Monteen Stover came. What is the evidence?

"The evidence uncontradicted discloses that Mary Phagan ate her dinner at 11:00 o'clock, and the evidence of the street car men was that she caught the 11:30 car which was due at the corner of Forsyth & Marietta Streets at 12:07½. The distance from this place to the Pencil Factory is about one-fifth of a mile. It required from 4 to 6 minutes to walk to the Factory, and especially would the time be enlarged, because of the crowds on the streets on Memorial Day.

"While the street car men swear the car was on time, and while George Epps, a witness for the State, who rode with Mary Phagan, swears he left her about 12:07 at the corner of Forsyth and Marietta Streets, there is some evidence to the effect that the car arrived according to custom, but might have arrived two or three minutes before scheduled time. If so, the distance would have placed Mary Phagan at the Pencil Factory at some time between 12:05 and 12:10. Monteen Stover looked at the clock and says she entered at 12:05. A suggestion is made that the Time Clocks, which were punched by the employees, might have been fast. This proposition was met by W. W. Rogers, who accompanied the Detectives to the scene of the murder on Sunday morning, and who testified, "I know that both clocks were running, and I noticed both of them had the exact time." Therefore, Monteen Stover must have arrived *before* Mary Phagan, and while Monteen Stover was in the room it hardly seems possible under the evidence, that Mary Phagan was at that time being murdered.

"Under our law, the only authority who can review the merits of the case and question the justice of a verdict which has any evidence to support it, is the trial judge. The Supreme Court is limited by the Constitution and [to] the correction of errors of law. The Supreme Court found in the trial no error of law and determined as a matter of law, and correctly in my judgment, that there was sufficient evidence to sustain the verdict.

"But under our judiciary system, the trial judge is called upon to exercise his wise discretion, and he cannot permit a verdict to stand which he believes to be unjust. A suggestion in the order over-ruling a motion for a new trial, that the judge was not satisfied with the verdict, would demand a reversal by the Supreme Court.

"In this connection Judge Roan declared orally from the bench that he was not certain of the defendant's guilt—

that with all the thought he gave on this case, he was not thoroughly convinced whether Frank was guilty, or innocent—but that he did not have to be convinced—that the jury was convinced and that there was no room to doubt that—that he felt it his duty to order that the motion for a new trial be over-ruled.

"This statement was not embodied in the motion overruling a new trial.

"Under our statute, in cases of conviction of murder on circumstantial evidence, it is within the discretion of the trial judge to sentence the defendant to life imprisonment (Code Section 63).

"The conviction of Frank was on circumstantial evidence, as the Solicitor General admits in his written argument.

"It will thus be observed that if commutation is granted, the verdict of the jury is not attacked, but the penalty is imposed for murder, which is provided by the State and which the Judge, except for his misconception, would have imposed. Without attacking the jury, or any of the courts, I would be carrying out the will of the Judge himself in making the penalty that which he would have made it and which he desires it shall be made.

"In any event, the performance of my duty under the Constitution, is a matter of my conscience. The responsibility rests where the power is reposed. Judge Roan, with that awful sense of responsibility, which probably came over him as he thought of that Judge before whom he would shortly appear, calls to me from another world to request that I do that which he should have done. I can endure misconstruction, abuse and condemnation, but I cannot stand the constant companionship of an accusing conscience, which would remind me in every thought that I, as Governor of Georgia, failed to do what I thought to be right. There is a territory "beyond A REASONABLE DOUBT and absolute certainty," for which the law provides in allowing life imprisonment instead of execution. This case has been marked by doubt. The trial Judge doubted. Two Judges of the Supreme Court of Georgia doubted. One of the three Prison Commissioners doubted.

"In my judgment, by granting a commutation in this case, I am sustaining the jury, the judge, and the appellate tribunals, and at the same time am discharging that duty which is placed on me by the Constitution of the State.

"Acting, therefore, in accordance with what I believe to be my duty under the circumstances of this case, it is

ORDERED: That the sentence in the case of Leo M. Frank is commuted from the death penalty to imprisonment for life.

"This 21st day of June, 1915.

/S/John M. Slaton
GOVERNOR"

Slaton called his secretary, Jesse Parry, early Sunday and handed him the order of commutation as well as a statement for the press. He wanted these published Monday, and warned Parry about the need for secrecy until Frank was safely in the Milledgeville Prison Farm, two hundred miles away. Then the Governor summoned Sheriff Mangum to his offices.

"I have commuted the sentence," he told the bearded sheriff. "Can you assure me of his safety?"

"If we want to save him from lynching," replied Mangum, "we will have to smuggle him out tonight." Promptly, Mangum deputized three of the Governor's assistants to help him transfer the prisoner. He did not want one of Frank's regular guards to reveal the commutation to the press.

Mangum closed the Tower to all visitors and reporters at noon. He even had the switchboard disconnected. But the reporters remained a special problem. They were alert to the possibility that Slaton might commute Frank's sentence, and they posted a twenty-four-hour guard around the Fulton Tower, knowing any commutation would entail Frank's transfer. To deceive them, Mangum kept a crew working all day on the gallows, making needless repairs and testing it over and over again with a two-hundred-pound weight.

At nine o'clock that evening, Deputy Sheriff Plennie Miner sauntered over to the reporters clustered around Britt Craig and offered them all some whiskey in one of the rooms off the main floor of the jail. The reporters accepted.

While Miner distracted these men, Mangum went to Frank's cell at 10:00 P.M. and told him the governor had commuted his sentence. Frank took the news with the same cool calm he reserved for any change in his situation. Without handcuffing his prisoner, the sheriff and his three new deputies left by one of the side doors and made their way through Atlanta to the railroad terminal, where they boarded the 12:01 P.M. Central of Georgia bound for Macon.

Before they reached Macon, however, one of the train conductors recognized Frank and telephoned a Macon newspaper from a wayside station. When Mangum, Frank, and the deputies alighted at Macon, they were surrounded by newsmen—George Griffin, news editor of the Associated Press, George Sparks, a reporter for the Macon *Telegraph,* and a half-dozen others. They verified the news for themselves. Slaton had spared Georgia's most famous criminal.

Earlier in the day, Mangum had dispatched another deputy to Macon, who now waited in a car. Wasting no time, the sheriff and Frank sped the remaining thirty-two miles to the prison farm, where Warden Smith, just notified of Frank's arrival, received the prisoner.

Back in Atlanta, the reporters emerging from the jailhouse, found the Macon papers already on the streets with the news. But these Atlanta reporters got to work. One of the headlines to appear that Monday was "Frank Practically Free."

Wheeler Mangum, with Frank released from his charge, came back that Monday noon to an Atlanta where no one's life was safe. He could read the placards: "Slaton, King of the Jews!" was one—and he could feel the amazing anger of the slowly-gathering mob. He knew this was only the beginning. Nightfall would bring more terrorizing by some of the mill hands who were not yet through for the day, and the rednecks would soon begin to arrive in the city from their rural areas. In fact, Deputy Sheriff Plennie Miner wasn't sure Mangum's own life was safe.

A large crowd began congregating in the hall of the House of Representatives. They firmly believed Frank had either been spirited from Atlanta days before or that he had been secured in the governor's mansion. Mangum went to the hall, and from the speaker's rostrum he detailed all the incidents of the past night's trip to Milledgeville, even offering to exhibit the records of transfer to a committee appointed by these angry, unreasoning Atlantans.

As yet the mob was aimless. Deprived of its sacrificial victim, Leo Frank, it had not yet decided on whom to vent its fury.

All the papers carried the text of the Governor's statement:

> "All I wish now is that the people of Georgia withhold judgement until they have given calm and careful consideration to the statement I have prepared on the case. I am sure that my action has been the right one, the just one and the one that all patriotic Georgians will agree with. Of course I care for the public approbation, but should I have failed to commute Frank I would have been guilty, as I see it, of murder. I can plow and hoe and live in obscurity if necessary, but I could not afford not to commute him. It was a plain case of duty as I saw it, and I believe the people will realize that this was my only course."

The people realized no such thing.

Allen Henson, Slaton's Assistant Attorney General recalls making his way through the frenzied mob outside the capitol to the Governor's now deserted offices. The last order the Governor had given him was that under no circumstances did he want to employ the state militia. But Henson watching that mob, sensing its hysteria, began to worry that it might re-assemble around the Buckhead mansion where the Governor lived. Without arguing further with himself, Henson picked up the telephone and told Major John Grice, second-in-command of the Governor's Horse Guard, that an executive order called his squadron to riot duty about the Slaton home. In doing this without the Governor's knowledge, Henson knew that he had gone far beyond his duties as Assistant Attorney General. He was to write later: "It was treason and I knew it." [3]

3 Henson, *op. cit.*, p. 72.

CHAPTER TWENTY–EIGHT

IF THE THRONGS in Atlanta needed any more inspiration for their anger over Slaton's betrayal, they could find it in the headlines. The Columbus *Sentinel*, for example, went into exquisite detail about Frank's future, describing the special kindnesses he would receive and the privileges that would be his until, "a future governor gives him a final pardon."

When he left the rostrum in the legislative chambers, the alarmed Sheriff Wheeler Mangum sought out several of Atlanta's leading Jews and warned them of the incipient riot. He asked them to close their stores and stay off the streets. In fact, he authorized several of them to carry firearms. The Jews did not need this warning. They already anticipated a catastrophe. While the mob centered itself in front of the capitol building awaiting Governor Slaton's arrival, the Jewish residential district of Atlanta, the South Side, was still a signal target.

By noon, all the Jewish businessmen had closed shop, and on the South Side people had sent their colored servants home. Jews locked their homes and in the afternoon began checking into the hotels, the Winecoff, the Kimball House, the Georgia Terrace, and the Piedmont. Many of the Jewish men took their families to the railroad station and sent their wives and children to relatives outside the state. Today, a retired schoolteacher recalls her parents putting her aboard a train bound for Chattanooga, where her uncle and aunt had a store. She says, "As

far as I can remember other people sent their children from
Atlanta, too. A classmate of mine went to Birmingham. Quite a
few young children left Atlanta that day."

Dispersing the crowd was the responsibility of Police Chief
John Beavers. He had his hands full. The crowd stubbornly refused to move from the State House lawn. Beavers put every
patrolman and officer on twenty-four-hour duty. One of the
reasons the police proved powerless was that the sympathies of
the patrolmen lay with the mob. Beavers lost his temper during
the day when he found one of his officers, J. A. Bozemen, actually
conspiring with the agitators.

At one point, a determined group of vigilantes stormed the
capitol building wanting to see, "that Jew-loving Slaton, face to
face." They were persuaded to leave only when one of Slaton's
ashen-faced secretaries showed them that the Governor's office
was empty.

Near sundown, it was obvious to the milling array that Slaton
was not coming to the capitol. The mob numbered over 5,000
now. It began to drift down Peachtree Street, which would take
it through the South Side district and on toward Slaton's Buckhead mansion. As it went along, it kept gaining momentum and,
crashing into the South Side, the mob was filled with flaming
anger when it found the homes darkened and the streets pa-
trolled by Mangum's deputies.

Most of Atlanta's Jews remained in their hotel rooms Monday
night, Tuesday, Wednesday, and Thursday, venturing home on
Friday to attend Sabbath services. There are Jews in Atlanta
today who experienced that Monday night, and when they discuss it among themselves they refer to it as "crystal night."

Finding deserted streets, sealed and darkened homes on the
South Side, then and there the mob elected a substitute—
John M. Slaton. These Georgians were sure Slaton was a Jewish
agent. The Buckhead mansion, where the Governor maintained
residence, was no more than two miles away. Five thousand
people began to march on it. They were armed with old-
fashioned pepper-box revolvers—revolvers with cap and lock.

They carried saws and hatchets. Some had rifles. One group struggled with a large basket of dynamite sticks.

At Buckhead itself, the Governor and his friends could hear the howls as the mob streamed through the city streets.

That Monday several of the Governor's friends had heard the lynch talk that centered on John Slaton. Logan Bleckley, chief clerk of the Supreme Court, and Judge Arthur Powell constituted themselves a counterforce and made their way to the mansion, Bleckley carrying a Springfield rifle and Powell a shotgun. Justice Beck of the Supreme Court came puffing up the walk to join them. He had a sawed-off shotgun and a pocketful of shells. Slaton's friends wanted to station themselves around the piazza, but the Governor dissuaded them. Instead, he invited them in to join his dinner guests. None of them were aware that Assistant Attorney General Henson had already alerted the Horse Guards and that Major Grice and Colonel Orville Hall were desperately mobilizing these militiamen. Even if Bleckley, Powell, and Beck had known it, still they wouldn't have enjoyed their dinner.

One of the Governor's dinner guests was a young actor, Sidney Blackmer, just beginning a distinguished career, playing Romeo to Adrienne Battey's Juliet that summer at Atlanta's Grant Field. Mrs. Slaton was particularly interested in a theatre project at Georgia Tech, and often gave the young performers a lawn party and a picnic on the grounds of the Governor's residence. Occasionally an actor or an artist was invited to dinner, and Blackmer was a guest on that fateful evening. He remembers vividly standing in the foyer with Mrs. Slaton while the Governor walked through the front door to face the mob when it formed a torch-lit semicircle: "As the Governor faced the mob that night, Mrs. Slaton went alone, but well controlled, up to her rooms in the mansion. But the one memory that has never left me is that of Governor Slaton facing the mob, then slowly turning into the house to join his guests," writes Blackmer.[1]

---

[1] Letter from Sidney Blackmer to Harry Golden, June 8, 1965.

There was no talking, no reasoning. First of all, Slaton could not make himself heard above the chant, "Slaton, Slaton, King of the Jews." Nor did the members of the mob have any intention of listening. They were working themselves up into the frenzy they would need to lynch this man who faced them. The fear that reasonable men have of mobs is that its passions will sweep them up into it; to be the object of those passions, to struggle against envelopment, is as futile as struggling against the elemental force of an enveloping maelstrom.

That mob would have taken Slaton. But the Horse Guard burst through and ringed the house before any of the vigilantes could advance. The militia corralled twenty-three of the most desperate, all of whom carried either blackjacks or firearms, and these horsemen penned them into a carriage house in the rear. Quickly the militia formed a cordon and, using their bayonets, advanced. The mob threw bricks and bottles, and some stood their ground and fought with their fists and teeth, but the Horse Guards kept up the steady, tedious advance, though thirteen of their number received serious injuries.

By midnight the mob was under control and by dawn completely dispersed, swallowed up into the city and the factories and the surrounding farms. It was the first and only time a governor of one of our states had to call upon his own militia to save his life for an official act.

Watching from his study with a reporter who had bluffed his way into the mansion, Slaton said, "It's not the people of Georgia out there yelling, not the people. It's the ragtag element. I want to tell you their demonstration doesn't mean an expression by the State, sir." [2]

It may not have been all Georgia storming Slaton's home, but it was a representative part. Georgia now hated John Slaton. It was through with him. Though the Horse Guard disbanded the mob, Slaton's ordeal was far from over.

Virtually every newspaper outside the South applauded John

---

[2] "A Courageous Governor," *Outlook Magazine*, August 25, 1915, p. 109.

Slaton's order of commutation. All the big city editors proph-
esied Slaton would make an excellent Senator. No outside
editor understood the implications of Slaton's act. They were
not reading Tom Watson, who struck with a pathological
fury.

"Our Grand old Empire State has been raped!

"We have been violated, and we are ashamed!

"The Great Seal of the State has gone, like a thief in the
night, to do for an unscrupulous law firm, a deed of darkness
which dared not bask in the sun. We have been betrayed! the
breath of some leprous monster has passed over us, and we feel
like crying out, in horror and despair, 'Unclean! UNCLEAN!' " [3]

In his fever, Watson was both inflammatory and libelous.

Some months before Slaton left office, his law firm had arranged a consolidation with Luther Rosser's; the two firms once
merged were to be called Rosser, Brandon, Slaton, and Phillips.
Slaton had specified, in his agreement with Rosser, that the two
firms would not share in any of the fees nor participate in any
of the cases pending until he left office.

Watson charged, however, that John Slaton was a secret
counsel for Leo Frank, that he had received huge bribes from
the Jews, that he was the "Traitor Governor of Georgia."
Watson, of course, failed to inform the rabble that Hugh
Dorsey's sister was married to Luther Rosser, not that it would
have made any difference. This charge of collusion weighed
heavily against Slaton. It was preposterous, but the world has
too often witnessed the sad empirical truth that the big lie
succeeds best.

There has always been something magical about the United
States Senate. Wealthy men have spent fortunes to win a seat in
this most exclusive club in the world. It is unthinkable that
even the poorest of the poor could be bribed *not* to become a
United States Senator, let alone a wealthy man like John Slaton.
Within the week, however, the rednecks and the mill hands and

[3] *Jeffersonian*, June 23, 1915.

many otherwise reasonable people firmly believed that the Jews had "bought" Slaton.

From a Southern viewpoint, Watson did more than libel the Governor of Georgia. He libeled and besmirched the honor and dignity of Mrs. Slaton. He impugned her morals and her family. He nicknamed her "Chief Justice Sally" and "Sally Fanny," and insisted in his editorials it was she who persuaded John Slaton to commute Frank's sentence: "Whereupon, as Slaton told the joyous New York reporters, Sally Fanny flung her arms around the neck of her troubled Jack and persuasively said, 'Jack, let's commute.' This was at 3 o'clock of a Sunday morning and all the rich Jews who had celebrated the commutation at Frank's house the evening before, were abed, sleeping it off." [4]

An anonymous politician wrote his impressions of these tirades two years later: "Watson made of Mrs. Slaton's private sorrows a subject of sarcastic comment. I say it in shame that not a scabbard was emptied in her defense and scarce a voice was raised in protest in that fine Southern land where the unwritten law presumes to make the name and dignity of women sacred. So hypnotized was the multitude, such a condition of seething hysteria prevailed, that even boasted Southern chivalry was cowed into inaction." [5]

Nor was Watson alone in his abuse. A. H. Henslee, one of Frank's jurors whose prejudice Rosser had exposed, published a statement in the three Atlanta papers condemning the Governor in flaming terms, declaring that the daughters, wives, mothers, and sisters of Georgians were still in danger. Yet Henslee, without question an anti-Semite, had been the only juror to doubt Frank's guilt on the first ballot.

Slaton's friends begged him to leave the State.

"I will have nothing to do with such a course of action,"

---

[4] *Jeffersonian*, August 15, 1915.
[5] "Why Frank Was Lynched," by A Public Man of Georgia, *The Forum*, December, 1916, p. 689.

Slaton said. "My term ends Saturday and I will discharge my duties as Governor until that time."

To fulfill these duties, it was necessary for Slaton to maintain martial law in Atlanta for the entire week. Despite the presence of the militiamen, he was hanged in effigy all over the city. In the rural areas the demonstrations were more intense and more vicious. Farmers pumped shotgun shell after shotgun shell into his effigy. To schoolchildren he became the bogeyman.

On Tuesday, Slaton sent a message to the Georgia Senate and the House informing both of his order of commutation. One of the House members, Pat Harrelson, representing Georgia's Fortieth District, made a motion to read Tom Watson's editorials instead. Later in the week, Harrelson introduced a bill curtailing the investigative powers of the prison board and the governor and limiting the governor's power to commute or pardon to those instances where the board of prison commissioners were in the majority about the commutation or where the solicitor general and a majority of the jury recommended clemency.

On Friday night Police Chief Beavers closed all the saloons and clamped down on the bootleggers. Thousands of Georgians were pouring into Atlanta for the inauguration of the new Governor, Nathaniel Harris. Wheeler Mangum went to Slaton's offices and determinedly told this sad man that the police and the Horse Guards were not enough. The mood in the city was ugly and frightening. The sheriff prevailed upon Slaton to call up the Fifth National Guard Regiment of Atlanta and the Second Regiment of Macon.

The guardsmen formed a cordon around the State Capitol, and several of them served as a personal bodyguard for the outgoing Governor. There was no disturbance when Slaton and Nat Harris entered the capitol and made their way to the Hall of Representatives. Harris gave a short inaugural address, and Slaton rose to present the new Governor with the Seal of the State.

The entire chamber erupted with hisses and boos and catcalls.

Slaton ignored the interruption and, handing over the Seal, said to Harris, "Governor, I know that during my term of office this great Seal of our State has not been dishonored."

"Lynch him!" cried the excited crowds as Slaton left.

"Remember Mary Phagan!"

"Jew lover!"

The soldiers maneuvered Slaton to his automobile, several platoons fighting off the men who wanted to overturn it. Slaton's chauffeur drove off in the direction of the railroad station, and then, at last, the mob broke past the soldiers and chased the car. Fortunately, Slaton went to a luncheon in honor of Governor Harris at the Piedmont Hotel. The New York train, which left Atlanta at one o'clock, was still there, and the mob raced through it, convinced Slaton was aboard. The military followed closely and prevented any damage to the station or harm to the passengers.

That following Monday Slaton left Georgia with his wife. There was no incident. The Slatons went to New York for a brief stay in the Adirondacks, after which Slaton began an expanded hegira—to the Far West, to the Pan-American Exposition in California, to Alaska—which occupied him for several years. He was an exile from the State in which he had been born and which he had served so honorably.

Upon Slaton's departure, Governor Nat Harris withdrew the troops and explained to his constituents he had retained martial law that weekend at Sheriff Wheeler Mangum's request. "I am fixed in my belief," said the new Governor, "that no one, however aggrieved he may feel himself to be, has the right to take the law into his own hands or force the State to stand guard against violent assaults upon the person or property of any of its citizens. I trust there will be an immediate cessation of all efforts at violent or riotous demonstrations over the matter. This is the first request I make of my people as their Governor, and I do sincerely hope that I will have their unanimous cooperation to the end that the honor and good name of the State may be preserved."

When a reporter for *The New York Times* asked the Governor if Slaton would be assassinated if he returned, Harris sadly replied, "I can't tell. I hope not. I hope the time hasn't come in Georgia when one of her Governors can't safely return to her soil."

The *Times* noted editorially that Harris would venture nothing more than "hope."

A few weeks later, Mayor James Woodward of Atlanta, attending a conference of mayors in San Francisco, delivered a more venomous directive: " 'Keep Out of Georgia,' Woodward Tells Slaton," read the headlines in many of the nation's newspapers. Said Woodward:

"People throughout the United States have obtained their ideas of the Frank case from a poisoned and subsidized press. There is not a member of the jury that tried Leo M. Frank who would change his decision if put to the test again. Georgia's people cannot be classed with tramps, hoodlums, bandits, and lawbreakers. But every avenue of law had been exhausted and the judgements of the courts set aside by one man and the people felt it was up to them to take the law into their hands. We people of Georgia deplore this deed, but when it comes to a woman's honor there is no limit we will not go to avenge and protect. I have known Jack Slaton thirty years. I have been friends with him, and, while I hate to say it, I would not advise him to return to Georgia for a year, if ever. The bulk of the people may believe he did what he thought was right, but I am afraid there are some who will resent his acts throughout all the years to come."

"When mobs are no longer possible," Tom Watson was writing, "Liberty will be dead." Slaton had gone, but Georgia was still a hurricane. The eye of that hurricane, deadly still, spun around the Milledgeville Prison where the "Silent Man of the Tower," Leo Frank, was now a convict.

CHAPTER TWENTY–NINE

"I HAD BEGUN TO THINK I would never get to see this place," said Leo Frank to Warden J. T. Smith. It was 4:35 on the morning of June 22, and Sheriff Wheeler Mangum had just turned over the prisoner. Frank became Number 965.

The convicts were already up. Marching in quickstep to the mess hall, they could see the crowd of newspapermen at the front gate, could count the doubled guards patrolling the fence, could feel the place alive with a special atmosphere.

Warden Smith admitted two of the reporters at 7:45 A.M. Frank had consented to an interview. He walked with a firm step into the large, airy office of the warden. But as he faced these two newspapermen, they could see that the muscles of his face were twitching and his eyes were red with fatigue from the long cross-country journey.

He told the reporters, "I am grateful beyond words to the Governor for the way he handled the case. I felt confident all the while that it would turn out as it has. Somehow I just felt I would not hang. Of course, I am unsettled as you can see from the tremendous nerve-wracking experience through which I have been drawn, especially during the last trying hours of this ordeal. And I am not composed enough at this time to give you an intelligent and connected conversation. Just say that I feel more than I can express in words and am happy that my life is saved. Time will prove as I have often told you the fact of my absolute innocence."

That afternoon Frank quickstepped past the barbed wire into the fields with the other convicts as a laborer. The warden assigned him to the fields rather than to the office because he had been incarcerated in the Fulton Tower for so long a time that outdoor work would serve his health best.

The Milledgeville Prison Farm was called the Georgia State Penitentiary, but it was only a penitentiary by courtesy. Georgia had recently abolished the convict-lease system and had yet to construct a maximum security prison. Milledgeville resembled more an army camp with a string of barracks, a mess hall, and administrative offices, all surrounded by barbed wire. White and colored prisoners lived in segregated areas. New prisoners, like Frank, wore stripes, and the older prisoners, as a reward for good behavior, wore gray.

Frank went about his duties with the field gangs obediently, almost cheerfully. In his letters to his wife, he talked about vindication and the day on which it would come. He never thought his vindication illusory, but then he didn't live long enough to lose hope. The Governor's life had been in precarious balance the day before; it was too much to expect that the central figure in this tragedy, even on an isolated prison farm, would be any safer.

Warden Smith and his superintendent, L. Burke, assured the adjutant general of the National Guard, J. Van Holt Nash, that they could protect and defend Frank. The prison ammunition room had more than enough rifles for the guards to hold off attackers. But Nash, on two occasions, had Smith and Burke watching the Milledgeville roads for a lynch party. Both alarms had proved false.

On July 1, Frank wrote defense counsel Luther Rosser:

"At this writing my health is much better, my cold having left me. I am sleeping fine and my appetite is good.

"The warden and his staff are very kind and solicitous.
"Will you please send me J. M. Slaton's present mail address. I would like to write to him.
"I have been given some chores in and about the prison building commensurate with my present physical condition. I go to bed at eight-thirty P.M. and rise at four-thirty A.M. My work consumes about 5-7 hours a day. Of course I must be ready to do any other work, beside the routine work, on call. Even at that I have several hours a day for reading, writing or any reasonable form of exercise or diversion. The sunshine and atmosphere here are great. I have plenty of opportunity to view plant life and my field for observation in the crimino-psychological field is practically limitless."

Rosser had been promised a fee of $15,000 for defending Frank, which he waived when the appeals proved so expensive. His practice had been crippled by the notoriety he received as Frank's chief counsel. What really saddened him, he wrote back to Frank, was that his best work hadn't been good enough. He said he was proud to have defended Frank, a client who never once lied to him. He still believed in Frank's innocence and he counseled patience and resignation. (Rosser's fee and all other fees and expenses were eventually paid in full with money provided by A. D. Lasker.)

But Frank needed more than patience and resignation. On the night of July 17, a twice-convicted murderer, William Creen, who worked in the prison kitchen, secreted a long knife in his trousers, and while Frank lay sleeping crept upon him and slashed his throat almost from ear to ear. Creen would have killed Frank with the second swipe, but Frank reached out with both hands and clasped the knife blade. The other convicts in the barracks, awakened by Creen's maniacal screaming, disarmed him.

Creen had only partially severed the jugular vein, but Frank would have bled to death in his cot had the warden not summoned another convict, J. W. McNaughton, a surgeon serving a life term for murder. McNaughton had been convicted of administering arsenic to one Fred Flanders and had been sentenced to hang. Slaton had commuted the sentence to life imprisonment.

When Frank came out of the anesthesia, he looked questioningly at McNaughton. "Am I going to die?" he asked.

"Fifty-fifty," answered the doctor.

"I am not afraid," said Frank. "There is nothing between me and God."

His neck and hands bandaged, Frank lay for two weeks between life and death in the prison hospital before he began to rally.

Throughout Georgia, petitions circulated asking Governor Harris to pardon Creen. His office was inundated with telegrams urging Creen's immediate release. Harris himself led an investigation into the attack and asked Creen why he had assaulted a fellow convict. Creen replied, "I was afraid the prison would be attacked. I was afraid I would be killed when the guards started shooting back at the men who would rescue Frank."

After the Creen assault, Tom Watson fell to his nadir.

"Let the Jews of Georgia remember that *we* did not start this thing: *let them beware how they threaten us!*

"Note: the man Creen, who slashed Frank's throat, *is a Roman Catholic*, the ward or god-son of a priest.

"The butcher knife the Catholic used had been in operation during the day *killing hogs.*

"Nathan Straus can make a memorandum of *that.*

"Kosher!" [1]

This is probably as cruel a thing as Watson ever said in all his writings against Catholics, Negroes, and Jews.

In late June, after the commutation, a group of over one hundred men, calling themselves the Knights of Mary Phagan,

[1] *Jeffersonian*, July 22, 1915.

met over the little girl's grave and, improvising a ritual, pledged themselves to avenge her. From their number, the Knights chose twenty-five to execute the vengeance. None of these twenty-five was riffraff. Not one was a drunk, and all were responsible fathers, wage-earners and church-goers. One was, sadly enough, a clergyman. These twenty-five elected a single leader and swore blind obedience to his orders, resolving to accept on their individual shoulders whatever burden might befall in hanging Leo Frank. These men never thought of themselves as lynchers but as men bound to do justice in a holy cause.

They would have seized Frank before Creen knifed him, but in July the rumor of their impending attack leaked from Marietta, and Governor Harris ordered the militia in readiness. The county police spent July 1 and 2 scouring the roads between Fulton and Cobb counties on the lookout for automobiles from Marietta. The Knights postponed their abduction. They spent the intervening weeks acquainting themselves with the back routes from Marietta to Milledgeville, studying the barbed wire entanglements and the telephone and telegraph wires.

On July 25, the Confederate veterans of Marietta raised a monument over Mary Phagan's grave. That evening, after the ceremonies, the Knights convened and resolved to seize Frank and lynch him as soon as he was released from the prison hospital. They only had three weeks to wait.

The name, Knights of Mary Phagan, first appeared in the *Jeffersonian*, in the issue of June 24, the issue that condemned Slaton's commutation. Tom Watson in each issue thereafter professed to see the great "Invisible Power" of these Knights. He made no secret of what he expected. Each issue of the *Jeffersonian* reviewed the Frank case and lamented that justice was frustrated as long as the Sodomite Jew lived. Watson even included a defense of lynch law, declaring in a July editorial, "The Voice of the People is the Voice of God. If Democracy does not mean exactly that let us abandon our Republican form of Government, kiss the toe of the Pope and ask him to appoint a 'divine right' king to rule over us." He made it even clearer in his issue of August 12: "THE NEXT JEW WHO DOES WHAT FRANK DID IS GOING TO GET EXACTLY THE SAME THING WE GIVE NEGRO RAPISTS."

By August 6, Frank had rallied enough to write Dan Lehon, William J. Burns's Atlanta director: "I was cheered and inspired by your good words. Thanks be to God I am recovering nicely and am well on the way to regain the good health I was enjoying. I believe I will have no other bad effect from the murderous attack than a not-too-conspicuous scar on my neck. Healing is progressing rapidly." [2]

Lucile Frank had come to see her husband when he was well enough to have visitors. The officials returned Frank to the barracks on August 15, and Lucile started back to Atlanta on the morning of the 16.

That afternoon, the advance guard of the Knights of Mary Phagan left Marietta bound for Milledgeville, where they would begin cutting the telephone wires at 10:00 P.M. It was a Monday, and the lynch cars left Marietta one by one, inconspicuously. There were eight cars in the caravan. Outside the dirt road that led to the Milledgeville Prison Farm, the lynchers rendezvoused.

J. W. Turner, a trusty, was the first to see their headlights bearing upon the prison. He ran to one of the three guards on duty and said, "They are coming for Frank. Get him out the back way."

The guard turned away. With another trusty named Bruce, Turner ran to the warden's office. The guard there sent him and Bruce back to their barracks. Official Georgia had had enough of Leo Frank. Frank meant a shooting war, and the prison officials had apparently decided to have none of it.

The invaders broke the front gates, and the twenty-five men,

---

2 Leo M. Frank letters quoted here, through courtesy of American Jewish Archives, Cincinnati campus, Hebrew Union College–Jewish Institute of Religion.

only three of them masked, split into four groups, each precisely drilled in its duties. The first group went to the prison garage and started emptying the gasoline from all the cars. Another group stormed the home of Warden Smith. As soon as Smith opened the door, they put a rifle in his face, and one man snapped handcuffs on the warden. "We have come for Leo Frank," said the leader. "You will find him tomorrow on Mary Phagan's grave. You can come with us, if you want."

"Damned if I go any place with you," said Smith.

A third group invaded Superintendent Burke's home. He, too, was handcuffed and, prodded by a shotgun, led the men to the prison administrative office, where the last guard was quickly overpowered.

A fourth group, exactly apprised of Frank's barracks, burst upon it and ran to the second floor where Frank lay asleep. One man grabbed him by his hair, and the others took his arms and legs and pulled him from his bed. They got him to his feet, and Frank groaned in pain. They handcuffed him and half-carrying, half-pushing their victim, they ran from the building. They were methodical and quick, awakening only one of the sleeping convicts.

From the prison office, Superintendent Burke could see them rushing Frank across the compound. One of the cars moved forward, and the lynchers thrust Frank to the floor and climbed in after him. Burke saw one of them brandish a noose in Frank's face. Then they were gone. It had taken them no more than ten minutes, and they had acted with such precision that the three commissioners of the prison board, Patterson, Rainey, and Davison, who were asleep that night at Burke's house, did not know until the following morning that the most famous convict in America had been kidnaped.

The vanguard that had preceded the main party had cut all the wires from Milledgeville to the outside world save one—a long-distance wire to Augusta which they did not know was in use.

A Negro prisoner ran to the home of Mr. Satterfield, the prison bookkeeper, and woke him. The bookkeeper could not get through to anyone by phone, and Warden Smith dispatched him as a courier to Macon. Then Superintendent Burke found the unbroken wire to Augusta and notified the police there that Frank was gone. Throughout Georgia the belief had gained currency that a Jewish conspiracy had every intention of rescuing Frank. It took Warden Smith some thirty minutes to convince other policemen that friends had not saved Frank, that the lynch party was indeed headed for Marietta. The Macon police alerted the sheriffs in a fifty-mile radius. Still, the lynch party had a one-hour start.

A posse started up from Milledgeville. The lynch party, the first on record ever to use automobiles in the South, had sped away in the direction of Eatontown. The sheriffs and police expected the caravan would skirt the towns of any considerable size on their journey back. They thought it would pursue a route as follows: from Milledgeville toward Eatontown, then westward to the corner of Baldwin County, on through the upper part of Jones County and into Jasper toward the village of Hillsboro, then cross the Ocmulgee River by toll bridge, detour Jackson and enter the main highway somewhere in the vicinity of Locust Grove near the Marietta graveyard. The Atlanta police were alerted to intercept them there.

But the lynchers were by now aware they had missed that one wire. At the swampy banks of the Little River, the caravan changed directions, the leader having decided they would not hang Frank in the graveyard but elsewhere in Marietta, on the other side of the town. They headed now for Frey's gin on the Roswell Road. Frey's gin was near the house where Mary Phagan had been born. They approached Marietta from an opposite direction.

Ex-Sheriff William Frey saw the autos pass him. He thought he recognized Leo Frank, now sitting, crammed between two men. Prudently he did not follow; instead he walked into

Marietta to find out what had happened the night before in Milledgeville. It was near seven on Tuesday morning.

Several men on their way to the railroad tracks to begin surveying work came around a turn on Roswell Road and saw eight cars pulling to a stop beside an oak grove. From one of the cars an unmasked man leaped waving a revolver at them and ordered them to walk the other way. They complied.

From the opposite direction, a farmer named Chandler was driving his team to his fields. He, too, saw the cars, and he saw the men pulling Leo Frank from the back seat. Frank, clad only in a nightshirt, his hands manacled in front, marched off into the grove between two of the lynchers. One of the lynchers approached Chandler and pointed a rifle at him. "Stay there," he ordered.

Throughout the long night neither Frank nor his lynchers talked. Frank was still weak from loss of blood, and he was in pain from the rough handling he had received. He was pretty well convinced that what little luck he had was now played out. He said nothing until these rough men marched him through the grove and halted before a big oak.

The leader of the party, once a Marietta police officer, waited for the others to assemble and then said: "Mr. Frank, we are going to do what the law said to do—hang you by the neck until you are dead. Do you want to say anything before you die?"

Frank answered with one word: "No."

"We want to know whether you are guilty or innocent of the murder of Mary Phagan."

"I think more of my wife and mother than I do of my own life. Would you return my wedding ring?"

They got on with the business. One of the men took the wedding ring from Frank's finger. Another produced a piece of brown canvas and tied it around Frank's waist, then fastened a handkerchief over his eyes. The noose was a brand-new three-quarter-inch manila rope, tied with a professional hangman's knot so as not to throw Frank's head back or his chin up. Two of the lynchers looped it now over a high branch that faced in the direction of Mary Phagan's home. Two others hoisted Frank atop a table, and kicked it from under him.

The drop opened up Creen's wound in his neck, and Frank's blood spilled over his shoulder. Quickly now the lynchers withdrew, leaving Frank's body swaying in the early light. Ironically, as Frank dangled in the lonely grove, the graveyard some miles away was ringed with Georgians, awaiting his appearance.*

"He's there!" shouted the farmer Chandler. "They got him. He's in the grove by Frey's gin." From the Marietta village square, the people began to stream out. Cars started up and men leaped on their running boards from the street. No one asked directions. Everyone was going to the same place.

Blood still poured from the wound when the first of the crowd reached the oak. They knew it was Leo Frank. The hands were scarred where they had wrestled with Creen's knife. The black hair was still combed. Above the breast on the nightgown were the initials L. M. F.

Frank hung four feet off the ground, a piece of hemp binding his feet. A man in the crowd rushed to cut it away, splitting it up for souvenirs. Some of the men began to hack away at the sleeves of Frank's nightshirt.

Still they came. Automobiles, horse-drawn carriages, wagons, pedestrians; by eight o'clock one thousand people crowded around the grove for a look at Leo Frank's last agony. The sight made some of the women sick. They groaned and fainted. Others, with babes in arms, pushed through the crowd and stared up at Frank in fascination. The excitement increased.

Bob Howell, the man who had almost succeeded in having William J. Burns lynched, arrived and started screaming. A notorious drunk and once convicted of manslaughter, he had been purposely excluded from the lynch party. "Well, now we've

---

* This and much of what follows are eyewitness reports, compiled and printed in the issues of The New York Times, and the Georgian, August 20, 21, 1915. There was no mystery as to the identity of the lynchers, but the reporters, to get the story, promised anonymity.

got you," shouted Howell. "You won't murder any more little
girls. We've got you! We've got you!"

His gestures increased in violence. He fanned the fever. Others
began to shout too. "They won't put any monument over you.
They are not going to get you. There won't be a piece of you
left as big as a cigar."

In frenzy some of the people pushed closer.

Judge Newton Morris, who had saved Burns from lynching,
rushed to quiet another mob. He had been in court at Alfreta
early that morning when he heard of Frank's abduction. He
called his office in Marietta. No answer. He asked the operator
what happened. She told him. She said, "I am the only person
left in Marietta." Morris and Lawyer John Woods drove out
to Frey's gin as fast as they could. Morris was a short, thickset
man with steely blue eyes. In a commanding voice he said,
"Men, hear me."

The noise fell away.

"Whoever did this thing——" began the judge.

"God bless him," shouted Howell.

Morris turned and put a stern arm on Howell's shoulder.
"Whoever did this thing did a thorough job."

"They shore did," came the chorus.

"Whoever did it left nothing more for us to do; little Mary
Phagan is avenged. In the good name of our county, let the
undertaker have this body."

Howell shrieked, "We will not let the undertaker have it. We
are going to burn this dirty thing."

"Don't do anything to this body," said the judge. "This man
has a father and a mother, and whatever we think of him, they're
entitled to the body of their son. Men, I appeal to you in the
good name of Cobb County: all in favor, say aye."

The crowd said aye.

By this time Lawyer Woods had summoned the Negro undertaker in Marietta, who was on his way. Before the undertaker
could rescue the corpse, a man climbed the tree and with a

penknife cut the rope from which Frank dangled. The body dropped with a thud, and the crowd packed around it, Howell standing at Frank's head.

The undertakers arrived. The Negro ran through the crowd and said. "Here I am, Judge, and there's the wagon." Two other Negroes opened the back of the wagon and drew out a large basket.

The crowd gave way. When the two Negroes picked up the body, Howell struck at them. Again Leo Frank's corpse tumbled to the ground. Howell stamped upon its face and drove his heel into the dead flesh. He stamped again and again.

"Stop him, for God's sake, stop him," ordered the Judge.

Two men pulled Howell off.

The Negroes retrieved the body, dumped it into the basket and hurried to their wagon. Morris cut the rope around Frank's neck and tossed it to the crowd. The souvenir-hunters were quick. They sliced it up immediately.

With that, Morris helped put the basket in the wagon and ran to Woods' car. John Woods guided the wagon through the grove to Roswell Road. Both he and Morris could hear the crowd behind them. It suddenly realized it had been robbed. It was a race to Atlanta. Gaining a little distance, Morris and Woods transferred the basket from the wagon to their Ford. It projected from both sides of the car.

"Now drive like hell to Atlanta," said Morris.

All the way to the city, Morris and Woods passed streams of cars, bumper to bumper, headed for Frey's gin. When two policemen stopped Woods for speeding, Morris said he and his friend would gladly submit to arrest if the policemen would take Leo Frank's body off their hands.

"Good God, no," said the policemen. So Morris impressed them as an escort, and by ten that morning, Morris delivered the corpse of the now mutilated Leo Frank to the Greenberg and Bond Funeral Home.

Before someone cut Frank down, an amateur photographer

had taken two snapshots of the dangling body. For the next fifteen years, that photograph decorated the store fronts of rural
markets, and any tourist could buy a postcard of the hanging
Frank for a nickel in many Georgia drugstores.

In Marietta, those who did not follow the body to Atlanta
could gather around the courthouse and listen to Fiddlin' John
Carson, a lanky, toothless mountaineer. Fiddlin' John had appeared at the Atlanta courthouse every day of the trial. He had
composed a ballad about Mary Phagan that was soon to be recorded and is still sung at folk-song festivals in the Deep South.
The author heard it less than ten years ago at an *All Night Sing*
in Charlotte, North Carolina. That Tuesday, Fiddlin' John
played the ballad on his fiddle over and over, recounting the
fate that befell little Mary Phagan.* Each time, the crowd
cheered. When he tired of the repetition, Fiddlin' John switched
momentarily to "Annie Laurie," "Give Me That Old Time
Religion," and "Little Old Log Cabin by the Lane."

On the day Frank died, thousands of men lost their lives in
the trenches on the Eastern and Western fronts as senselessly as
Frank lost his. But something about the way Frank had died
made his death as significant as the death of any one of them,
even though he was a nervous, myopic, slightly unpleasant–but
ultimately brave–young man.

The press understood. On the day Frank was lynched the
Germans captured Kovno, cut the Petrograd railroad, encircled
the Russian army; a Zeppelin raid over London killed ten
civilians, and wounded thirty-six; a storm swept southeastern
Texas, killing one hundred people in Galveston and Texas
City. But the front page headline in most of the metropolitan
dailies reported the lynching of Leo Frank at Marietta, Georgia.
In many ways, this lynching had a more profound effect on
America, and cost it more, than all these other events.

At two-thirty in the afternoon, of August 17, the Greenberg
and Bond Funeral Home admitted Atlantans to see Leo Frank's
_____
* Appendix D.

corpse. More people had queued up to see his bruised and scarred body than had queued up to see the body of Mary Phagan. They had kept coming until well past midnight.

Even in death Leo Frank had had to suffer this last indignity at their hands—the reward they had demanded for not having destroyed his body.

This, then, was the final proof of an undeniable truth, beyond appeal—a truth the man whom Atlantans called the Silent Man in the Tower expressed in one of his rare addresses, and his last, to the Court:

"The issues at bar were lost. The poison of unspeakable things took their place."

On August 19 the body of Leo Frank was released by authorities to Rabbi David Marx, who had arranged to ship it to New York. The Rabbi accompanied Mrs. Frank on the trip North. The lynching prostrated Rhea Frank and her husband Rudolph. When a large, curious crowd gathered in front of the Brooklyn residence, the police moved them back until the parents had time to move Frank's body to a funeral parlor. When the reporters gathered at their home at 152 Underhill Avenue in Brooklyn, Mr. Frank whispered, "I can't talk. I can't talk." Mrs. Frank said through her tears, "Thank God, he is dead and through with his trouble. If he had lived, his life would have been a torture to him and they might have killed him in a worse way."

There were fewer than twenty mourners present at Frank's simple, dignified burial services, Thursday, the twentieth, in Mount Carmel Cemetery in Cypress Hills, New York. Rabbi Alexander Lyons of Brooklyn's Eighth Avenue Temple, who had known Frank since boyhood, and Rabbi Marx conducted the services.

EPILOGUE

GOVERNOR NAT HARRIS made a public apology for the lynching. He said, "The penitentiary was not built to keep people out but to keep them in." He offered a reward for the conviction of any of the lynch party, and for this was immediately subjected to a cascade of threatening letters. The Governor knew no policeman would uncover the identity of these men, and if one did, no grand jury would ever indict, or solicitor general prosecute. But the press of America was livid with indignation, and Nat Harris was doing the best he could.*

The Governor discussed the lynching with a reporter from *The New York Times:*

"Let a strong man make use of his strength to force a helpless woman to yield to him and there is something that arouses the tiger in Southern men. It goes with a white man's skin and I have even seen it in some cases among niggers. I went through the State prison and a Negro man came up to me and said: 'Boss, I'm dying of tuberculosis; won't you pardon me and let me go home and die with my people?' I said, 'What's your

---

* This author sold newspapers as a boy in New York City. Like other newsboys, I had one location all mine—the corner of Norfolk and Delancey Streets. But on the morning of August 18, 1915, I ran through the whole of the Lower East Side, as did the other boys, shouting, "Leo Frank dead!" We all knew the word "lynched" would not have immediacy to the Yiddish-speaking readers. I sold the *Jewish Daily Forward* that morning, the paper that had covered the trial and kept abreast through a special correspondent of all aspects of the case. It was the first time I had ever seen a paper with a full-page headline in red ink.

crime?' He said, 'Murder.' I said, 'I can't let you out of here, even though you are dying, if you committed a crime as that. Did you really kill a man?' He said, 'Yes, I killed a man who seduced my wife.' I said, 'Old man, you shall go home and die with your people.' No, sir, you can't argue these things. They are too deep for reason to reach." [1]

Later in the week, O. B. Keeler, a reporter for the Atlanta *Georgian* who lived in Marietta, had a visitor. A man he had never seen before handed him an envelope and ran away. Inside, Keeler found a wedding ring and a note which read: "Frank's dying request was that this his wedding ring be given his wife. Will you not see this bequest is carried out? This note will be delivered to you by a man you do not know and who does not know you. Make no effort to find out his identity. You are expected to destroy this after reading it."

Tom Watson referred to Frank's death as an "execution" and never used the word "hanging" or "lynching." The August 26 issue of the *Jeffersonian* reported the hanging in full. His front page bore two headlines: "The Wages of Sin is Death," and "Frank Virtually Confessed: Ceased to Claim Innocence." He was never to sell more copies than he sold that day. Intelligent men fought their way to newsboys and paid from 25 to 50 cents a copy for the first issue of Watson's paper. Cultured women leaned from fine automobiles and purchased copies and rode away smiling over Watson's screams of delight in the act of a squad of men taking a half-dead, defenseless human being, undressed, over 175 miles of roads and hanging him to a tree.

Watson wrote: "In putting the Sodomite murderer to death the Vigilance Committee has done what the Sheriff would have done, if Slaton had not been the same mould as Benedict Arnold. LET JEW LIBERTINES TAKE NOTICE! Georgia is not for sale to rich criminals." [2]

---

[1] *The New York Times*, August 21, 1915.
[2] *Jeffersonian*, August 26, 1915.

The grand jury that considered the Frank lynching decided to take no action and was discharged at the end of September. This was the last official act of the State of Georgia in the terrible tragedy which saw mob violence triumph over law and justice.

In Marietta, the Knights of Mary Phagan stood a twenty-four-hour guard over the oak from which they had hanged Leo Frank, lest someone cut it down or the Governor order it destroyed. Two months to the day after they had lynched Frank, the Knights climbed to the bald top of Stone Mountain outside Atlanta and burned a huge cross, visible throughout the city.

Five weeks later, on Thanksgiving Day, one William Joseph Simmons led fifteen of the Knights of Mary Phagan to the top of Stone Mountain, where they conducted the first initiation ceremony of the "reincarnated Klan."

The frenzy generated by the Frank case presented a valuable opportunity to the promoters of the "Invisible Empire." A historian of the Klan writes: "The lynching of the Jewish factory owner, Leo Frank, helped shape and prepare the way for the (modern) Ku Klux Klan." [3]

Harry Rose, a salesman of Elberton, Georgia, was in Toccoa, on business. A mob composed of men who knew him well came to the store he was calling on. They had ropes and guns and threatened to lynch him, "because I was a Jew but the sheriff was an old friend, and he saved me, talked to the mob and managed to disperse it." [4]

Joseph Cohen had a dry goods store at Canton, Georgia. He had been there for 21 years. On August 16, 1915, a mob came into Cohen's store and ordered him to leave town. Mr. Cohen wrote a letter to Governor Nat Harris.

The Governor replied that he couldn't do anything; the best thing for Cohen to do was to "leave Canton till things cool off." [5]

---

[3] David M. Chalmers, *Hooded Americanism* (Doubleday, New York, 1965), p. 71.
[4] Letter, *New York Times*, August 19, 1915.
[5] Interview with Mr. Cohen at Hotel Martinique, New York, *New York Times*, August 21, 1915.

Almost immediately after the Frank lynching, Tom Watson became obsessed with the delusion that Nathan Straus would assassinate him.

"His days and nights bring him unending terror [wrote a contemporary]. He is ever haunted by the delusion that somebody wants to assassinate him. He never leaves his home except on compulsion and never rides on a railroad train. He resides in a fine mansion and in his intimate life affects all the airs of a man of wealth and culture. He is inclined to the grandiose, and forces those who deal with him to treat him as if he were lord of a manor. His place is guarded like that of a king, and even his friends find difficulty in getting to him." [6]

In January, 1916, the United States Attorney General began proceedings against Watson for his articles on the Frank case. Attorney General Thomas W. Gregory hoped to ban the *Jeffersonian* from the mails, and he wanted to try Watson on a federal charge. This time, the Justice Department initiated a court petition to try Watson outside Georgia. Twice before they had started proceedings against Watson because of his obscene anti-Catholic articles, only to find both juries bringing in acquittals.

Hearing of the government move, Tom Watson called a mass meeting of his followers at Thomson.

"I tell the Attorney General to his teeth [he shouted], you cannot remove me from the Southern District of Georgia. If I have to give up my life for having incurred the savage hatred of the Roman priests and rich Jews, it will be given up right here in the same region where my ancestors gave up theirs. I don't intend to budge an inch. The cause is yours as well as mine. And I will die on my threshold." [7]

---

[6] "A Public Man of Georgia," *op. cit.*, p. 691.
[7] C. Vann Woodward, *op. cit.*, pp. 448–49.

Watson might bluff defiance to his admirers, but he was discreet enough to persuade Governor Harris to talk with the Attorney General. Harris was successful. He persuaded Gregory to drop the prosecution but not before Gregory said: "I don't understand you Georgia politicians. When you come up here you tell me you hate Tom Watson and when I propose to silence him you take his part."

"I did not answer him according to the inquiry," wrote the Governor in his account of the interview, "but contented myself with telling him that I wanted him to let Mr. Watson alone for the sake of the honor of my own state and people." [8]

In the 1917 elections, however, Watson turned with a vengeance on Harris, calling him a Slaton man. Watson backed the ambitious Hugh Dorsey, whom he characterized as "the fearless, incorruptible Solicitor General who won the great fight for LAW AND ORDER and the PROTECTION OF WOMANHOOD in the Leo Frank case. *The Jeffersonian is for him tooth and nail.*"

Watson also announced his support of A. H. Henslee for the Prison Commission: *"He is the juror who was outrageously DENOUNCED BY LUTHER ROSSER IN THE FRANK CASE! Henslee stood firm and true, for LAW, for JUSTICE, for WOMANHOOD."*

The Watson candidates ran on the issue of Leo Frank. All of them won. How powerful was the Leo Frank issue? It strengthened the county unit system of counting votes, made it a keystone in Georgia politics. The county unit system kept the political power in the hands of the rural politicians, and barred Atlanta men from the governorship. There was one exception— Hugh Dorsey. Dorsey's success emphasized the rural-urban conflict in the Frank case and furnished the successful pattern of prejudice, albeit most of it against the Negro, which became the route for success in Georgia politics until the 1960s.

---

[8] C. Vann Woodward, *op. cit.,* p. 450.

Now in control of the Georgia State Legislature, Watson instructed it to enact a law forbidding the federal government to extradite citizens from Georgia for trial elsewhere.

In 1920, after his second term, Hugh Dorsey went to Hickory Hill and told Watson he would like to try for the United States Senate. Watson said no. Watson would run himself. In September, he beat Dorsey badly, 117,723 to 72,885. While Dorsey in his campaign had tried to get what mileage he could out of the Frank case, Watson did far better on the issue since he had been continuously writing about Leo Frank for six years.

On the Senate floor Watson could be counted on for a fiery speech on behalf of the rural farmer and anything else that might strike his frenzied fancy. His last speech was against the confirmation of William Howard Taft as Chief Justice of the United States. Watson went back to the rhetoric of his early Populist days and talked about "Big Money," "Wall Street," and the "Railroad Trust."

An old man now, grossly overweight and coarse and more than occasionally drunk, Watson succumbed to bronchial asthma on the dark, pre-dawn morning of September 26, 1922. He was dead, his power ended at last. He had been in his time on every side of every issue, not caring about his contradictions, inconsistencies, or specious logic. Now some people found it hard to sum up what Tom Watson had meant.

President Warren Harding sent a simple telegram of condolences to Mrs. Watson. Several of Watson's colleagues in the Senate had nothing at all to say about his demise.

Some of the native Georgians were warmer. James A. Holloman, the political writer for the Atlanta *Constitution*, wrote a front-page obituary:

> "The position of prosecuting attorney was offered him when a young man and he declined it.
> " 'If I err in the practice of law,' said he, 'I shall err on the side of mercy,' and there is no man living in Georgia

today who has torn the chains of felony from more men
charged with infraction of laws.

" 'I suspect some of them were guilty,' he said once to
me, 'but I would rather free a thousand guilty men than
to have the consciousness of having convicted an innocent
man.' "

The *Journal* devoted its editorial to the disease which killed
Watson. The best the editors could think to say of him was
that his career had been "remarkable" and that he was a politician of "unusual magnetism."

Georgia's Secretary of State, S. G. McLendon, rose to the occasion by comparing Watson to Voltaire:

> "If like Voltaire, the common people's tribune, it is still
> more like Voltaire, the bitter satirist, that the Georgia Sena-
> tor is best characterized. It is in this role that he has be-
> come the best loved and the worst hated man in the South.
> His lance of ridicule has been thrust into the most con-
> ventional beliefs and traditions of the church. Catholic be-
> lief he has waged bitter war against, and Protestant prac-
> tices he has fought. Politicians, office-holders, teachers—
> men in every walk of life—have felt the lash of the Watson
> satire."

Another admirer, though not a particularly voluble one, was
the young, vigorous Congressman from Georgia, Representative Carl Vinson, who said, "Watson's death removes from
Congress one of its ablest members and statesmen."

Forty years later, Watson still remains an anomaly. When
Representative Robert Stephens of Georgia suggested to the
Post Office Department that it issue a stamp to honor Watson's
memory as the father of Rural Free Delivery, the Postmaster
General hesitated. In the end, the Post Office Department ruled
Watson was not well known enough. The department conse-
quently issued one stamp commemorating basketball and an-

other honoring the memory of Frederick Remington, the painter.

Among the flowers that accompanied Watson's funeral cortege through Atlanta, a small bouquet of roses came from his friend of the 1890s, Eugene V. Debs, America's leading Socialist, and a large cross of flowers from the Ku Klux Klan. Nothing sums the man up better than the polar opposites represented by these two floral tributes.

Hugh Dorsey returned to private practice in 1921. Five years later, he was appointed Judge of Atlanta's City Court, the same court over which his father had presided. Nine years later, in 1935, he became Judge of the Fulton County Superior Court and stayed there until poor health forced his resignation in March, 1948. In June of the following year, he died at the age of seventy-seven.

There were some anomalies about Hugh Dorsey, too. In 1921, he published an indignant pamphlet scoring Georgia for its treatment of the Negro. He was noted as an early liberal on the race issue. Certainly he was a dedicated public servant, for it is rare for a former governor to accept judgeships when he can make much more money in private practice.

Dorsey lived long enough to swear in his two sons, Hugh, Jr. and James, as members of the Georgia Bar. Despite a lifetime of public service, Georgia saved one humiliation for Hugh Dorsey. In 1947, some friends in the State Legislature tried to pass a bill which would allow Dorsey to claim a pension in his old age and ill health; he hadn't quite enough service to qualify for existing pensions. But Dorsey's friends couldn't muster the two-thirds majority. The bill failed.

To the end of his life, Dorsey remained convinced of Leo Frank's guilt. He told A. L. Henson, shortly before he died, that his own files indubitably proved Leo Frank murdered Mary Phagan. Where those files are today is anyone's guess.

Dorsey's portrait, unveiled by his two sons on March 7, 1963, hangs in the Fulton Superior Court beside that of Rufus T., his father.

After the United States entered the war in 1917, John Marshall Slaton served as chief of the Red Cross in Romania. When the war ended he returned to Atlanta, but his political life was over. His friends entered him in the senatorial contest of 1924, but he fared so badly that thereafter the former Governor devoted all his time to his law practice.

For the next forty years he taught a Sunday School class in his church. He also served twenty-seven consecutive years as Chairman of the State Board of Bar Examiners. In the 1940s his wife, Sally, died and until January 11, 1955, when he himself died of a circulatory failure, John Slaton walked to the cemetery every morning to place a rose on her grave. After his death the Slaton mansion alone brought a price of $1,356,000.

In 1957, the Georgia State Legislature authorized the John Marshall Slaton Memorial. On behalf of the state of Georgia, Governor Ernest Vandiver accepted the marble bust in an impressive ceremony. Virlyn B. Moore, Senior Judge of Atlanta's Judicial Circuit, delivered the memorial address, calling Slaton, "The Incomparable Georgian."

In 1916, Fanny Phagan Coleman, Mary's mother, brought a suit against the National Pencil Company charging that it was liable for damages in her daughter's murder. The court awarded her several thousand dollars, agreeing the company was negligent in not affording Mary Phagan personal protection. The Montags and the other shareholders turned to their insurance company, the Travelers of Hartford. But the Travelers said it wasn't liable for these damages since the National Pencil Company had not notified it promptly of Mary Phagan's murder. The Travelers and the National Pencil Company eventually agreed to a compromise settlement of $1250.

But the notoriety and the loss of business doomed the National Pencil Company. A few years after the lynching of Leo Frank, M. A. Ferst bought the pencil-making machines, and some of the other company assets and organized the firm which flourishes today as Scripto.

Fanny Phagan Coleman died at seventy-five in August of 1947. She was laid to rest in a grave beside that of her murdered daughter, Mary.

George Epps filed a suit in a federal court in Rome, Georgia, in 1956 against Dell Publishing Company and the American News Company of Atlanta, charging that the Samuelses' book, *Night Fell on Georgia*, falsely referred to him as an unmitigated liar. He asked $55,000 in damages in each of the two suits. He claimed he was an upstanding member of the Cedartown, Georgia, community and a Methodist church member, and that as a result of the book he had become "the butt of jokes and ridicule."

Judge Frank Hooper dismissed the suit against Dell on November 1. Epps had failed to file certain other necessary forms with the court, which probably meant he intended to let the suit die.

The Knights of the Ku Klux Klan initiated a notorious career of terror which lasted for the next decade. There is no evidence, C. Vann Woodward remarks, that Tom Watson launched the modern Klan: "Yet if any mortal man may be credited (as no man may rightly be) with releasing the forces of human malice and ignorance and prejudice, which the Klan merely mobilized, that man was Thomas E. Watson." [9]

Once he seized upon the Frank case, Watson articulated for the poverty-stricken Southerners the principles which lent significance to their nativist program: the protection of white womanhood; the determination not to let the "foreigner" intrude upon the homogeneous composition of the South; the

[9] C. Vann Woodward, *op. cit.*, p. 290.

defiance against encroaching industrialization; and the anti-Catholic and anti-Negro attitudes, of course, which only needed clever exploitation.

At the time of Frank's lynching, the movie *Birth of A Nation* was showing to excited audiences all over the country. William J. Simmons, the new Grand Wizard of the Invisible Empire of the Knights of the Ku Klux Klan, needed nothing more. D. W. Griffith, Tom Watson, and Leo Frank had generated the spontaneity with which to revive the hooded secret order dedicated to protecting "patriotism," which they interpreted in terms of white supremacy and nativism. Simmons was an itinerant salesman, who reveled in organizing fraternal orders. He had successfully promoted Masonry, the Knights Templar, and Woodmen of the World, but he was proprietor of none. He was a Southerner, born and bred, "just the man," John Higham remarks, "to revive a vanished sectional institution as an instrument of modern American nationalism. His cloudy wits spun with the myths and history of the South; his heart exuded Southern sentiment as a plum does juice." [10]

For the next five years, Simmons recruited no more than five thousand into his Invisible Empire. But in 1920, he formed a partnership with Edward Y. Clarke and Mrs. Elizabeth Tyler, experienced fund raisers. Within a year the Klan began exercising an iron control over local politics in the South and in some of the non-southern states, especially in Indiana, New Jersey, and Illinois. It would be a mistake to think the Klan ever dictated any policies on the national level, but it came perilously close once or twice in such attempts, for many congressmen and senators were dependent upon its support.

The death of the little factory girl, Mary Phagan, called up the power of the modern Klan. Ironically, as DeWitt Roberts concludes in his monograph for the Anti-Defamation League, the death of another girl destroyed that power. In 1926, D. C.

---

[10] John Higham, *Strangers in the Land* (Rutgers University Press, 1955), p. 287.

Stephanson, the Klan's Imperial Wizard, was convicted of second degree murder in the death of Madge Oberholtzer. Stephanson, in consort with other Klansmen, had kidnapped and raped this young woman, who took poison in a Chicago hotel room. Womanhood wasn't so safe after all.

If Leo Frank gave impetus to the Ku Klux Klan, he also lent the same impetus to the Anti-Defamation League. "The Trial of Leo Frank," writes Dore Schary, the fourth national chairman of the ADL, "had a galvanic effect on the men who created the league. Certainly the B'nai B'rith would have founded the league sooner or later, but the story of Leo Frank struck the American Jewish community like nothing before in its experience. It was Frank's destiny to give the league a sense of urgency that characterizes its operations to this day."

More than influencing the Jews, the Leo Frank case had profound influence on the way many Americans interpreted their civil liberties. John P. Roche, in his excellent interpretation of the Frank case, says the trial and lynching of Leo Frank helped end once and for all, "the notion, profoundly Jeffersonian, that the rural yeoman is the paradigmatic democratic citizen and that the cities are a source of civic degeneracy, a malignant cancer on the body politic." [11]

Leo Frank's widow, Lucile, became a fixture in the Jewish community of Atlanta for the next forty years, and a constant reminder as well. She never remarried, and for many years worked quietly in one of the city's leading fashion shops. For the rest of her life, she signed all her checks and papers, "Mrs. Leo M. Frank."

When the author met her in 1951, he had been warned beforehand not to mention the case. She never replied to offers from national magazines to write her story. She died at the age of sixty-nine, on April 23, 1957.

---

[11] John P. Roche, "The Curbing of the Militant Majority," *The Reporter*, July 18, 1963, p. 34.

Another crisis descended upon this Jewish community of Atlanta in 1958, with the bombing of the Reform Temple in the wake of the Negro's civil rights struggle. The outrage had results quite unexpected to the perpetrators of the crime. There was no fear this time. The overwhelming sympathy and support of the entire Atlanta community from every level of its religious, official, business, and social structure came out for the Jewish community.

The new liberal spirit was really born in the late 1930's when the New Deal began to make life somewhat easier for the farmer and industrial worker.

In Atlanta today massive skyscrapers are the landmarks of the commercial and financial leadership of the South. All the major New York stock brokers and advertising agencies have offices there. Even the El Al Israel Airlines has a branch office to take care of the Baptists, Methodists, and Presbyterians who want to fly to the Holy Land. And Ralph McGill, a tower of strength for an enlightened South, has been telling the uncomfortable truths and the people have been listening.

What has happened in those fifty years since Leo Frank was dragged from his cell and hanged from an oak outside Marietta?

Years ago the power lay in the hands of the rural sections of the state. From the county courthouse the Tom Watsons pulled the strings, laid down the law for state legislatures and members of the Congress.

It was absurd, of course, but it was not until the mid-1940s that anyone ever attempted to challenge it.

More than any one person, the man who can claim credit for that great Southern challenge was an Atlanta lawyer, Morris Abram, son of a Jewish merchant, an immigrant from Romania.

In 1946 Morris Abram began a sixteen-year struggle which eventually led to a political miracle for Atlanta and the State of Georgia. Candidate Helen Douglas Mankin had beaten her opponent in the popular vote, for the Democratic nomination for Fifth District Congressman. But her opponent, patrician

Judge James C. Davis, a politician of the old school, won the county-unit votes and the nomination. Abram took the case to court.

For the next sixteen years Abram wrote, spoke, debated, filed new writs for additional clients, until the issue finally reached the United States Supreme Court. Pat Watters of the Atlanta *Journal*, wrote of the Abram presentation: ". . . the two-hour Abram argument was good to the soul to hear, partly because of the conviction of the man speaking and partly because it was a sounding of truths that brought alive the greatness and the glory of the concepts of self-government."

Two days later the court decided that Abram's viewpoint was correct, and the rural domination of the state of Georgia was dead.

The "climate" that killed Leo Frank and kept its stranglehold on Georgia politics for decades had lifted and the man who helped engineer the change of climate was the son of a Jewish immigrant, Morris Abram.

Jim Conley served less than a year on the chain gang after Judge Leonard Roan sentenced him as an accessory after the fact in the murder of Mary Phagan. He was released from prison on the day Judge Ben Hill sentenced Leo Frank for the third time.

In 1919 Conley was arrested again. The newspapers said he was involved in a "melee," which probably involved a killing, because he was sentenced to fourteen years on the chain gang.

He served his time and was released. Then he disappeared.

On the night of October 20, 1941, James A. Belflower, a veteran police reporter for the Atlanta *Journal*, came down to the precinct house to write a routine story about a police raid on a lottery game in the Negro district. Belflower had covered the original trial of Leo Frank, and he recognized the name of one of the prisoners. That one was an old man with silver hair, but it was the same Jim Conley. Belflower posted *a certiorari* appeal for Conley and interviewed him.

Conley said he had been leading an honest life for the past seven years, working as a truck driver. Belflower asked him about the Frank case.

"That's gone and forgotten," Conley said. "I'll talk about anything else. Not that."

In 1947, Conley turned up at the police station, this time on the minor charge of drunkenness. His name didn't appear again in the Atlanta newspapers until 1962, in an obituary.

He told at least three people he killed Mary Phagan. He told his lawyer, William Smith; he told a fellow convict, who gave a deposition to that effect some ten years later; and he told Annie Maude Carter. A fourth person also knew Conley had killed the girl. That was a Negro friend who played checkers with Conley in the basement that morning of April 26, 1913. Whoever he was, he may well have witnessed the murder.

Jim Conley was lucky. He might have told all Atlanta he murdered Mary Phagan; it was obvious that Tom Watson and Hugh Dorsey would never have believed him. Nor probably would 1913 Atlanta. An average of four Negroes were lynched every month in those years. The people of Georgia needed a different atonement for the murder of the pretty but sad little girl, Mary Phagan.

In 1916 the Marietta Camp #763 of the United Confederate Veterans erected a monument over the grave of Mary Phagan, and in 1960, the white supremacists tried to exploit the tragedy. A Robert Bowling of Atlanta was chairman of the *Remember Mary Phagan Committee*. The circular he issued urging citizens to visit the little girl's grave, claimed, ". . . the Jews are behind the Supreme Court's decision to destroy the white race."

Once there were elaborate plans in Marietta to build a white brick wall around the oak tree from which Leo Frank was hanged. For nearly fifty years after the lynching, the area around Frey's gin on the Roswell Road was known as Leo Frank's Woods. Now the lynch site is gone. It lies buried under four lanes on Interstate Highway 75, which bypasses Marietta.

APPENDICES

APPENDIX A

Mr. Justice Holmes, dissenting: *

MR. JUSTICE HUGHES and I are of the opinion that the judgment should be reversed. The only question before us is whether the petition shows on its face that the writ of habeas corpus should be denied, or whether the district court should have proceeded to try the facts.

The allegations that appear to us material are these: The trial began on July 28, 1913, at Atlanta, and was carried on in a court packed with spectators and surrounded by a crowd outside, all strongly hostile to the petitioner. On Saturday, August 23, this hostility was sufficient to lead the judge to confer in the presence of the jury with the chief of police of Atlanta and the colonel of the Fifth Georgia Regiment, stationed in that city, both of whom were known to the jury. On the same day, the evidence seemingly having been closed, the public press, apprehending (346) danger, united in a request to the court that the proceedings should not continue on that evening. Thereupon the court adjourned until Monday morning. On that morning, when the solicitor general entered the court, he was greeted with applause, stamping of feet and clapping of hands, and the judge, before beginning his charge, had a pri-

---

* No. 775 Leo M. Frank, Appt. *v.* C. Wheeler Mangum, Sheriff of Fulton County, Ga.

vate conversation with the petitioner's counsel in which he expressed the opinion that there would be "probable danger of violence" if there should be an acquittal or a disagreement, and that it would be safer for not only the petitioner but his counsel to be absent from court when the verdict was brought in. At the judge's request they agreed that the petitioner and they should be absent, and they kept their word. When the verdict was rendered, and before more than one of the jurymen had been polled, there was such a roar of applause that the polling could not go on until order was restored. The noise outside was such that it was difficult for the judge to hear the answers of the jurors, although he was only 10 feet from them. With these specifications of fact, the petitioner alleges that the trial was dominated by a hostile mob and was nothing but an empty form.

We lay on one side the question whether the petitioner could or did waive his right to be present at the polling of the jury. That question was apparent in the form of the trial and was raised by the application for a writ of error; and although, after the application to the full court, we thought that the writ ought to be granted, we never have been impressed by the argument that the presence of the prisoner was required by the Constitution of the United States. But habeas corpus cuts through all forms and goes to the very tissue of the structure. It comes in from the outside, not in subordination to the proceedings, and although every form may have been preserved, opens the inquiry whether they have been more than an empty shell.

(347) The argument for the appellee in substance is that the trial was in a court of competent jurisdiction, that it retains jurisdiction although, in fact, it may be dominated by a mob, and that the rulings of the state court as to the fact of such domination cannot be reviewed. But the argument seems to us inconclusive. Whatever disagreement there may be as to the scope of the phrase "due process of law," there can be no

doubt that it embraces the fundamental conception of a fair trial, with opportunity to be heard. Mob law does not become due process of law by securing the assent of a terrorized jury. We are not speaking of mere disorder, or mere irregularities in procedure, but of a case where the processes of justice are actually subverted. In such a case, the Federal court has jurisdiction to issue the writ. The fact that the state court still has its general jurisdiction and is otherwise a competent court does not make it impossible to find that a jury has been subjected to intimidation in a particular case.

The loss of jurisdiction is not general, but particular, and proceeds from the control of a hostile influence.

When such a case is presented, it cannot be said, in our view, that the state court decision makes the matter res judicata. The state acts when, by its agency, it finds the prisoner guilty and condemns him. We have held in a civil case that it is no defense to the assertion of the Federal right in the Federal court that the state has corrective procedures of its own—that still less does such procedure draw to itself the final determination of the Federal question. Simon v. Southern R. Co. 236 U.S. 115, 122, 123, ante, 492, 497, 35 Sup. Ct. Rep. 255. We see no reason for a less liberal rule in a matter of life and death. When the decision of the question of fact is so interwoven with the decision of the question of constitutional right that the one necessarily involves the other, the Federal court must examine the facts. Kansas City Southern R. Co. v. C. H. Albers Commission Co. 223 U.S. 573, 591, 56 L. ed. 556, 565, 32 Sup. Ct. Rep. 316; Norfolk & W. R. Co. v. Conley, (348) March 8, 1915 (236 U.S. 605, ante, 745, 35 Sup. Ct. Rep. 437). Otherwise, the right will be a barren one. It is significant that the argument for the state does not go so far as to say that in no case would it be permissible, on application for habeas corpus, to override the findings of fact by the state courts. It would indeed be a most serious thing if this court were so to hold, for we could not but regard it as a removal of what is perhaps the most important guaranty of the Federal Constitution. If, however, the argument stops short of this, the whole structure built upon the state procedure and decisions falls to the ground.

To put an extreme case and show what we mean, if the trial and the later hearing before the supreme court had taken place in the presence of an armed force known to be ready to shoot if the result was not the one desired, we do not suppose that this court would allow itself to be silenced by the suggestion that the record showed no flaw. To go one step further, suppose that the trial had taken place under such intimidation, and that the supreme court of the state, on writ of error, had discovered no error in the record, we still imagine that this court would find a sufficient one outside of the record, and that it would not be disturbed in its conclusion by anything that the supreme court of the state might have said. We therefore lay the suggestion that the supreme court of the state has disposed of the present question by its judgment on one side, along with the question of the appellant's right to be present. If the petition discloses facts that amount to a loss of jurisdiction in the trial court, jurisdiction could not be restored by any decision above. And notwithstanding the principle of comity and convenience (for, in our opinion, it is nothing more, United States v. Sing Tuck, 194 U.S. 161, 168, 48 L. ed. 917, 920, 24 Sup. Ct. Rep. 621) that calls for a resort to the local appellate tribunal before coming to the courts of the United States for a writ of habeas corpus, when, as here, that resort has been had in vain, the power to secure fundamental rights (340) that had existed at every stage becomes a duty, and must be put forth.

The single question in our minds is whether a petition alleging that the trial took place in the midst of a mob savagely and manifestly intent on a single result is shown on its face unwarranted, by the specifications, which may be presumed to set forth the strongest indications of the fact at the petitioner's command.

This is not a matter for polite presumptions; we must look facts in the face. Any judge who has sat with juries knows that, in spite of forms, they are extremely likely to be impregnated by the environing atmosphere. And when we find the judgment of the expert on the spot—of the judge whose business it was to preserve not only form, but substance—to have been that if one juryman yielded to the reasonable doubt that he himself later expressed in court as the result of a most anxious deliberation, neither prisoner nor counsel would be safe from the rage of the crowd, we think the presumption overwhelming that the jury responded to the passions of the mob.

Of course we are speaking only of the case made by the petition, and whether it ought to be heard. Upon allegations of this gravity in our opinion it ought to be heard, whatever the decision of the state court may have been, and it did not need to set forth contradictory evidence, or matter of rebuttal, or to explain why the motions for a new trial and to set aside the verdict were overruled by the state court.

There is no reason to fear an impairment of the authority of the state to punish the guilty. We do not think it impracticable in any part of this country to have trials free from outside control. But to maintain this immunity it may be necessary that the supremacy of the law and of the Federal Constitution should be vindicated in a case like this.

It may be that on a hearing a different complexion would be given to the judge's alleged request and expression of fear.

But supposing the alleged facts to be true, we are (350) of opinion that if they were before the supreme court, it sanctioned a situation upon which the courts of the United States should act; and if, for any reason, they were not before the supreme court, it is our duty to act upon them now, and to declare lynch law as little valid when practised by a regularly drawn jury as when administered by one elected by a mob intent on death.

APPENDIX B

Governor John M. Slaton's Commutation Order: *

EXECUTIVE OFFICE

JUNE 21ST, 1915

In Re Leo M. Frank, Fulton Superior Court. Sentenced to be executed, June 22, 1915.

Saturday, April 26th, 1913, was Memorial Day in Georgia and a general holiday. At that time Mary Phagan, a white girl, of about 14 years of age was in the employ of the National Pencil Company located near the corner of Forsyth and Hunter Streets in the City of Atlanta. She came to the pencil factory a little after noon to obtain the money due her for her work on the preceding Monday, and Leo M. Frank, the defendant, paid her $1.20, the amount due her and this was the last time she was seen alive.

Frank was tried for the offense and found guilty the succeeding August. Application is now made to me for clemency.

This case has been the subject of extensive comments through the newspapers of the United States and has occasioned the transmission of over 100,000 letters from various States requesting clemency. Many communications have been received from citizens of this State advocating or opposing interference with the sentence of the court.

I desire to say in this connection that the people of the State

---

* Courtesy of the Department of Archives and History, Atlanta, Georgia

of Georgia desire the esteem and good will of the people of every State in the Union. Every citizen wishes the approbation of his fellows and a State or Nation is not excepted. In the preamble to the Declaration of Independence, Thomas Jefferson wrote that "When in the course of human events, it becomes necessary for one people to dissolve the political bonds which have connected them with another, and to assume among the powers of the earth the separate and equal station to which the Laws of Nature and of Nature's God entitles them, a decent respect to the opinions of mankind requires that they should declare the causes which impel them to the separation."

Many newspapers and multitudes of people have attacked the State of Georgia, because of the conviction of Leo M. Frank and have declared the conviction to have been through the domination of a mob and with no evidence to support the verdict. This opinion has been formed to a great extent by those who have not read the evidence and who are unacquainted with the judicial procedure in our State.

I have been unable to even open a large proportion of the letters sent me, because of their number and because I could not through them gain any assistance in determining my duty.

The murder committed was a most heinous one. A young girl was strangled to death by a cord tied around her throat and the offender deserves the punishment of death. The only question is as to the identity of the criminal.

The responsibility is upon the people of Georgia to protect the lives of her citizens and to maintain the dignity of her laws, and if the choice must be made between the approbation of citizens of other States and the enforcement of our laws against offenders whether powerful or weak, we must choose the latter alternative.

MOBS.

It is charged that the court and jury were terrorized by a Mob and the jury were coerced into their verdict.

I expect to present the facts in this case with absolute fairness and to state conditions with regard only to the truth.

When Frank was indicted and the air was filled with rumors as to the murder and mutilation of the dead girl, there was intense feeling and to such extent that my predecessor, Governor Brown, stated in argument before me that he had the Military ready to protect the defendant in the event any attack was made. No such attack was made and from the evidence that he obtained none was contemplated.

Some weeks after this, defendant was put on trial. Georgia probably has the broadest provisions for change of venue in criminal cases that exist in any State. Our law permits the Judge to change the venue on his own motion, in the event he thinks a fair trial cannot be given in any county. The defendant can move for a change of venue on the same ground, and if it be refused, the refusal of the judge is subject to an immediate appeal to the Supreme Court, and in fact, the entire genius of our law demands a fair trial absolutely free from external influence.

Frank went to trial without asking a change of venue and submitted his case to a jury that was acceptable to him. He was ably represented by counsel of conspicuous ability and experience.

During the progress of the case, after evidence had been introduced laying the crime with many offensive details upon Frank, the feeling against him became intense. He was the general superintendent of the factory and Mary Phagan was a poor working girl. He was a Cornell graduate and she dependent for her livelihood upon her labor. According to a witness, whose testimony will subsequently be related more completely, when this girl came to get her small pay, since she only worked one day in the week, because of lack of material, this general superintendent solicited her to yield to his importunities and on her refusal slew her.

The relation of these facts anywhere and in any community would excite unbounded condemnation.

If the audience in the court room manifested their deep resentment toward Frank, it was largely by this evidence of feeling beyond the power of a court to correct. It would be difficult anywhere for an appellate court, or even a trial court, to grant a new trial in a case which occupied thirty days, because the audience in the court room upon a few occasions indicated their sympathies. However, the deep feeling against Frank which developed in the progress of the evidence was in the atmosphere and regardless of the commission of those acts of which the court would take cognizance, the feeling of the public was strong.

Since Governor Brown has related secret history in his public argument before me, I may state that Friday night before the verdict was expected Saturday, I had the Sheriff call at the Mansion and inquired whether he anticipated trouble. This was after many people had told me of possible danger and an editor of a leading newspaper indicated his anticipation of trouble. The Sheriff stated he thought his deputies could avert any difficulty. Judge Roan telephoned me that he had arranged for the defendant to be absent when the verdict was rendered. Like Governor Brown, I entered into communication with the Colonel of the Fifth Regiment, who stated he would be ready if there were necessity.

I was leaving on Saturday, the day the verdict was expected, for Colorado Springs to attend the Congress of Governors, and did not wish to be absent if my presence were necessary. I have now the original order prepared by me at the time, in the event there were a necessity for it. I became convinced there would be slight chance for any use of force and therefore filled my engagement in Colorado.

Judge Roan, in the exercise of precaution, requested that both counsel and defendant be absent when the verdict was rendered, in order to avoid any possible demonstration in the event of acquittal.

The jury found the defendant guilty and with the exception

of demonstration outside the court room, there was no disorder.

Hence, it will be seen that nothing was done which courts of any State could correct through legal machinery. A court must have something more than an atmosphere with which to deal, and especially when that atmosphere has been created through the processes of evidence in disclosing a horrible crime.

Our Supreme Court, after carefully considering the evidence as to demonstrations made by spectators, declared them without merit, and in this regard the orderly processes of our tribunals are not subject to criticism.

RACIAL PREJUDICE.

The charge against the State of Georgia of racial prejudice is unfair. A conspicuous Jewish family in Georgia is descended from one of the original colonial families of the State. Jews have been presidents of our Boards of Education, principals of our schools, Mayors of our cities, and conspicuous in all our commercial enterprises.

THE FACTS IN THE CASE.

Many newspapers and non-residents have declared that Frank was convicted without any evidence to sustain the verdict. In large measure, those giving expression to this utterance have not read the evidence and are not acquainted with the facts. The same may be said regarding many of those who are demanding his execution.

In my judgment, no one has a right to an opinion who is not acquainted with the evidence in the case, and it must be conceded that the jury who saw the witnesses and beheld their demeanor upon the stand are in the best position as a general rule to reach the truth.

I cannot, within the short time given me to decide the case, enter into the details outlined in thousands of pages of testimony. I will present the more salient features, and have a right to ask that all persons who are interested in the determination of the matter, shall read calmly and dispassionately the facts.

THE STATE'S CASE.

The State proved that Leo M. Frank, the General Superintendent of the Factory, was in his office a little after 12 o'clock on the 26th day of April, 1913, and he admitted having paid Mary Phagan $1.20, being the wages due her for one day's work. She asked Frank whether the metal had come, in order to know when she could return for work. Frank admits this and so far as is known, he was the last one who saw her alive. At three o'clock the next morning (Sunday), Newt Lee, the night watchman, found in the basement the body of Mary Phagan strangled to death by a cord of a kind kept generally in the Metal Room, which is on Frank's floor. She had a cloth tied around her head which was torn from her underskirt. Her drawers were either ripped or cut and some blood and urine were upon them. Her eye was very black, indicating a blow, and there was a cut $2\frac{1}{2}$ inches in length about four inches above the ear and to the left thereof, which extended through the scalp to the skull. The County Physician who examined her on Sunday morning declared there was no violence to the parts and the blood was characteristic of menstrual flow. There were no external signs of rape. The body was not mutilated, the wounds thereon being on the head and scratches on the elbow, and a wound about two inches below the knee.

The State showed that Mary Phagan had eaten her dinner of bread and cabbage at 11:30 o'clock and had caught the car to go to the pencil factory which would enable her to arrive at the factory within the neighborhood of about thirty minutes. The element of exact time will be discussed later.

Dr. Harris, the Secretary of the State Board of Health, and an expert in this line, examined the contents of Mary Phagan's stomach ten days after her burial and found from the state of the digestion of the cabbage and bread, that she must have been killed within about thirty minutes after she had eaten the meal.

Newt Lee, the Negro night watchman, testified that Frank had "told me to be back at the factory at 4 o'clock Saturday afternoon," and when he "came upstairs to report, Frank rubbing his hands" met Newt Lee and told him to "go out and have a good time until 6 o'clock," although Lee said he would prefer to lie down and sleep. When Lee returned, Frank changed the slip in the time clock, manifesting nervousness and taking a longer time than usual.

When Frank walked out of the front door of the factory, he met a man named Gantt, whom he had discharged a short time before. Frank looked frightened, his explanation being that he anticipated harm. Gantt declared he wished to go upstairs and get two pairs of shoes which permission Frank finally granted, stating that he thought they had been swept out.

About an hour after this occurrence, Frank called up Lee over the telephone, a thing he had never done before, and asked him if everything was all right at the factory. Lee found the double inner doors locked, which he had never found that way before. Subsequently, when Lee was arrested and Frank was requested by the Detectives to go in and talk to him in order to find what he knew, Lee says that Frank dropped his head and stated, "If you keep that up, we will both go to hell."

On Sunday morning at about 3 o'clock, after Newt Lee, the night watchman, had telephoned the Police Station of the discovery of the dead body and the officers had come up to the factory, they endeavored to reach Frank by telephone, but could not get a response. They telephoned at 7:00 Sunday morning and told Frank that they wanted him to come down to the factory, and when they came for him, he was very nervous and trembled. The body at that time had been taken to the undertakers, and according to the evidence of the officers who took Frank by the undertaker's establishment to identify the girl, he (Frank) showed a disinclination to look at the body and did not go into the room where it lay, but turned away at the door.

Frank had made an engagement on Friday to go to the baseball game on Saturday afternoon with his brother-in-law, but broke the engagement, as he said in his statement, because of the financial statement he had to make up, while before the Coroner's Jury, he said he broke the engagement because of threatening weather.

The contention of the State, as will hereafter be disclosed, was that Frank remained at the factory Saturday afternoon to dispose of the body of Mary Phagan, and that that was the reason he gave Newt Lee his unusual leave of absence.

The cook's husband testified that on Saturday, the day of the murder, he visited his wife at the home of Mr. Selig, defendant's father-in-law, where Frank and his wife were living, and that Frank came in to dinner and ate nothing. The Negro cook of the Selig's was placed upon the stand and denied that her husband was in the kitchen at all on that day. For purposes of impeachment, therefore, the State introduced an affidavit from this cook taken by the Detectives, and as she claimed under duress, which tended to substantiate the story of her husband and which affidavit declared that on Sunday morning after the murder, she heard Mrs. Frank tell her mother that Mr. Frank was drinking the night before and made her sleep on a rug and called for a pistol to shoot himself, because he (Frank) had murdered a girl. This affidavit was relevant for purposes of impeachment, although, of course, it had no legal probative value as to the facts contained therein. On the stand, the cook declared that she was coerced by her husband and detectives under threat of being locked up unless she gave it, and it was made at the Station House. The State proved it was given in the presence of her lawyer and said that her denial of the truth of the affidavit was because her wages had been increased by the parents of Mrs. Frank. No details are given as to where the conversation occurred between Mrs. Frank and her mother, nor is there any explanation as to how she happened to hear the conversation. It will be easily seen that the effect of the affidavit upon the jury might be great.

It is hard to conceive that any man's power of fabrication of minute details could reach that which Conley showed, unless it be the truth.

The evidence introduced tended to show that on Sunday morning Frank took out of the time clock the slip which he had admitted at that time was punched for each half hour, and subsequently Frank claimed that some punches had been missed. The suggestion was that he had either manipulated the slip to place the burden on Lee, or was so excited as to be unable to read the slip correctly.

The State introduced a witness, Monteen Stover, to prove that at the time when Mary Phagan and Frank were in the Metal Room, she was in Frank's office and he was absent, although he had declared he had not left his office. The State showed that the hair of Mary Phagan had been washed by the undertaker with pine tar soap, which would change its color and thereby interfere with the ability of the doctor to tell the similarity between the hair on the lathe and Mary Phagan's hair.

The State further showed a cord of the character which strangled Mary Phagan was found in quantities on the Metal Room floor, and was found in less quantities and then cut up in the basement. As to this Detective Starnes testified, "I saw a cord like that in the basement, but it was cut up in pieces. I saw a good many cords like that all over the factory."

Holloway testified: "These cords are all over the building and in the basement."

Darley testified to the same effect.

However, this contradicts the testimony that was presented to the jury for solution.

The State claimed to the jury that witnesses for the defendant, under the suggestion of counsel in open court, would change their testimony so that it might not operate against the defendant.

I have not enumerated all the suspicious circumstances urged by the State, but have mentioned what have appeared to me the most prominent ones. Where I have not mentioned the more prominent ones, an inspection of record fails to maintain the contention.

It is contended that a lawyer was engaged for Frank at the Station House before he was arrested. This is replied to by the defense that a friend had engaged counsel without Frank's knowledge, and the lawyer advised Frank to make a full statement to the detectives.

JIM CONLEY.

The most startling and spectacular evidence in the case was that given by a Negro, Jim Conley, a man 27 years of age, and one who frequently had been in the chain gang. Conley had worked at the factory for about two years and was thoroughly acquainted with it. He had worked in the basement about two months and had run the elevator about a year and a half.

On May 1st he was arrested by the detectives.

Near the body in the basement had been found two notes, one written on brown paper and the other on a leaf of a scratch pad. That written on white paper in a Negro's handwriting showed the following:

"He said he wood love me and land doun play like night witch did it but that long tall black negro did buy hisslef."

On the brown paper, which was the carbon sheet of an order blank headed "Atlanta, Ga._____, 190____," which hereafter becomes important, was written in a Negro's handwriting the following:

"Mam that negro hire doun here did this i went to make water and he push me doun that hole a long tall negro black that hoo it was long sleam tall negro i wright while play with me."

The detectives learned about the middle of May that Conley could write, although at first he denied it. He made one statement and three affidavits which are more fully referred to in stating the defendant's case. The affidavits were introduced by the defendant under notice to produce.

By these affidavits there was admitted the substance of the evidence that he delivered on the stand, which in brief was as follows:

Conley claimed that he was asked by Frank to come to the factory on Saturday and watch for him, as he previously had done, which he explained meant that Frank expected to meet some woman and when Frank stamped his foot Conley was to lock the door leading into the factory and when he whistled, he was to open it.

Conley occupied a dark place to the side of the elevator behind some boxes, where he would be invisible.

Conley mentioned several people, including male and female employees, who went up the steps to the second floor where Frank's office was located. He said that Mary Phagan went up the stairs and he heard in a few minutes footsteps going back to the Metal Room, which is from 150 to 200 feet from the office. He heard a scream and then he dozed off. In a few minutes Frank stamped and then Conley locked the door and then Frank whistled, at which time Conley unlocked the door and went up the steps. Frank was shivering and trembling and told Conley "I wanted to be with the little girl and she refused me and I struck her and I guess I struck her too hard and she fell and hit her head against something, and I do not know how bad she got hurt. Of course, you know I ain't built like other men."

Conley described Frank as having been in a position which Conley thought indicated perversion, but the facts set out by Conley do not demand such conclusion.

Conley says that he found Mary Phagan lying in the Metal Room some 200 feet from the office, with a cloth tied about her neck and under the head as though to catch blood, although there was no blood at the place.

Frank told Conley to get a piece of cloth and put the body in it and Conley got a piece of striped bed tick and tied up the body in it and brought it to a place a little way from the dressing room and dropped it and then called on Frank for assistance in carrying it. Frank went to his office and got a key and unlocked the switchboard in order to operate the elevator, and he and Conley took the body in the elevator down to the basement, where Conley rolled the body off the cloth. Frank returned to the first floor by the ladder, while Conley went by the elevator and Frank on the first floor got into the elevator and went to the second floor on which the office is located. They went back into Frank's private office and just at that time Frank said, "My God, here is Emma Clark and Corinthia Hall," and Frank then put Conley into the wardrobe. After they left Frank let Conley out and asked Conley if he could write, to which Conley gave an affirmative reply. Frank then dictated the letters heretofore referred to. Frank took out of his desk a roll of greenbacks and told him, "Here is $200," but after a while requested the money back and got it.

One witness testified she saw some Negro, whom she did not recognize, sitting at the side of the elevator in the gloom. On the extraordinary motion for new trial, a woman, who was unimpeached, made affidavit that on the 31st of May, through newspaper report, she saw that Conley claimed he met Frank by agreement at the corner of Forsyth and Nelson Streets on the 26th of April, 1913, and she became satisfied that she saw the two in close conversation at that place on that date between 10:00 and 11:00 o'clock.

Frank put his character in issue and the State introduced ten witnesses attacking Frank's character, some of whom were factory employees, who testified that Frank's reputation for lasciviousness was bad and some told that he had been seen making advances to Mary Phagan, whom Frank had professed to the detectives either not to have known, or to have been slightly acquainted with. Other witnesses testified that Frank had improperly gone into the dressing room of the girls. Some witnesses who answered on direct examination that Frank's reputation for lasciviousness was bad, were not cross-examined as to details, and this was made the subject of comment before the jury.

The above states very briefly the gist of the State's case, omitting many incidents which the State claims would confirm Frank's guilt when taken in their entirety.

DEFENSE.

The defendant introduced approximately one hundred witnesses as to his good character. They included citizens of Atlanta, collegemates at Cornell, and professors of that college.

The defendant was born in Texas and his education was completed at the institution named.

The admission of Conley that he wrote the notes found at the body of the dead girl, together with the parts he admitted he played in the transaction, combined with his history and his explanation as to both the writing of the notes and the removal of the body to the basement, make the entire case revolve around him. Did Conley speak the truth?

Before going into the varying and conflicting affidavits made by Conley, it is advisable to refer to some incidents which cannot be reconciled to Conley's story. Wherever a physical fact is stated by Conley, which is admitted, this can be accepted, but under both the rules of law and of common sense, his statements cannot be received, excepting where clearly corroborated. He admits not only his participation as an accessory, but also glibly confesses his own infamy.

One fact in the case, and that of most important force in arriving at the truth, contradicts Conley's testimony. It is disagreeable to refer to it, but delicacy must yield to necessity when human life is at stake.

The mystery in the case is the question as to how Mary Phagan's body got into the basement. It was found 136 feet away from the elevator and the face gave evidence of being dragged through dirt and cinders. She had dirt in her eyes and mouth. Conley testified that he and Frank took the body down to the basement in the elevator on the afternoon of April 26, 1913, and leaves for inference that Frank removed the body 136 feet toward the end of the building, where the body was found at a spot near the back door which led out towards the street in the rear. Conley swears he did not return to the basement, but went back up in the elevator, while Frank went back on the ladder, constituting the only two methods of ingress and egress to the basement, excepting through the back door. This was between one and two o'clock on the afternoon of April 26th.

Conley testified that on the morning of April 26th he went down into the basement to relieve his bowels and utilized the elevator shaft for the purpose.

On the morning of April 27th at 3 o'clock, when the detectives came down into the basement by way of the ladder, they inspected the premises, including the shaft, and they found there human excrement in natural condition.

Subsequently, when they used the elevator, which everybody, including Conley, who had run the elevator for 1½ years, admits, only stops by hitting the ground in the basement, the elevator struck the excrement and mashed it, thus demonstrating that the elevator had not been used since Conley had been there. Solicitor General Dorsey, Mr. Howard and myself visited the pencil factory and went down this elevator and we found it hit the bottom. I went again with my secretary with the same result.

Frank is delicate in physique, while Conley is strong and powerful. Conley's place for watching, as described by himself, was in the gloom a few feet from the hatchway, leading by way of ladder to the basement. Also he was in a few feet of the elevator shaft on the first floor. Conley's action in the elevator shaft was in accordance with his testimony that he made water twice against the door of the elevator shaft on the morning of the 26th, instead of doing so in the gloom of his corner behind the boxes where he kept watch.

Mary Phagan in coming down stairs was compelled to pass within a few feet of Conley, who was invisible to her and in a few feet of the hatchway. Frank could not have carried her down the hatchway. Conley might have done so with difficulty. If the elevator shaft was not used by Conley and Frank in taking the body to the basement, then the explanation of Conley, who admittedly wrote the notes found by the body, cannot be accepted.

In addition there was found in the elevator shaft at 3 o'clock Sunday morning, the parasol, which was unhurt, and a ball of cord which had not been mashed.

Conley in his affidavits before the detectives testified he wrapped up the body in a crocus sack at the suggestion of Frank, but on the trial, he testified he wrapped up the body in a piece of bed-tick "like the shirt of the Solicitor General." The only reason for such a change of testimony, unless it be the truth, was that a crocus sack unless split open would be too small for the purpose. If he split open the crocus sack with a knife, this would suggest the use of a knife in cutting the drawers of the girl.

So the question arises, whether there was any bed-tick in the pencil factory? and no reason can be offered why bed-tick should be in a pencil factory. It has no function there. Had such unusual cloth been in the factory, it certainly must have been known, but nobody has ever found it.

Conley says that after the deed was committed, which everybody admits could not have been before 12:05, Frank suddenly said: "Here comes Emma Clark and Corinthia Hall," and he put Conley in a wardrobe.

The uncontradicted evidence of these two witnesses, and

they are unimpeached, was they reached the factory at 11:35 a.m. and left it at 11:45 a.m., and therefore this statement of Conley can hardly be accepted.

Conley says that when they got the body to the bottom of the elevator in the basement, Frank told him to leave the hat, slipper and piece of ribbon right there but he "taken the things and pitched them over in front of the boiler" which was 57 feet away.

Conley says that Frank told him when he watched for him to lock the door when he (Frank) stamped and to open the door when he whistled. In other words, Frank had made the approach to the girl and had killed her before he had signaled Conley to lock the door.

Conley says, "I was upstairs between the time I locked the door and the time I unlocked it. I unlocked the door before I went upstairs." This explanation is not clear, nor is it easy to comprehend the use of the signals which totally failed their purpose.

It is curious during the course of the story that while Frank explained to Conley about striking the girl when she refused him and Conley found the girl strangled with a cord, he did not ask Frank anything about the use of the cord, and that subject was not mentioned.

The wound on Mary Phagan was near the top of the head and reached the skull. Wounds of that character bleed freely. At the place Conley says he found blood, there was no blood. Conley says there was a cloth tied around the head as though to catch the blood, but none was found there.

One Barrett says that on Monday morning he found six or seven strands of hair on the lathe with which he worked and which were not there on Friday. The implication is that it was Mary Phagan's hair and that she received a cut by having her head struck at this place. It is admitted that no blood was found there. The lathe is about $3\frac{1}{2}$ feet high and Mary Phagan is described as being chunky in build. A blow which would have forced her with sufficient violence against the smooth handle of the lathe to have produced the wound must have been a powerful one, since the difference between her height and that of the lathe could not have accounted for it. It was strange, therefore, that there was a total absence of blood and that Frank, who was delicate, could have hit a blow of such violence.

Some of the witnesses for the State testified the hair was like that of Mary Phagan, although Dr. Harris compared Mary Phagan's hair with that on the lathe under a microscope and was under the impression it was not Mary Phagan's hair. This will be the subject of further comment.

Barrett and others said they thought they saw blood near the dressing room, at which place Conley said he dragged the body.

Chief of Police Beavers said he did not know whether it was blood.

Detective Starnes said, "I do not know that the splotches I saw were blood."

Detective Black says, "Mr. Starnes, who was there with me, did not call my attention to any blood splotches."

Detective Scott says: "We went to the Metal Room where I was shown some spots supposed to be blood spots."

A part of what they thought to be blood was chipped up in four or five chips and Dr. Claude Smith testified that on one of the chips he found, under a microscope, from three to five blood corpuscles, a half drop would have caused it.

Frank says that the part of the splotch that was left after the chips were taken up was examined by him with an electric flash lamp, and it was not blood.

Barrett, who worked on the Metal floor, and who several witnesses declare claimed a reward because he discovered the hair and blood, said the splotch was not there on Friday, and some witnesses sustained him.

There was testimony that there were frequent injuries at the factory and blood was not infrequent in the neighborhood of the ladies' dressing room. There was no blood in the elevator.

Dr. Smith, the City Bacteriologist, said that the presence of blood corpuscles could be told for months after the blood had dried. All of this bore upon the question as to whether the murder took place in the Metal Room, which is on the same floor of Frank's office. Excepting near the Metal Room at the place mentioned where the splotches varied, according to Chief Beavers' testimony, from the size of a quarter to the size of a palm leaf fan, there was no blood whatever. It is to be remarked that a white substance called haskoline used about the factory was found spread over the splotches.

CONLEY'S AFFIDAVITS.

The defense procured under notice one statement and three affidavits taken by the detectives from Conley and introduced them in evidence.

The first statement, dated May 18, 1913, gives a minute detail of his actions on the 26th day of April and specifies the saloons he visited and the whiskey and beer he bought, and minutely itemized the denomination of the money he had and what he spent for beer, whiskey, and pan sausage. This comprehends the whole of Affidavit #1.

On May 24, 1913, he made for the detectives an affidavit in which he says that on Friday before the Saturday on which the murder was committed, Frank asked him if he could write. This would appear strange, because Frank well knew he could write and had so known for months, but according to Conley's affidavit Frank dictated to him practically the contents of one of the notes found by the body of Mary Phagan. Frank, then, according to Conley's statement, took a brown scratch pad and wrote on that himself, and then gave him a box of cigarettes in which was some money and Frank said to him that he had some wealthy relatives in Brooklyn, and, "Why should I hang."

This would have made Frank guilty of the contemplated murder on Friday which was consummated Saturday and which was so unreasonable, it could not be accepted.

On May 28th, 1913, Conley made for the detectives another affidavit, which he denominates as "second and last statement." In that he states that on Saturday morning after leaving home he bought two beers for himself and then went to a saloon and won 90 cents with dice, where he bought two more beers and a half pint of whiskey, some of which he drank, and he met Frank at the corner of Forsyth and Nelson Streets and Frank asked him to wait until he returned.

Conley went over to the factory and mentioned various people whom he saw from his place of espionage going up the stairs to Mr. Frank's office. Then Frank whistled to him and he came upstairs and Frank was trembling and he and Frank went into the private office when Frank exclaimed that Miss Emma Clark and Corinthia Hall were coming and concealed Conley in the wardrobe. Conley said that he stayed in the wardrobe a pretty good while, for the whiskey and beer had gotten him to sweating. Then Frank asked him if he could write and Frank made him write at his dictation three times and Frank told him he was going to take the note and send it in a letter to his people and recommend Conley to them. Frank said, "Why should I hang?"

Frank took a cigarette from a box and gave the box to Conley, and when Conley got across the street, he found it had two paper dollars and two silver quarters in it, and Conley said, "Good luck has done struck me." At the Beer Saloon he bought one-half pint of whiskey and then got a bucket and bought 15 cents worth of beer, 10 cents worth of stove wood, and a nickle's worth of pan sausage and gave his old woman $3.50. He did not leave home until about 12:00 o'clock Sunday. On Tuesday morning Frank came upstairs and told him to be a good boy. On Wednesday Conley washed his shirt at the factory and hung it on the steam pipe to dry, occasioning a little rust to get on it. The detectives took the shirt and, finding no blood on it, returned it.

On the 29 of May, 1913, Conley made another affidavit, in which he said that Frank told him that he had picked up a girl and let her fall and Conley hollered to him that the girl was dead, and Frank told him to go to the cotton bag and get a piece of cloth, and he got a big wide piece of cloth and took her on his right shoulder, when she got too heavy for him and she slipped off when he got to the dressing room. He called Frank to help and Frank got a key to the elevator and the two carried the body downstairs and Frank told him to take the body back to the sawdust pile, and Conley says he picked the girl up and put her on his shoulder, while Frank went back up the ladder.

It will be observed that the testimony and the appearance of the girl indicated that she was dragged through the cinders and debris on the floor of the basement, yet Conley says he took her on his shoulder.

The affidavit further states that Conley took the cloth from around her and took her hat and slipper, which he had picked up upstairs, right where her body was lying and brought them down and untied the cloth and brought them back and "throwed them on the trash pile in front of the furnace." This was the time that Conley says Frank made the exclamation about Emma Clark and Corinthia Hall.

An important feature in this affidavit is as follows:

Conley states in it that Mr. Frank said: "Here is $200, and Frank handed the money to him."

All of the affidavit down to this point is in typewriting, the original was exhibited to me. At the end of the affidavit in hand-writing is written the following: "While I was looking at the money in my hands, Mr. Frank said, 'Let me have that and I will make it all right with you Monday, if I live and nothing happens,' " and, "He took the money back and I asked him if that was the way he done, and he said he would give it back Monday."

It will be noticed that the first question which would arise would be, what became of the $200? This could not be accounted for. Therefore, when that query presumably was propounded to Conley, the only explanation was that Frank demanded it back.

The detectives had Conley for two or three hours on May 18th trying to obtain a confession, and he denied he had seen the girl on the day of the murder. The detectives questioned him closely for three hours on May 25th, when he repeated this story. On May 27th, they talked to him about five or six hours in Chief Lanford's office.

Detective Scott, who was introduced by the State, testified regarding Conley's statement and affidavits as follows:

"We tried to impress him with the fact that Frank would not have written those notes on Friday, that that was not a reasonable story. That it showed premeditation and that would not do. We pointed out to him why the first statement would not fit. We told him we wanted another statement. He declined to make another statement. He said he had told the truth.

"On May 28th, Chief Lanford and I grilled him for five or six hours again, endeavoring to make clear several points which were farfetched in his statement. We pointed out to him that his statement would not do and would not fit, and he then made the statement of May 28th, after he had been told that his previous statement showed deliberation and could not be accepted. He told us nothing about Frank making an engagement to stamp and for him to lock the door, and told nothing about Monteen Stover. He did not tell us about seeing Mary Phagan. He said he did not see her. He did not say he saw Quinn. Conley was a rather dirty Negro when I first saw him. He looked pretty good when he testified here.

"On May 29th, we talked with Conley almost all day. We

pointed out things in his story that were improbable and told him he must do better than that. Anything in his story that looked to be out of place, we told him would not do. We tried to get him to tell about the little mesh bag. We tried pretty strong. He always denied ever having seen it. He denied knowing anything about the matter down in the basement in the elevator shaft. He never said he went down there himself between the time he came to the factory and went to Montags. He never said anything about Mr. Frank having hit her, or having hit her too hard, or about tiptoes from the Metal Department. He said there was no thought of burning the body.

"On May 18th we undertook in Chief Lanford's office to convince him he could write, and we understood he said he could not write and we knew he could. We convinced him that we knew he could write and then he wrote."

In his evidence before the jury in the re-direct examination, Conley thought it necessary to account for the mesh bag, and for the first time, said that "Mary Phagan's mesh bag was lying on Mr. Frank's desk and Mr. Frank put it in the safe." This is the first mention of the mesh bag.

The first suggestion that was made of Frank being a pervert was in Conley's testimony. On the stand, he declared Frank said, "He was not built like other men."

There is no proof in the record of Frank being a pervert. The situation in which Conley places him and upon Conley's testimony must that charge rest, does not prove the charge of perversion if Conley's testimony be true.

On argument before me, I asked what motive Conley would have to make such a suggestion and the only reason given was that someone may have made him the suggestion because Jews were circumcised.

Conley in his evidence shows himself amenable to a suggestion. He says, "If you tell a story, you know you have got to change it. A lie won't work and you know you have got to tell the whole truth."

Conley in explaining why his affidavits varied said: "The reason why I told that story was I do not want them to know that these other people passed by me for they might accuse me. I do not want people to think that I was the one that done the murder."

AUTHOR OF THE NOTES.

Conley admits he wrote the notes found by the body of Mary Phagan. Did Frank dictate them? Conley swears he did. The State says that the use of the word "did" instead of "done" indicates a white man's dictation. Conley admits the spelling was his. The words are repeated and are simple, which characterizes Conley's letters. In Conley's testimony, you will find frequently that he uses the word "did" and according to calculation submitted to me, he used the word "did" over fifty times during the trial.

While Conley was in jail charged with being an accessory, there was also incarcerated in the jail a woman named Annie Maude Carter, whom Conley had met at the Court House. She did work in the jail and formed the acquaintaince of Conley, who wrote to her many lengthy letters. These letters are the most obscene and lecherous I have ever read. In these letters, the word "did" is frequently employed. It will be observed that in Conley's testimony, he uses frequently the word "Negro," and in the Annie Maude Carter notes, he says: "I have a Negro watching you."

The Annie Maude Carter notes, which were powerful evidence in behalf of the defendant, and which tended strongly to show that Conley was the real author of the murder notes, were not before the jury.

The word "like" is used in the Mary Phagan notes, and one will find it frequently employed in Conley's testimony. The word "play" in the Mary Phagan notes, with an obscene significance, is similarly employed in the Annie Maude Carter notes. The same is true as to the words "lay" and "love."

In Conley's testimony, he uses the words "make water" just as they are used in the Mary Phagan notes.

In Conley's testimony he says the word "hisself" constantly.

It is urged by the lawyers for the defense that Conley's characteristic was to use double adjectives.

In the Mary Phagan notes, he said "long tall negro, black," "long slim, tall negro."

In his testimony Conley used expressions of this sort. "He was a tall, slim build heavy man." "A good long wide piece of cord in his hands."

Conley says that he wrote four notes, although only two were found. These notes have in them 128 words, and Conley swears he wrote them in $2\frac{1}{2}$ minutes. Detective Scott swears he dictated eight words to Conley and it took him about six minutes to write them.

The statement is made by Frank, and that statement is consistent with the evidence in the record, that the information that Conley could write came from Frank when he was informed that Conley claimed he could not write. Frank says he did not disclose this before, because he was not aware Conley had been at the factory on the 26th day of April, and therefore the materiality of whether Conley could write any more than any other Negro employee, had not been suggested to him. Frank says that he gave the information that Conley had signed receipts with certain jewelers, with whom Conley had dealings.

WHERE WERE THE NOTES WRITTEN.

At the time of the trial, it was not observed that the Death Note written on brown paper was an order blank, with the date line "Atlanta, Ga. _____, 190__." Subsequently, the paper was put under a magnifying glass and in blue pencil, it was found that one Becker's name was written there. He had been employed at the factory on the fourth floor. Investigation was made and Becker testified that he worked for the pencil factory from 1908 until 1912, and the order blank was #1018. During that entire time, he signed orders for goods and supplies. The brown paper on which the Death Note was written bears his signature, and at the time he left Atlanta in 1912, the entire supply of blanks containing the figures 190___, had been exhausted, and the blanks containing the figures "191___," had already been put in use. Becker makes affidavit that before leaving Atlanta, he personally packed up all of the duplicate orders which had been filled and performed their functions, and sent them down to the basement to be burned. Whether the order was carried out, he did not know.

In reply to this evidence, the State introduced on the extraordinary motion, the testimony of Philip Chambers, who swears that unused order blanks entitled "Atlanta, Ga., _____, 191___," were in the office next to Frank's office and that he had been in the basement of the factory and found no books or papers left down there for any length of time, but some were always burned up.

This evidence was never passed upon by the jury and developed since the trial. It was strongly corroborative of the theory of the defense that the death notes were written, not in Frank's office, but in the basement, and especially in view of the evidence of Police Sergeant Dobbs, who visited the scene of the crime on Sunday morning, as follows:

"This scratch pad was also lying on the ground close to the body. The scratch pad was lying near the notes. They were all right close together. There was a pile of trash near the boiler where this hat was found, and paper and pencils were down there, too."

Police Officer Anderson testified:

"There are plenty of pencils and trash in the basement."

THE TIME QUESTION.

The State contended that Mary Phagan came to the office of Leo M. Frank to get her pay at some time between 12:05

and 12:10 and that Frank had declared that he was in his office the whole time.

It is true that at the coroner's inquest held on Thursday after the murder (Page 364), he said he might have gone back to the toilet, but did not remember it. However, in some of his testimony, Frank said he had remained the whole time in his office. Monteen Stover swears that she came into Frank's office at 12:05 and remained until 12:10, and did not see Frank or anybody. She is unimpeached, and the only way to reconcile her evidence would be that she entered Frank's office, as she states for the first time in her life, and did not go into the inner room, where Frank claimed to have been at work. If Frank were at work at his desk, he could not be seen from the outer room. Monteen Stover said she wore tennis shoes and her steps may not have attracted him.

Darley testified: "I have seen all kinds of paper down in the basement. The paper that note is written on is a blank order pad. That kind of paper is likely to be found all over the building for this reason, they write an order and sometimes fail to get a carbon under it, and at other times, they change the order and it gets into the trash. That kind of pad is used all over the factory.

Over the boiler is a gas jet.

Another feature which was not known at the trial and which was not presented to the jury, but came up by extraordinary motion, was regarding the hair alleged to have been found by Barrett on the lathe. The evidence on the trial of some of the witnesses was that the hair looked like that of Mary Phagan. It was not brought out at the trial that Dr. Harris had examined the hair under a microscope and by taking sections of it and comparing it with Mary Phagan's hair, thought that on the lathe was not Mary Phagan's hair, although he said he could not be certain of it.

This, however, would have been the highest and best evidence.

The evidence as to the probability of the blank on which the death note was written being in the basement, and the evidence as to the hair, would have tended to show that the murder was not committed on the floor on which Frank's office was located.

However, the pertinency of Monteen Stover's testimony is that Mary Phagan had to come to get her pay and Frank had gone with her back to the metal room and was in process of killing her while Monteen Stover was in his office, and this was at a time when he had declared he was in his office.

The evidence loses its pertinency if Mary Phagan had not arrived at the time Monteen Stover came. What is the evidence?

The evidence uncontradicted discloses that Mary Phagan ate her dinner at 11:30 o'clock, and the evidence of the streetcar men was that she caught the 11:50 car, which was due at the corner of Forsyth and Marietta Streets at 12:07½. The distance from this place to the pencil factory is about one-fifth of a mile. It required from 4 to 6 minutes to walk to the factory, and especially would the time be enlarged, because of the crowds on the streets on Memorial Day.

While the streetcar men swear the car was on time, and while George Epps, a witness for the State, who rode with Mary Phagan, swears he left her about 12:07 at the corner of Forsyth and Marietta Streets, there is some evidence to the effect that the car arrived according to custom, but might have arrived two or three minutes before schedule time. If so, the distance would have placed Mary Phagan at the pencil factory sometime between 12:05 and 12:10. Monteen Stover looked at the clock and says she entered at 12:05. A suggestion is made that the time clocks, which were punched by the employees, might have been fast. This proposition was met by W. W. Rogers, who accompanied the detectives to the scene of the murder on Sunday morning, and who testified (Page 200), "I know that both clocks were running, and I noticed both of them had the exact time." Therefore, Monteen Stover must have arrived before Mary Phagan, and while Monteen Stover was in the room, it hardly seems possible under the evidence, that Mary Phagan was at that time being murdered.

Lemmie Quinn testifies that he reached Frank's office about 12:20 and saw Mr. Frank. At 12:30, Mrs. J. A. White called to see her husband at the factory where he was working on the fourth floor, and left again before one o'clock.

At 12:50, according to Denham, Frank came up to the fourth floor and said he wanted to get out. The evidence for the defense tends to show that the time taken for moving the body, according to Conley's description, was so long that it could not have fitted the specific times at which visitors saw Frank. It will be seen that when Mrs. White came up at 12:30, the doors below were unlocked.

Another feature of the evidence is that the back door in the basement was the former means of egress for Conley, when he desired to escape his creditors among the employees. On Sunday morning, April 27th, the staple of this door had been drawn. Detective Starnes found on the door the marks of what he thought were bloody fingerprints, and he chipped off two pieces from the door, which looked like "bloody finger prints." The evidence does not disclose further investigation as to whether it was blood or not.

The motive of this murder may be either robbery, or robbery and assault, or assault.

There is no suggestion that the motive of Frank would be robbery. The mesh bag was in Mary Phagan's hands and was described by Conley, in his re-direct examination, at the trial for the first time. The size of the mesh bag I cannot tell, but since a bloody handkerchief of Mary Phagan's was found by her side, it was urged before me by counsel for the defense, that ladies usually carried their handkerchiefs in their mesh bags.

If the motive was assault, either by natural or perverted means, the physician's evidence, who made the examination, does not disclose its accomplishment. Perversion by none of the suggested means could have occasioned the flood of blood. The doctors testified that excitement might have occasioned it under certain conditions. Under the evidence, which is not so set forth in detail, there is every probability that the virtue of Mary Phagan was not lost on the 26th day of April. Her mesh bag was lost, and there can be no doubt of this. The evidence shows that Conley was as depraved and lecherous a Negro as ever lived in Georgia. He lay in watch and described the clothes and stockings of the women who went to the factory.

His story necessarily bears the construction that Frank had an engagement with Mary Phagan, which no evidence in the case would justify. If Frank had engaged Conley to watch for him, it could only have been for Mary Phagan, since he made no improper suggestion to any other female on that day, and it was undisputed that many did come up prior to 12:00 o'clock, and whom could Frank have been expecting except Mary Phagan under Conley's story. This view cannot be entertained, as an unjustifiable reflection on the young girl.

Why the Negro wrote the notes is a matter open to conjecture. He had been drinking heavily that morning, and it is possible that he undertook to describe the other Negro in the building so that it would avert suspicions.

It may be possible that his version is correct.

The testimony discloses that he was in the habit of allowing men to go into the basement for immoral purposes for a consideration, and when Mary Phagan passed by him close to the hatchway leading into the basement and in the gloom and darkness of the entrance, he may have attacked her. What is the truth we may never know.

JURY'S VERDICT.

The jury which heard the evidence and saw the witnesses found the defendant, Leo M. Frank, guilty of murder. They are the ones, under our laws, who are chosen to weigh evidence and to determine its probative value. They may consider the demeanor of the witness upon the stand and in the exercise of common sense will arrive with wonderful accuracy at the truth of the contest.

JUDICIARY.

Under our law, the only authority who can review the merits of the case and question the justice of a verdict which has any evidence to support it, is the trial judge. The Supreme Court is limited by the Constitution and the correction of errors of law. The Supreme Court found in the trial no error of law and determined as a matter of law, and correctly in my judgment, that there was sufficient evidence to sustain the verdict.

But under our judicial system, the trial judge is called upon to exercise his wise discretion, and he cannot permit a verdict to stand which he believes to be unjust. A suggestion in the order overruling a motion for a new trial, that the judge was not satisfied with the verdict, would demand a reversal by the Supreme Court.

In this connection Judge Roan declared orally from the bench that he was not certain of the defendant's guilt—that with all the thought he had put on this case, he was not thoroughly convinced whether Frank was guilty, or innocent—but that he did not have to be convinced—that the jury was convinced and that there was no room to doubt that—that he felt it his duty to order that the motion for a new trial be overruled.

This statement was not embodied in the motion overruling new trial.

Under our statute, in cases of conviction of murder on circumstantial evidence, it is within the discretion of the trial judge to sentence the defendant to life imprisonment (Code Section 63).

The conviction of Frank was on circumstantial evidence, as the Solicitor General admits in his written argument.

Judge Roan, however, misconstrued his power, as evidenced
by the following charge to the jury in the case of the State
against Frank:

"If you believe beyond a reasonable doubt from the evidence
in this case that the defendant is guilty of murder, then, you
would be authorized in that event to say, 'We, the jury, find the
defendant guilty.' Should you go further, gentlemen, and say
nothing else in your verdict, the court would have to sentence
the defendant to the extreme penalty of murder, to-wit: 'To be
hanged by the neck until he is dead.' "

Surely, if Judge Roan entertained the extreme doubt indicated by his statement and had remembered the power granted
him by the Code, he would have sentenced the defendant to life
imprisonment.

In a letter written to counsel he says, "I shall ask the Prison
Commission to recommend to the Governor to commute Frank's
sentence to life imprisonment. . . . It is possible that I showed
undue deference to the jury in this case, when I allowed the verdict to stand. They said by their verdict that they had found
the truth. I was in a state of uncertainty, and so expressed myself. . . . After many months of continued deliberation, I am
still uncertain of Frank's guilt. This state of uncertainty is
largely due by the character of the Conley testimony, by which
the verdict was largely reached.

"Therefore, I consider this a case in which the Chief Magis-
trate of the State should exert every effort in ascertaining the
truth. The execution of any person, whose guilt has not been
satisfactorily proven, is too horrible to contemplate. I do not
believe that a person should meet with the extreme penalty of
the law, until the Court, Jury, and Governor shall have all been
satisfied of that person's guilt. Hence, at the proper time, I shall
express and enlarge upon these views, directly to the Prison
Commission and Governor.

"However, if for any cause I am prevented from doing this,
you are at liberty to use this letter at the hearing."

It will thus be observed that if commutation is granted, the verdict of the jury is not attacked, but the penalty is imposed for murder, which is provided by the State and which the Judge, except for his misconception, would have imposed. Without attacking the jury, or any of the courts, I would be carrying out the will of the Judge himself in making the penalty that which he would have made it and which he desires it shall be made.

In the case of Hunter, a white man charged with assassinating two white women in the City of Savannah, who was found guilty and sentenced to be hung, application was made to me for clemency. Hunter was charged together with a Negro with having committed the offense, and after he was convicted the Negro was acquitted. It was brought out by the statement of the Negro that another Negro who was half-witted committed the crime, but no credence was given to the story, and he was not indicted.

The Judge and Solicitor General refused to recommend clemency, but upon a review of the evidence, and because of the facts and at the instance of the leading citizens of Savannah, who were doubtful of the guilt of defendant, I commuted the sentence, in order that there should be no possibility of the execution of an innocent man. This action has met with the entire approbation of the people of Chatham County.

In the case of John Wright in Fannin County, two men went to the mountain home of a citizen, called him out and shot him and were trampling on his body, when his wife, with a babe in her arms, came out to defend her husband. One of the men struck the babe with his gun and killed it. Wright was tried, found guilty and sentenced to death. Evidence was introduced as to his borrowing a gun. His threats, his escape after the shooting occurred at the time he was an escapee from the Fannin County Jail under indictment for felony.

I refused to interfere unless the judge, or solicitor, would recommend interference, which they declined to do. Finally, when on the gallows the Solicitor General recommended a reprieve, which I granted, and finally on the recommendation of the Judge and Solicitor General, as expressed in my Order, I reluctantly commuted the sentence to life imprisonment. The doubt was suggested as to the identity of the criminal and as to the credibility of the testimony of a prejudiced witness. The crime was as heinous as this one and more so.

In the Frank case three matters have developed since the trial which did not come before the jury, to-wit: The Carter notes, the testimony of Becker, indicating that the death notes were written in the basement, and the testimony of Dr. Harris, that he was under the impression that the hair on the lathe was not that of Mary Phagan, and thus tending to show that the crime was not committed on the floor of Frank's office.

While defense made the subject an extraordinary motion for a new trial, it is well known that it is almost a practical impossibility to have a verdict set aside by this procedure.

The evidence might not have changed the verdict, but it might have caused the jury to render a verdict with the recommendation to mercy.

In any event, the performance of my duty under the Constitution is a matter of my conscience. The responsibility rests where the power is reposed. Judge Roan, with that awful sense of responsibility, which probably came over him as he thought of that Judge before whom he would shortly appear, calls to me from another world to request that I do that which he should have done. I can endure misconstruction, abuse and condemnation, but I cannot stand the constant companionship of an accusing conscience, which would remind me in every thought that I, as Governor of Georgia, failed to do what I thought to be right. There is a territory "beyond A REASONABLE DOUBT and absolute certainty," for which the law provides in allowing life imprisonment instead of execution. This case has been marked by doubt. The trial judge doubted. Two judges of the Court of Georgia doubted. Two judges of the Supreme

Court of the United States doubted. One of the three Prison Commissioners doubted.

In my judgment, by granting a commutation in this case, I am sustaining the jury, the judge, and the appellate tribunals, and at the same time am discharging that duty which is placed on me by the Constitution of the State.

Acting, therefore, in accordance with what I believe to be my duty under the circumstances of this case, it is

ORDERED: That the sentence in the case of Leo M. Frank is commuted from the death penalty to imprisonment for life.

This 21st day of June, 1915.

/S/ John M. Slaton
GOVERNOR

APPENDIX C

THE LEO M. FRANK CASE *

By a Reporter Who
Studied the Tragedy

San Francisco, California
June 23, 1915

———————————————————————————————

HERE IS A PERSONAL ACCOUNT of the Frank case from the viewpoint of a newspaper reporter who covered the story.

It is an unbiased account of what really happened, following the murder of little Mary Phagan, and shows the whole famous and dramatic chain of incidents as seen by a man trained in gathering correct impressions and deducing correct conclusions from tangled evidence for publication in the paper.

The fact that reporters are by education and experience superior to the professional detective in searching out the truth in such a tangled case as that of the Frank prosecution gives an added value and interest to the account of this young man, who covered it for Atlanta papers at the time the incidents related happened.

* Courtesy of the American Jewish Archives, on the Cincinnati campus of the Hebrew Union College—Jewish Institute of Religion

By HAROLD W. ROSS
Formerly reporter on the Atlanta *Journal,* who "covered" the
Frank case from the time of the murder until Frank's conviction.

One who saw Leo M. Frank as he looked upon the mutilated
and abused body of Mary Phagan in the morgue at Atlanta
three hours after her remains had been found, who talked to
him afterward, who observed his conduct in detention and under arrest, who listened to his remarkable statement at his trial
and heard his intensely dramatic appeal when the death sentence was passed upon him for the first time, can not today believe him guilty.

Without making the assertion that Frank is innocent, it may
be said that his conduct from the outset was that of an innocent man, that he did not have a fair trial, that the evidence
against him was not conclusive and that it did not prove him
guilty beyond that "reasonable doubt" required by law.

He begins his life sentence in prison after two years of sus-
pense, a possible—perhaps probable—victim of circumstances,
and, incidentally the living proof of the assertion that if juries
convict men upon evidence such as was adduced against him,
and judges uphold them, no man is absolutely safe from paying
the penalty for a crime he did not commit. Because the evidence
against Frank might, conceivably, grow up about any man.

The murder of Mary Phagan was the most brutal crime in the
annals of the South. After the unfolding of the details the police
did what they always do in Georgia—arrested a Negro. Newt
Lee, the nightwatchman, who found her body in the shadowy
basement of the National Pencil factory and reported it to the
police, was the first and the most logical suspect. So he was made
a prisoner.

But this time the public—always excitable in the South—was
not satisfied. The furor did not die down in two or three days
as it had in the cases the police had to deal with in the past.

Baffled in their hunt for the real slayer, they at the same time realized that something else must be done. So they arrested more Negroes. But this did not stop the clamor.

The crime was an abnormal one; it outshadowed all previous ones. The police realized the truth which determined their whole future course of action:

The murder of Mary Phagan must be paid for with blood. And a Negro's blood would not suffice.

Finally Frank was arrested. It was five or six days after the murder. He was taken into custody only after much consideration. They knew that once they arrested him they could not turn back; they would have to prosecute him to the end. They could not put him in a cell, question him, sweat him and then turn him loose like they could a Negro. He admitted giving the girl her week's pay in the almost-deserted pencil factory on a half-holiday; he admitted being the last to see her alive.

He was taken to the city prison and held. The next day he was formally placed under arrest. And there was no turning back, no deviating. Frank had been accused, he had been arrested, he must be found guilty! Every bit of evidence was shaped to this end. Weeks after this arrest there came a surprise. Among the Negroes at first arrested was Jim Conley. Conley, almost forgotten for a month, at whom the detectives shook their heads and said, "He don't know anything," made a confession!

He said he had written the notes found by the side of Mary Phagan's body. He said he had done it on a Friday afternoon, the day before the crime, at Frank's dictation. The grand jury met that day and Conley was rushed before it. Frank was indicted.

Later, in calmer reflection, it became apparent that the crime was not a premeditated one, that the notes could not have been written on the Friday in question. Conley made another confession, in which he said the notes were written on Saturday. This was real evidence. Conley made two more confessions on consecutive days, each repudiating, wholly or partially, those preceding it. The amazing things about the confessions is that they eventually dovetailed into the theory of the prosecution. If such and such a certain act, say in the second confession, was incongruous with the evidence already developed, the conflict was remedied in the third confession. The defense at the trial called this process "schooling."

Finally Conley was taken from the city prison to the county jail.

"He has told all he knows," the detectives said. About this time whispers that Frank was a pervert began to be circulated.

Conley, at the county jail, was available to reporters for the first time. I was, I think, the first newspaper man to talk to him after his series of confessions.

"Is Frank a pervert?" I asked flatly.

"No," was the reply. Moreover the Negro exhibited surprise at the question. Obviously he had never even thought of such a thing before.

Yet, a week later, when the police thought he was talking too much to newspaper reporters and he was taken back to the city jail and secluded, he made still another confession in which he said Frank was a pervert and a month later at the trial he got on the witness stand and testified to that effect, reciting a series of alleged acts of perversion.

But the testimony of Conley did not alone convict Frank. Nor did the circumstantial evidence. It was a combination of these with the outside influences. There was a strong religious prejudice against Frank. The atmosphere in the courtroom was obviously hostile. The trial was conducted in a hot, crowded inadequate room. For twenty-six days evidence was introduced amid the wrangles of lawyers—a volume of evidence which no human mind could assimilate and weigh.

The jury did not try the case on its merits. It could not. Unable, as all human minds would be, to grasp and digest the testimony, the jurors unknowingly, perhaps, based their verdict upon the superficial impressions they had gained.

Frank, of course, could not be hanged for the murder of Mary Phagan. It was apparent from the first that someone, no matter how distasteful the duty, would have to step in and reverse the decision of the jury. The higher courts could find shelter in legal technicalities. The Georgia boards of pardons hesitated and finally placed the matter squarely up to Governor Slaton. And Governor Slaton, realizing the large element of existing doubt, was duty bound to save him from the gallows. And his act will receive the endorsement of the American people, with a notable exception perhaps in his own state.

APPENDIX D

THE BALLAD OF MARY PHAGAN

Little Mary Phagan
She went to town one day;
She went to the pencil factory
To get her weekly pay.
She left her home at eleven,
She kissed her mother goodbye;
Not one time did that poor girl think
She was going off to die.

Leo Frank he met her
With a brutish heart and grin;
He says to little Mary,
"You'll never see home again."
She fell down on her knees
To Leo Frank and pled.
He picked up a plank from the trash pile
And beat her o'er the head. . . .

Her mother sits a-weeping,
She weeps and mourns all day;
And hopes to meet her darling
In a better world some day.

I have an idea in my mind,
When Frankie comes to die,
And stands examination
In the courthouse in the sky

He'll be so astonished
To what the angels say,
How he killed little Mary
Upon that holiday.
Judge Roan passed the sentence;
He passed it very well;
The Christian doers of heaven
Sent Leo Frank to hell. . . .

                     FROM OLIVE W. BURT COLLECTION *

---

* Four other versions in *American Murder Ballads*, Olive Woolley Burt
(Oxford University Press, 1958; Paperback, Citadel Press, 1964).

SELECTED BIBLIOGRAPHY

Alexander, Henry A., *Some Facts About the Murder Notes in the Phagan Case,* privately printed (Atlanta, Georgia). No date.

American Jewish Committee. Extracts from the Minutes of the Executive Committee, Re: Frank Case (New York).

Arnett, Alex Mathews, *The Populist Movement in Georgia;* Columbia University Press. (New York, 1922).

Asbury, Herbert, "Hearst Comes to Georgia," *American Mercury* Magazine (New York, January, 1926).

Atlanta *Georgian,* files, April 27, 1913 to September 9, 1915, courtesy Los Angeles Public Library (Los Angeles, California) ; Atlanta *Constitution* and Atlanta *Journal,* courtesy of the publishers (Atlanta, Georgia).

Brewton, William W., *The Life of Thomas E. Watson,* published by the author (Atlanta, Georgia, 1926).

Bricker, L. O., D.D., "A Great American Tragedy," *Shane Quarterly,* April, 1943. Vol. 4, No. 2. Butler University (Indianapolis, Ind.).

Buck, Solon J., *The Agrarian Crusade,* Yale University Press (New Haven, Conn., 1920).

Carter, Hodding, *The Angry Scar,* Doubleday and Company (New York, 1959).

Chalmers, David M., *Hooded Americanism,* Doubleday (New York, 1965).

Connolly, C. P., *The Truth About the Frank Case*, Vail-Ballou (New York, 1915).

"A Courageous Governor," *The Outlook* Magazine (New York, August 25, 1915).

Engel, Irving M. Personal correspondence on Leo Frank Case (New York, 1953–59).

Fay v. Noia (March 1963), 423, U.S. 107 (U.S. Supreme Court).

Faulkner, Harold U., *Politics, Reform and Expansion*, Harper Brothers (New York, 1959).

Frank v. Mangum, 237, U.S. 309 (U.S. Supreme Court).

Frank v. State, 83, S. E. Rep. 645 (Georgia Supreme Court).

Greene, Ward, *Death in the Deep South*, Stackpole (New York, 1936).

Gunther, John, *Taken at the Flood*, Harper Brothers (New York, 1960).

Henson, Allen Lumpkin, *Confessions of a Criminal Lawyer*, Vantage Press (New York, 1959).

Hicks, John D., *The Populist Revolt*, University of Minnesota Press (Minneapolis, 1931).

Higham, John, *Strangers in the Land*, Rutgers University Press, (New Brunswick, N. J., 1955).

Jeffersonian, The (weekly), edited by Thomas E. Watson. January 30, 1913 through June 30, 1919 (Thomson, Georgia).

Lawson, John D. *American State Trials*, Vol. X, F. H. Thomas Law Book Company (St. Louis, Missouri, 1918).

Marshall, Louis. Correspondence. American Jewish Archives, (Cincinnati, Ohio).

McGill, Ralph, "Tom Watson: The People's Man," *New Republic* (New York, August 23, 1948), pp. 16–20.

New York Times, The, August 17–22, 1915 (New York).

"The Passing of Tom Watson," *The Outlook* Magazine (New York, October 11, 1922).

Pfeffer, Leo, *This Honorable Court*, Beacon Press (Boston, Mass., 1965).

Powell, Arthur G., *I Can Go Home Again,* University of North
Carolina Press (Chapel Hill, 1943) .

"A Review of the Frank Case," *B'nai B'rith News,* April, 1914,
reprinted from the Chicago *Examiner* (Chicago, Illinois,
March 9, 1914) .

Roberts, DeWitt, *The Story of Mass Hysteria,* Report to the
Anti-Defamation League, New York (Atlanta, Georgia,
1948) .

Roche, John P., "The Curbing of the Militant Majority," *The
Reporter* (New York, July 18, 1963) .

Samuels, Charles and Louise, *Night Fell on Georgia,* Dell Publishing (New York, 1956) .

Slaton, John Marshall. Personal papers, Courtesy Georgia Department of Archives and History (Atlanta, Georgia) .

Van Paassen, Pierre, *To Number Our Days,* Charles Scribner's
Sons (New York, 1964) .

"Why Frank Was Lynched," by "A Public Man of Georgia."
Forum magazine (New York, December, 1916) .

Woodward, C. Vann, *Tom Watson: Agrarian Rebel,* Macmillan
Company (New York, 1938) .